Dear Reader:

The book you are about to read is the latest bestseller from the St. Martin's True Crime Library, the imprint the *New York Times* calls "the leader in true crime!" Each month, we offer you a fascinating account of the latest, most sensational crime that has captured the national attention. St. Martin's is the publisher of bestselling true crime author and crime journalist Kieran Crowley, who explores the dark, deadly links between a prominent Manhattan surgeon and the disappearance of his wife fifteen years earlier in THE SURGEON'S WIFE. Suzy Spencer's BREAKING POINT guides readers through the tortuous twists and turns in the case of Andrea Yates, the Houston mother who drowned her five young children in the family's bathtub. In Edgar Award–nominated DARK DREAMS, legendary FBI profiler Roy Hazelwood and bestselling crime author Stephen G. Michaud shine light on the inner workings of America's most violent and depraved murderers. In the book you now hold, DEADLY AMERICAN BEAUTY, veteran scribe John Glatt details the sordid underside of a "perfect" marriage gone horribly wrong . . .

St. Martin's True Crime Library gives you the stories behind the headlines. Our authors take you right to the scene of the crime and into the minds of the most notorious murderers to show you what really makes them tick. St. Martin's True Crime Library paperbacks are better than the most terrifying thriller, because it's all true! The next time you want a crackling good read, make sure it's got the St. Martin's True Crime Library logo on the spine—you'll be up all night!

Charles E. Spicer, Jr.
Executive Editor, St. Martin's True Crime Library

ST. MARTIN'S TRUE CRIME LIBRARY TITLES BY JOHN GLATT

For I Have Sinned

Evil Twins

Cradle of Death

Blind Passion

Internet Slavemaster

Cries in the Desert

Twisted

Deadly American Beauty

DEADLY
AMERICAN
BEAUTY

A True Story of Passion, Adultery, and Murder

John Glatt

St. Martin's Paperbacks

DEADLY AMERICAN BEAUTY

Copyright © 2004 by John Glatt.

Cover photograph courtesy AP/Wide World Photos.

ISBN: 0-312-98419-7

Printed in the United States of America

St. Martin's Paperbacks edition / March 2004

10 9 8 7 6 5 4 3 2 1

For Gail Freund

Acknowledgments

This book is the result of over a year's work and intensive interviews with many of the key people involved in the Kristin Rossum Case. I owe a great debt to the de Villers' family civil lawyers Craig McClellan and Cindy Lane for their unstinting patience and invaluable advice. I would also like to thank Jon and Sharon Van de Grift and their children Jacob and Jenna for being my point people in San Diego and guiding me around the city.

I would like to thank Deputy DA David Hendren and public defender Alex Loebig for spending many hours giving me their own unique insights into the trial and background.

And much gratitude goes to: San Diego Court Reporter Thom Mantell, Daniel Anderson, Dr. Susan Gloch, Claire Becker, Kevin Cox, Meredith Dent, Dr. Milder, Officer Laurence Horowitz, Sgt. Bob Jones, Teddy and Karen Maya, Michael Christopher, Jenn Powazek, Dr. Frederick Reiders, Michael Robertson, Greg Schoonard, Gary Scott, and Elke at SDSU Library.

As always, I would like to thank my editor at St. Martin's Paperbacks, Charles Spicer, along with Joseph Cleemann and Josh Rubins, and my agent, Peter Miller, Nathan and Lisa.

Thanks also to: Roger Hitts, Daphna Inbar, Danny and Allie Trachtenberg, Cari Pokrassa, Benny Sporano, Virginia Randall, Jeff Samuels, Annette Witheridge and Wensley Clarkson.

Contents

Prologue

It was a perfect Sunday afternoon in June 2001, with temperatures in the low 80s, when Kristin Rossum set out from her San Diego apartment to score methamphetamine in Tijuana. Earlier she had called her Mexican drug dealer, a taxi driver named Armando, to arrange the deal, withdrawing $100 from her bank ATM. It was a routine she had followed numerous times over the last year.

During the short drive south on I-15 toward the San Ysidro border crossing, the beautiful 24-year-old hazel-eyed blonde's mind was racing in so many different directions.

Since her husband Greg's mysterious death eight months earlier from a massive fentanyl overdose, Kristin had become the prime suspect in his murder. As a toxicologist in the San Diego County Medical Examiner's Office, Homicide detectives knew she had access to the highly restricted pain-killing drug, a hundred times stronger than morphine. They also knew of Kristin's passionate affair with her dashingly handsome Australian boss, Dr. Michael Robertson. During an interview, she had admitted asking Greg for a separation two days before his death, saying that he had reacted angrily by threatening to expose her drug use and her unprofessional relationship with the chief toxicologist.

There were numerous unanswered questions surrounding 26-year-old Greg's untimely death the previous November.

Initially it had appeared to be a suicide. His body had been found on the floor of their modest student apartment surrounded by 30 red rose petals, their wedding picture by his head and Kristin's personal journal, chronicling her dissatisfaction with the marriage, conveniently open nearby. It all seemed too perfect, and detectives suspected that it had been staged.

On that Monday night, a hysterical Kristin had dialed 911, saying her husband had stopped breathing. She later told campus police that he had been sick all day and had taken some of her drugs, which he'd been secretly keeping for years.

Greg's death would have been ruled a tragic suicide but for his younger brothers Jerome and Bertram, who refused to believe Kristin's story. Greg had an almost pathological hatred of all drugs, and besides, as the ambitious business manager of a biotech start-up company, he was on a roll at work, and optimistically looking forward to the future and the prospect of starting a family.

Homicide detectives also noted Kristin's romantic streak and an obsession with roses, shared by her lover. She'd made no secret that her favorite movie was *American Beauty*, and the similarities between it and Greg's macabre death scene did not escape police attention. For eight months now they had been playing out an elaborate cat-and-mouse game with her and Robertson, hoping that one of them would break. Eventually Robertson had fled to Australia in May, leaving Kristin to face the music alone.

Kristin was well aware she was under suspicion, and that it was only a matter of time before she was arrested. Now, while proclaiming her innocence, she was making preparations for that eventuality.

But she felt confident of at least one more week of freedom. Her lawyer Michael Pancer had just left for a short vacation, assuring her that police would not make their move while he was out of town. So she had decided to have one final methamphetamine binge to de-stress. One week, deduced the beautiful toxicologist, should be more than enough time for her body to purge all traces of the drug.

"It was one of the most stressful times of my life," she would later explain.

As she walked through the metal turnstile of the border crossing, the exact same spot where she had first met Greg de Villers six years earlier during another drug run, Rossum tried to blend in with the other day-trippers and Mexican workers returning home. It was easy. Walking across the bridge into Mexico and returning to the United States carrying drugs had never been a problem either. That is, if you looked like *the* all-American girl, as Kristin did.

She walked briskly past the Mexican police chatting by their ramshackle headquarters and into Mexico. Up ahead she could see a bustling square full of drug stores advertising Viagra, HGH, and other prescription drugs sold over the counter, no questions asked. It was a busy Sunday afternoon and the square was in motion. Car horns blasted impatiently and everyone was in a hurry.

Kristin looked across a square and was relieved to see her dealer waiting for her by the edge of the taxi rank. She got into the back of his battered yellow cab for the ten-minute ride to Revolución Avenue, the main tourist drag in the center of Tijuana. There he would make the connection for what he cheerfully called "Christina"—the stuff her petite body so desperately craved. Although Rossum had been a sporadic methamphetamine addict since her early teens, she had never needed it more than now. For something told her it might be the last score she'd ever make.

The following morning, Kristin prepared some meth in a glass torch, smoking it before leaving for work. She had been "tweaking" through the night and had hardly slept a wink. But just as she was walking out the door, she received the call she had been dreading. Her lawyer Michael Pancer informed her that the San Diego Police Department had issued a warrant for her arrest and he urged her to surrender at police headquarters. Tearfully, Kristin agreed, but there was something she had to do first.

It was just a short drive from her apartment in Golden Hill to TriLink BioTechnologies in Sorrento Valley, where she had found a job as an assistant chemist, after being fired from the medical examiner's office along with Dr. Robertson. She arrived at 10:15 a.m., parking her white Toyota Cressida in the back lot. She looked terrible and knew it. Her current methamphetamine binge had ravaged her looks. She had scabs all over her face and she'd picked her nails to the quick.

Carefully applying her eye makeup in the car mirror to hide her bloodshot, teary eyes, Kristin composed herself and walked into the sleek white building. Then she breezed through front desk security and into the laboratory, sitting down at her work station.

"She was in a panic and was crying," remembered her best friend Claire Becker, who sat directly in front of her. "I asked her what was wrong, and she told me that she's just heard they had put out a warrant for her arrest. And she was freaking out."

Wiping her eyes, Kristin cleared her desk scooping up some gifts that she had proudly placed there several weeks earlier: a small stuffed koala bear, a card, some love letters and photographs.

"Please hang on to them," she begged Becker. "They're from Michael."

The English-born Becker had become her confidante in the last few months, and knew all about the murder investigation and her affair with Michael Robertson. It was common knowledge at TriLink that Kristin was under a cloud of suspicion, but her bosses were convinced of her innocence. They viewed her as a dedicated hard-worker, feeling very protective, and believed she had been persecuted by the police.

"We all believed her," said Becker. "Later I found out she was *two* very different people."

· · ·

Half an hour later, Kristin Rossum was still high when she returned to her apartment to find detectives waiting for her. She was then driven to police headquarters and arrested on suspicion of killing her husband. She sat impassively as she was read her Miranda rights before being fingerprinted and photographed. Later that day, in floods of tears, she was taken in handcuffs to Las Colinas Women's Detention Facility to await her fate.

Chapter 1

The Golden Girl

Kristin Rossum was the academic equivalent of an army brat, changing location numerous times during her childhood, as her ambitious father carved out a distinguished career as a nationally renowned expert in constitutional law and juvenile delinquency. Ralph Rossum was a self-made man, and strove for perfection, always placing high demands on his daughter and her two brothers. Highly intelligent and stunningly beautiful, Kristin would always try to please him, but always fall short.

Born on December 17, 1946, Ralph Rossum grew up on a small dairy farm in rural Alexandria in central Minnesota, the elder of two brothers. His hard-working father was a farmer who eked out a living from the land. There was little money in the household, so Ralph won a series of scholarships and got the best education possible.

He was the first in his family to ever go to college, securing a place at Concordia College in Moorhead, Minnesota. And in 1968, after paying his way through college with a variety of summer jobs, he graduated summa cum laude.

He then transferred to the University of Chicago, doing post-graduate work as an instructor of Behavioral Sciences for the Department of Police Academy Services, getting his M.A. in 1971.

A year later, Ralph fell in love with an attractive blonde

journalism student at Indiana University. Her name was Constance, and she was two years younger, intelligent and highly ambitious. Soon, they were married.

A year later, after getting his Ph.D. from the University of Chicago, Ralph moved his new wife to Grinnell, Iowa, where he got his first teaching job at Grinnell College as an instructor in the Department of Political Science. But before long, they moved to Memphis, Tennessee, so he could take up an assistant professorship at Memphis State University.

Soon after arriving in Memphis, Constance became pregnant, and on October 25, 1976, Kristin Margrethe Rossum was born. She was a beautiful baby and her parents were thrilled when they soon realized that she was exceptionally intelligent.

Ralph Rossum was now on the academic fast-track and making a national name for himself. In 1977, he was promoted to associate professor of the university's Department of Political Science and was granted tenure a year later. Constance was also busy, studying journalism and communications, and her sister Marguerite Zandstra would baby-sit on weekends. Kristin's Aunt Marge would later fondly recall how the cherubic little girl had had a passion for music and dancing from the beginning.

In early 1979, Constance gave birth to a baby boy named Brent, and Kristin's earliest memory is of her brother being born in the Memphis suburb of Germantown. From the beginning, Kristin bonded with Brent and they would always remain close.

A year later, the Rossums moved to the northern Chicago suburb of Wilmette, when Professor Rossum was appointed associate professor of Loyola University's Department of Political Science. Within a year he'd made associate dean of the graduate school, publishing well-received books and monographs on the American Constitution and the criminal justice system. Among his published works at that time were *Police, Criminal Justice, and the*

Community, and *The Politics of the Criminal Justice System*.

In Chicago, four-year-old Kristin's reading and writing skills were well advanced for her age. When she started school, she stood out from all the other little girls with her radiant beauty, natural curiosity and enthusiasm to learn.

One day her Aunt Marge came to school to collect Kristin for a trip to the circus.

"I noticed when I went into her classroom," recalled her aunt, "Kristin was in the front row with her hand real high, waving. She seemed to have a very good rapport with everyone."

That Christmas, Constance took her little daughter by train to downtown Chicago to see *The Nutcracker Suite* at Marshall Field's department store. Kristin was riveted by the glamorous ballerinas, deciding there and then to become one. Years later, she would dance a leading role in *The Nutcracker*, developing an obsession with the classic Tchaikovsky ballet.

"I was absolutely enchanted by the experience," she would later remember.

When Kristin was six, Constance launched her beautiful daughter into a modeling career. Success came quickly when the angelic blonde child was selected from hundreds of other children to star in a national advertising campaign for McDonald's.

Then, in 1983, the Reagan administration hand-picked Ralph Rossum for the U.S. Department of Justice, appointing him deputy director of the Bureau of Justice Statistics. His highly influential new position was equal on paper to that of deputy assistant attorney general. An acknowledged expert in the field, he was put in charge of compiling statistics on juvenile crime in America.

Once again the Rossum family was on the move, this time to Bethesda, Maryland, just outside Washington, DC. Constance, who now had degrees in Journalism, Political Science and Communications, found a job as a marketing manager for Marriott Host International. The Rossums were now part of the Washington, DC, elite, and seemed destined for success.

Within easy driving distance of the capital, and close to the Smithsonian Institution and other national monuments, Bethesda was a picture-perfect town. Everything from the trash receptacles to the street lights, the flower pots to the well-groomed trees lining the sidewalks, was dictated by the Montgomery County Planners. Soon after they arrived, a new extension of the Metro subway Red Line was opened, linking Bethesda to downtown Washington, DC. Bethesda was just the place to bring up young children.

Eight-year-old Kristin entered Seven Locks Elementary School in Bethesda, soon discovering a love of the sciences.

"I remember feeling like a big girl at the elementary school, and feeling so grown up," Kristin said years later. "Just becoming really interested in studying."

The Seven Locks School was affiliated with the American Ballet Company and Kristin began ballet lessons, displaying a raw natural talent. Her mother now saw her daughter's future career in professional ballet, persuading her to give up modeling and concentrate on dance.

"I loved it," Kristin would remember. "It was great fun."

She soon was selected for a small walk-on role as one of Rosalind's pages in the Joffrey Ballet's performance of Sergei Prokofiev's *Romeo and Juliet* at the Kennedy Center. Kristin was stagestruck.

"The experience of being backstage surrounded by such grace and beauty is something that has truly touched my spirit," she would later write. "Hearing the powerful score of Prokofiev, being brought to life each night by the orchestra. There is so much passion in his notes."

Professor Ralph Rossum was also busy building up an academic network. His influential friends in government soon included future U.S. Supreme Court Justice Antonin Scalia, who became his mentor. The ultra-conservative Scalia frequently visited the Rossum home, and the two men became close, later teaching courses together and co-authoring several articles.

An ardent Republican, Rossum instilled his values in his daughter, later creating in her a strange dichotomy of hedonism and conservatism. Kristin looked up to her father and was proud of his achievements, often boasting to school friends that Justice Scalia was a good friend of her family.

But just as Kristin was settling into her pampered new life in Bethesda, everything changed. This time the West Coast beckoned when Professor Rossum was recruited to the prestigious Rose Institute for State and Local Government at Claremont McKenna College outside Los Angeles.

In January 1984, he moved to California to take up his new post, leaving his wife and two children behind in Washington.

For the next eighteen months, Professor Rossum divided his time between Claremont and Washington. He was put in charge of a million-dollar training project for juvenile justice reform, a two-year program funded by the U.S. Department of Justice. The project's mission was to draft a juvenile justice code, which included organizing a national conference and various workshops and training sessions all over America.

Finally, in June 1985, Ralph Rossum summoned his wife and children to Claremont, where Kristin's idyllic, protected childhood would soon turn into a nightmare.

Chapter 2

Claremont

Inspired by England's Oxford University, Claremont is an intellectual oasis that has little in common with the rest of Southern California. Lying thirty miles west of Los Angeles, its six prestigious colleges are set like precious gems in the heart of the city. By and large Claremont exists in a vacuum, sheltering itself from the outside world to protect its rarefied cloistered existence. But nothing had quite prepared it for Kristin Rossum.

It was once home to the Cahuilla Indians, who roamed its lush plains in the shadow of the San Bernadino Mountains for centuries, prior to the arrival of the Spanish conquerors in 1771. The new settlers stole the tribe's lands, setting up Mission San Gabriel and forcing many of the Native Americans into working for the padres as shepherds. In 1883 two smallpox outbreaks decimated what remained of the unfortunate Cahuilla, virtually wiping them out.

Three years later Claremont was put on the map when the Santa Fe Railroad opened its new track between Chicago and Los Angeles. A year later Pomona College was founded, which would set the stage for the town's future academic life.

Then the citrus industry moved in, establishing water cooperatives to irrigate the groves. The city's architecture still bears the mark of early Spanish colonialists and the citrus industry.

Claremont's six cloistered college campuses, all complete with their own well-cultivated gardens, occupy 300 acres of land and are within walking distance of each other. After Pomona College, specializing in the arts and sciences, came Scripps College, teaching fine arts and humanities. In 1947 Claremont Men's College was founded for public affairs. The fourth one was Harvey Mudd College, teaching science, mathematics and engineering, followed by Pitzer for behavioral sciences. The last of the six to be built was Claremont Graduate School.

The city's social and cultural life revolves around the colleges, which organize an array of concerts, plays and exhibitions. The six colleges, which boast of combining an intimate academic environment with all the cultural advantages of a full-scale campus, are also Claremont's biggest employer, with an enormous influence on its 35,000 citizens.

In 1976, Claremont Men's College went co-ed, changing its name to Claremont McKenna and fast gaining a reputation as an influential conservative stronghold. When Professor Ralph Rossum arrived a few years later, he knew he'd finally found where he wanted to settle down permanently with his family.

Ten-year-old Kristin entered Conduit Elementary School on North Mountain Avenue in Claremont, with just a few weeks remaining of her third grade year. Constance, who had recently been promoted to director of marketing for the Marriott Corporation, had selected the school for its specialized dance classes. Kristin soon became a straight-A student, relentlessly competing with her new classmates for the best grades.

"I was expected to do well in school," she would later say. "I wanted to make my parents proud of me. I wanted to be the best in everything I did. I wanted to be perfect."

And Kristin excelled at everything she did with the exception of writing, which she did not consider her strong suit. She would later remember her mother telling her she couldn't write, after she had worked hard on a school project.

"I felt like a failure," Kristin remembered. "Instead of working to improve at my writing skills, I shifted my attention to math and science. I liked it in part because I was good at it, and in part because my parents weren't."

Kristin enjoyed being better than her parents at something, as she could take full credit. It also didn't hurt that it made her parents proud of her.

One semester at Conduit, Kristin's class attended the D.A.R.E. anti-drug program, where she first became aware of methamphetamine and other drugs. But it would be several years before she would start experimenting with them herself.

A few months after moving to Claremont, Constance Rossum became pregnant again, giving birth in 1986 to a second son they named Pierce. That summer Ralph Rossum, funded by a special grant from the National Endowment of the Humanities, conducted a three-week seminar for fifteen federal judges and law professors on the relevance of the American Constitution. The Rossums were now among the elite in Claremont, and they felt as if the sky was the limit.

When Kristin began her freshman year at Claremont Junior High School, her mother enrolled her in ballet classes at a dancing academy in Anaheim. Twice a week, her father would drive her to and from practices, and during the sixty-four-mile journey, they developed a close father–daughter bond.

"I got to know her," Professor Rossum would later remember. "I thought we had a very good relationship."

During the drive home they would listen to classic radio dramas, like "Box 13," starring Alan Ladd as Doc Holliday. Although Professor Rossum would get "irked" when the rehearsals ran overtime, he would always be supportive, constantly telling his daughter how she made him proud.

Kristin now set her sights on a dancing career, practicing for hours every day. Over the next few years, she would appear in local productions of her favorite ballet, *The Nutcracker Suite*. Each fall she would attend rehearsals daily, and her father would always ferry her there and back.

By now, Kristin was dancing competitively, and her world revolved around her blossoming dance career. But despite all the hours she spent on her ballet, Kristin maintained an A average at Claremont. Her studies seemed effortless, and her parents had high hopes for her future.

"I think that my conflicts surrounding ballet emerged around twelve or thirteen," she later wrote. "I was hypercritical of myself, my technique, my body [and] my inflexible back."

She felt frustrated by her physical limitations, and became jealous of her fellow ballet students, who she believed were physically better equipped. It distressed her that she did not possess the "God-given genetics" to be "the best . . . the prima ballerina."

But she still found time to make new friends at Claremont Junior High School, where her quick wit and bubbly personality made her a popular student. Soon after she arrived, she met another professor's daughter named Melissa Prager, Often the girls would overnight at each other's houses and Melissa got to know the Rossum family well. The two girls became part of a tight group of friends who hung out together after school, attending dances on weekends.

"Kristin was always one of the best students in the class," remembered Prager, "as far as sitting in the front of the classroom and [being] eager to answer any questions."

Kristin also became close friends with an English girl named Corrine Bright, whose father was also a professor at the Claremont Colleges. They were both at the top of their classes and competed ruthlessly with each other, both academically and socially.

"We were best friends and goody-two-shoes," Kristin would later write in her journal. "To completely love another person . . . completely and without reservation is perhaps the greatest gift life has to offer."

Despite her parents' strong Republican leanings, Kristin joined the school's Amnesty International Club, writing letters to political prisoners of conscience all over the world. She was in a club picture printed in the 1991 Claremont School Year Book, as a fresh-faced blonde sitting on a bench outside the school.

Friends from that time remember Kristin as a quiet, intelligent girl who kept to herself.

"She was incredibly thin, which was something I was always jealous of," recalled Jenn Powazek, who took ballet classes with Kristin. "She was pretty quiet . . . not gossipy or talkative like the rest of us, and an incredible ballerina."

During her first year at Claremont High, Kristin was selected by the Orange County Ballet Company to play the Sugar Plum Fairy in its production of *The Nutcracker*. She was ecstatic.

Initially Kristin was to understudy a professional dancer, but the company decided to allow the 14-year-old amateur to dance the main role. Her Cavalier was a professional dancer from the Houston Ballet.

"I felt like it was a dream come true," she said. "The role meant hours and hours of rehearsal and an enormous time commitment."

That Christmas, Kristin's proud family was in the audience to watch her perform, her father filming it for posterity. It was a triumph, and perhaps *the* greatest moment of Kristin's life.

But a few months later an injury would destroy her ballet career forever and send her into a tailspin.

In 1991, Ralph Rossum uprooted the family yet again when he was sent to Hampden-Sydney College in Virginia on a year-long sabbatical. Kristin was delighted to move back East, where there were better ballet-training opportunities. She was awarded a place at St. Katherine's School, as a border. It was an hour away from where her family was staying, and she would be able to dance with the prestigious Richmond Ballet.

Soon after arriving, during her sophomore year, Kristin was accidentally dropped by her dance partner, taking a bad fall and tearing ligaments in her ankle. For the next two months, she had a cast on her leg and could not dance. Desperate to resume her dancing, Kristin came back before her ankle was fully healed and soon re-injured herself, suffering a stress fracture to her foot that wouldn't heal. Her dreams of a successful ballet career were finally dashed forever.

Kristin became depressed and lost motivation. She began drinking beer, smoking cigarettes, even trying marijuana for the first time, which she said had little effect.

In summer 1992, Ralph Rossum completed his year sabbatical and the family returned to Southern California. They moved into a bigger, more expensive house in one of the best areas of Claremont. It had a big back yard where Brent, now an eighth-grader, and Pierce, who was in kindergarten, could play soccer.

Kristin re-enrolled at Claremont High School for her junior year, but she found everything had changed in the year she had been away. Her best friend Corinne had moved to England, and Kristin no longer related to her old friends. So she found a new set that her parents did not approve of.

Kristin had also gone through puberty during her year in Virginia, and begun dating a young man named Chris Elliott, who was five years older.

"She came back as a young woman," her father would later explain. "There was a real physical maturity that occurred during that time. [Now] she caught the eye of people that shouldn't have had contact with her."

In late October, before a big football game at Claremont High, one of Kristin's new girlfriends offered her a hit of crystal methamphetamine. She accepted, sniffing several lines of the white powder in her friend's car before they went to see the game.

"I remember it feeling good," she would later fondly recall. "[A] kind of euphoria. You feel very revved up and energetic and happy."

Kristin was so enamored with the drug that she sought out her friend's dealer, and began scoring regularly. But when her old Claremont High School friends heard she was snorting methamphetamine, they ostracized her, as they didn't approve of hard drugs.

"I lost friends," she later admitted. "Our social group did not approve of speed."

Kristin then started running with the "stoner" crowd at Claremont High, going to parties where she was introduced to other drugs like cocaine.

Over the next few months, her whole attitude to life changed as she became hooked on methamphetamine. She began neglecting her personal hygiene, developing sores on her face which she would scratch incessantly. She also became obsessed with her weight, developing an eating disorder and using a laxative to purge after meals.

Melissa Prager began to suspect that Kristin had developed a drug problem, and confronted her one day. Kristin looked hurt, totally denying that she was taking crystal methamphetamine. But Prager was not convinced.

Kristin's grades also began to suffer as she lost focus, finding it difficult to concentrate. By the second semester of her junior year, she was getting B's across the board. For the first time she started being late with class assignments, or missing them altogether.

"[I was] just worn out, tired," Kristin would later explain. "I had gotten to the point where what started off as a good feeling was just something I really needed to feel normal."

At first, her mother put Kristin's bad grades and behavioral changes down to "teenage angst" and her new set of friends, none of whom she ever brought home.

"She just didn't seem like our Kristin," Constance Rossum would later explain. "She had always been very neat and organized. That was no longer the case."

Every time she asked her daughter what was wrong, Kristin brushed it off, saying it was nothing and promising to get better grades in the future. And over winter 1992 Ralph and Constance Rossum had many discussions about what was wrong with their daughter.

"Ralph wanted to give her a bit of space," Constance would later say. "I had the Mommy antenna rising a little bit."

Professor Rossum, who is reported to have helped draft Nancy Reagan's "Just Say No" anti-drug program, later maintained that he had no idea Kristin was hooked on methamphetamine. But that would soon change.

"It's one of those situations," he would later testify, "when you understand what the issue is, the scales fall from your eyes. And suddenly, okay, now I understand a whole series of things that up to that point just didn't seem like Kristin."

Chapter 3

Trouble in Paradise

In March 1993, Ralph and Constance Rossum celebrated their twenty-first wedding anniversary with a week-long Caribbean cruise, leaving their sixteen-year-old daughter in charge of her two younger brothers. They left cash in an envelope for pizza, and a list of numbers to call in an emergency.

Soon after they had left, Kristin began inviting her friends, including her methamphetamine dealer, over to her house to party. She bought drugs from the dealer, using the money her parents had left for her brothers' food. During the week her parents were away, she would put the boys to bed and then smoke crystal meth downstairs, staying up all night, talking to friends and listening to music.

St. Patrick's Day was Pierce's birthday, so she threw a party for him. Word soon spread around Claremont High School that she was having a "rager" while her parents were away, and everyone was invited. It started quietly in the afternoon when some of her "good friends" came over to share a birthday cake and ice cream.

But later that night, it turned into an open-house, as a procession of seniors and football players arrived with beer and drugs, leading to complaints from the neighbors. Some of her drug buddies also rifled through the house, stealing a video camera, her parents' credit cards and a checkbook, which they later used. They also took the Rossum family car for a late night spin around Claremont.

When Kristin's parents returned the following Sunday, neighbors told them of the noisy party while they had been away. When they discovered the credit cards and checks missing, they confronted Kristin, who denied everything. But her parents were still suspicious and punished her by withdrawing her driving privileges. They also called Claremont police, filing a burglary report and giving names of their daughter's friends whom they didn't approve of.

The following Tuesday evening, her brothers, alarmed by Kristin's now-erratic behavior, searched her room. They found a glass crack pipe, a mirror, a razor blade and some Ex-Lax, and told their parents.

The Rossums were furious and confronted her as she tried to walk out at 7:00 p.m. carrying her backpack. Kristin claimed she was on her way to the library to study for a class, but her parents were suspicious. Her father demanded to see what was in the backpack, snatching it from her when she refused to give it to him. On opening it, he found a white box inside and demanded to know what it was. Kristin burst into tears, claiming it was a present for her mother. But when Rossum insisted on looking inside and saw drug paraphernalia, he immediately realized what was going on.

Then, frustrated by all her lies, he began smacking her on the arm as her mother looked on.

"He grabbed me real hard by my left arm," Kristin would later tell Claremont police. "He then started hitting me with his fist four or five times on my upper left arm."

Finally, according to Kristin's account, Professor Rossum let go of his daughter, picked up one of her sandals and began hitting her on her buttocks, as her mother slapped her in the face, calling her a worthless slut.

Hysterical, Kristin suddenly grabbed a kitchen knife, screaming that she was going to kill herself. Her father wrestled it away, and she ran upstairs, locking herself in the bathroom. When one of her brothers came down, saying that Kristin had some razor blades, Ralph Rossum dashed upstairs to discover her cutting her wrist in what he would later describe as a "melodramatic" suicide attempt.

"[It was] nothing too serious," Prof. Rossum later told police. "The razor blades were taken away from me."

Kristin eventually composed herself enough to come downstairs, where she tearfully admitted she had a drug problem, saying that she had taken crack three times. Feeling "mortified" and "devastated" that her parents had discovered she was on drugs, she promised to clean up.

"We all agreed to work on the situation," her father told police at the time."

The next morning, Kristin went to school and started acting strangely. She began pounding her fists against the school walls and lockers, threatening to kill herself. When her friends Melissa Yamaha and Kelly Jackson, who had been at her party, asked what was wrong, she told them her father had beaten her up, displaying her bruised arm.

"Melissa and I were very worried about Kristin," Kelly later told police. "She has really changed during the past week."

They were so concerned about Kristin's welfare that they went to a school counselor, saying they feared Kristin's parents were physically abusing her. The matter was then referred to the head teacher, Barbara Salyer, who summoned Kristin into her office to investigate. But Kristin refused to discuss what had happened.

On Friday morning, Salyer called in Claremont police, as she was mandated to under California law. Officer Laurence Horowitz was assigned to investigate the child-beating allegations, interviewing Kristin and her two friends in the head teacher's office.

"Kristin seemed depressed," Officer Horowitz later wrote in his report. "I observed that she had pulled all of her nails away. There were fresh wounds on her knuckles and she had appeared to have picked at old sores on the back of her hands."

Initially, Kristin refused to tell what had happened. But eventually she broke down in tears, telling him how her parents had beaten her after finding out about the party and that she had been using crack. She told him she had become so upset that she had considered cutting her wrists, but now things had improved at home.

The officer then examined her left arm, taking photographs of her extensive bruising.

"I think she minimized it significantly," he would later say. "She didn't want to get her mom and dad in trouble."

Officer Horowitz, a trained social worker who has worked with juvenile drug addicts, told Kristin to inform her parents about their interview, and that he would call them later that night.

Back at the Claremont police station, he contacted the Child Abuse Hotline, writing a report which he telephoned in to Child Welfare Services.

A few hours later, Kristin called the Claremont Police Department asking for Horowitz. She told him she wanted to fully explain what her father had done, claiming he had never hit her. She now said her heavy bruising had occurred when Professor Rossum had restrained her, after she had tried to flee the house. An hour later, Horowitz telephoned Constance Rossum, arranging to interview her and her husband at 8:00 a.m. the following morning.

When the officer arrived at the Rossums' plush Weatherford Court home, he immediately realized that Kristin was not the normal type of girl to be involved in hard drugs and family violence.

"She came from a very privileged background," he remembered. "The Rossums lived in a large, very upscale home in one of the more preferred necks of the woods. My guess is that they felt my involvement was not something they wanted."

Ralph and Constance Rossum were cordial, inviting the uniformed officer into their front room, where they explained how frustrated and angry they had become at the shock of finding their daughter involved with drugs.

"Ralph got mad and did hit her on the arm," Constance

said. "I admit that I slapped her in the face, but she tried to hit me first."

She hadn't taken her daughter to the hospital after she had cut her wrists, saying, "I was afraid of what would happen."

Her father also admitted striking Kristin "three or four times" for betraying his trust.

"I realize that there is a lot going on and that we need some help," he told Horowitz, going on to describe his work with the federal government developing its juvenile crime policy.

Horowitz advised them that a Child Services worker would be in contact, later filing a second report to the Child Welfare Services. Apparently no further action in the matter was ever taken, but three months later, one of the stolen checks surfaced with Kristin's name on it.

Soon after Kristin's run-in with Claremont police, her parents brought her to their family physician, Professor Richard Mabie, for a physical check-up, concerned about any damage from methamphetamine. They told the doctor they had "found this drug stuff," and, as Professor Mabie gave Kristin a full physical examination with her mother present, he delivered a stern lecture on drugs. He gave her a clean bill of health, assuring the Rossums that there had been no long-term damage.

The Rossums also consulted several other doctors for advice on how to deal with Kristin's drug problem, and Constance even called in the Betty Ford Clinic.

"We had a representative from the Betty Ford Center come to our house and discuss an intervention," Ralph Rossum would later testify. "We concluded that an intervention was not going to be helpful, first of all, because interventions work when people deny they have a problem. We all knew that Kristin knew and acknowledged that she was using meth."

He then enrolled Kristin in a Narcotics Anonymous

twelve-step program in Chino, well away from Claremont so they wouldn't be recognized. And for the next two months, Rossum attended the twice-weekly three-hour family meetings with Kristin, never missing a single one.

"She knew how important I thought this was that we get that problem behind her," said her father.

After completing the program, Kristin seemed to be back to her old self, proudly declaring that drugs were now in her past. Her parents were convinced she was cured and that they could get on with their lives.

Professor Rossum had now been made director of an annual week-long think-tank for fifteen federal judges, discussing the Constitution and the Bill of Rights. He was in charge of selecting the judges for the prestigious seminar at Claremont McKenna, chairing all the sessions.

That summer, Kristin stayed clean. She went to summer school and got a job in a local video store to make extra money. She was also an enthusiastic member of her school's a cappella choir, performing in several concerts.

But that fall, in her senior year she ran into one of her old drug friends, asking him to hook her up with a dealer. Before long, she was back into crystal methamphetamine, scoring regularly from a boy at school.

When her grades began to suffer, her father recognized the symptoms, immediately suspecting she had relapsed.

"We started to see that kind of picking behavior on her knuckles that we had seen before," he said. "I think we saw some weight loss. We were also getting progress reports in school. Kristin, who is brilliant when it comes to math, was doing very poorly in Calculus. That made no sense to us. So we knew there was a problem again."

For the rest of the year, there was tension in the Rossum household as her frustrated parents debated what to do. Kristin was now careful to keep her drugs and her paraphernalia well hidden, always vehemently denying that she was using and acting hurt that anyone would even question her about drugs.

She and her parents also argued about her choice of

friends. The strait-laced Rossums disapproved of many, and would try to prevent their daughter from seeing them. Kristin would staunchly defend them as good people, accusing her parents of trying to control her.

"Mr. and Mrs. Rossum don't like [us]," one of Kristin's high school friends told police at the time. "She is very curt with us and will not allow Kristin to talk with us. They don't seem like very friendly people."

On January 14, 1994, Kristin, now 17, went to see an evening performance of the musical *Oklahoma!* at Claremont High and was given some meth and a pipe from a male friend. After smoking some of the drug at the show, she took the rest home, getting high the following morning before going to school.

That afternoon she came home wearing her brother Brent's clothing, which Constance had warned her not to do.

"Kristin seemed agitated," her mother would tell police. "I began to suspect that she had been using speed again."

When Constance accused her daughter of using drugs, Kristin frantically grabbed her chest and tried to run away. But her mother restrained her, searched her bra and discovered a glass pipe. Then, at her wits' end, she telephoned Claremont police, asking them to come over and deal with Kristin.

By coincidence, Officer Laurence Horowitz got the call at 10:45 p.m., and drove to Weatherford Court with a female uniformed officer. His second encounter with the Rossums left such an impression, he could recall it vividly almost ten years later. As the father of three teenaged daughters who also went to Claremont High, he could easily relate to the Rossums' situation.

Horowitz was shocked at the sight of the drugged-out Kristin Rossum he saw that day. She seemed totally different from the polite, clean-cut girl he had interviewed at school nine months earlier.

"They were two different people," he recalled. "*Agitated* was about the only way I can describe her. Mom was also visibly distressed about the whole thing."

As soon as Horowitz arrived, Constance handed him Kristin's crack pipe and a little plastic bindle of meth, accusing her daughter of having a two-year drug problem. The officer immediately noticed in the well-lit front room that Kristin seemed to be under the influence of drugs. Her pupils were visibly enlarged, she had a dry mouth and was unable to express a clear thought or form complete sentences. He then checked her pulse, which was racing at 118 beats a minute, and measured her pupils.

Kristin then admitted she had smoked crystal in her bedroom that morning, even naming the Claremont High School boy who had supplied her.

"I have not used any speed since this morning," she declared. "I use the drugs to help me with school studies and other activities."

Then, as Horowitz arrested the tearful girl for possession of drug paraphernalia and being under the influence of a controlled substance, Constance Rossum voiced her frustration.

"This incident is the last straw, and something needs to be done about this," she told him. "My husband and I had first denied it. We have tried doctors and therapy, but nothing so far has worked."

After reading Kristin her rights, Horowitz handcuffed her and drove her to the Claremont police station, where she was photographed and gave a urine sample. Her mug shot reveals just how the beautiful teenager's looks had been ravished by drugs. Her emaciated 5'2" body weighed just 105 pounds, and her eyes were red and swollen from crying.

Later that night, Kristin was released into her parents' custody. As she had no previous convictions, the case never went to juvenile court.

When word got out at Claremont High School that Kristin had named names when she was arrested, she began to be harassed. Her life was threatened and her parents received telephone calls demanding money. One morning Professor Rossum went to his mailbox in front of his home and found a bag of methamphetamine, which he took straight to the police.

By the end of January, Kristin's parents decided to take her out of Claremont High School for a safer environment.

Chapter 4

Redlands

The perfect opportunity to give Kristin a fresh start came when Professor Rossum was offered a year-long teaching position at the University of Redlands.

Kristin had accumulated enough credits to graduate a semester early from Claremont High, and in February 1994, she enrolled at Redlands on a Presidential scholarship.

"Redlands seemed like a good place for school," Professor Rossum would later tell a jury. "Good school, good science program. [That semester] she just took two courses. She was getting herself ramped up to go full-time in the fall."

Situated thirty miles east of Claremont on I-10, the private liberal arts and sciences university was considered one of the best in America. It would also allow Professor Rossum, who had arranged for Kristin to take her two courses on the same days he was teaching, a chance to get reacquainted with his daughter, as he drove her to and from classes.

Her 1994 graduation photo in the Claremont High School Yearbook betrays no hint of Kristin's drug problem. Dressed in an off-the-shoulder black gown with a simple string of pearls, she looks like the all-American graduate, with more than a passing resemblance to movie star Gwyneth Paltrow.

But it was a tough first semester for Kristin, who came

down with mumps, later catching chickenpox on the day of her final exams. Despite having to postpone taking them, she still managed to get good grades. And during their three-times-a-week forty-five-minute drives to and from the campus, she and Professor Rossum enjoyed the kind of father–daughter talks they hadn't had since her ballet days.

That spring, Professor Rossum traveled to London to co-direct an international conference, comparing the English and American juvenile justice systems. For a few months, at least, family life in the Rossum household returned to normal; her parents were proud that Kristin had finally cleaned herself up.

"We thought we had our Kristin back," said her mother.

During her summer vacation, Kristin stayed in Claremont, resuming her friendship with Melissa Prager, whom her parents approved of. Melissa was dating the lead guitarist of Fat Finger, a local garage band, and one day she took Kristin to hear them practice.

Kristin was immediately attracted to the band's bass guitarist, Teddy Maya, and a few nights later she went to see them play at a party. Afterwards, some of the guests went hot-tubbing together and she and Maya struck up a conversation. Kristin told him how she loved the Grateful Dead and reggae music, and he was struck by her beauty and intelligence.

"She was sweet," remembered Maya, who felt drawn to the beautiful hazel-eyed blonde. "She was an upbeat, incredibly cheery person to be around, and really pretty. We started dating."

Raised in Claremont, Maya had just finished his first year as a Political Science major at UCLA. When Kristin brought him home, Constance Rossum was impressed and encouraged the relationship.

"Her parents were nice enough, but they were very conservative," he remembered. "I think that their lifestyle reflected their conservatism, and they had a nice, big house— over a million dollars. It had even a second storey, and that's pretty rare in Southern California."

Constance whipped up eggs Benedict for brunch, as she asked Maya about himself and his family. Maya remarked on numerous pictures of the Hamburglar proudly adorning the walls, and Constance explained how she had worked on the McDonald's Chicken McNugget marketing account.

One Sunday, Teddy brought Kristin to his house to meet his parents at brunch. From their first meeting, his psychologist mother, Karen Maya, felt there was something strange about Kristin, and that she was not what she appeared to be.

"I found her very guarded," Karen recalled. "A very careful young woman. We probably spent an hour together and I thought, 'Who is this girl?' She was enigmatic and something about her troubled me."

On their dates, the young couple would often discuss politics, and Maya was surprised by Kristin's ultra-conservative views.

"She did buy into her parents' mindset," he said. "She was proud of her dad's relationship with [Supreme Court Justice] Scalia, and that he was buying a new Lexus. Once, we got into an argument about welfare reform, which was the big issue of the day. And she was just talking about how horrible welfare is and how these homeless people are just lazy. I thought it was horrible that she believed the sort of traditional conservative, family value–type bullshit that her parents were feeding her."

In the fall semester, after her father's year-long assignment had finished, Kristin became a full-time border at the University of Redlands, moving into the Grossmont Dormitory on campus. Every weekend Teddy Maya would drive to Redlands from UCLA, collect Kristin and then drive her back to Claremont.

They would go for romantic dinners at T.G.I. Friday's or see a movie, and she once persuaded him to go bungee-jumping with her. By this time, he was in love with Kristin and they were discussing marriage. When they weren't together, they would talk on the telephone almost every night, discussing their future.

"She was always telling me how much she wanted to see me," he remembered. "But then at one point, she stopped answering the phone. I thought, 'Why can't I get hold of her? Where is she?' "

A few weeks into the fall semester, Kristin relapsed into drugs after being offered crystal meth at a party by a fellow student in her Advanced Calculus class. Soon she was getting high every day and her grades plummeted.

"I thought I could study harder, work better," she would later explain to a jury. "[I was] not realizing my limitations and how quickly that would snowball into more regular use."

On Tuesday, October 25, 1994, Kristin celebrated her eighteenth birthday with a family outing, and once again, her parents had no idea she was back into drugs. Ironically, Professor Rossum was now working on a major article for the *Pepperdine Law Review* entitled, "Holding Juveniles Accountable: Reforming America's 'Juvenile Justice System.' " In the scathing article, published a year later, Rossum labeled the juvenile justice system as a complete failure.

"The juvenile courts fail to teach juveniles that they will be held responsible for their criminal acts," he wrote. "As a consequence, serious juvenile crime is soaring while the public's confidence in juvenile justice is plummeting."

But even if the professor failed to spot his own juvenile criminal problem in his daughter, Teddy Maya suspected that some of the "pretty bad things" his Claremont friends had told him about Kristin might be true.

"I got into a big fight with one of my friends and I would not believe the things he was telling me," said Maya. "But at some point it became clear that these things were true."

Just before the Christmas holidays, Kristin was expelled from Redlands, after drugs were found in her room. But when Maya drove to Redlands on Friday, December 16, to spend the night, Kristin seemed upbeat, never mentioning that she had been asked to leave the university.

The next morning, Professor Rossum's birthday, Constance Rossum had arranged to drive to Redlands to bring Kristin back to Claremont for the Christmas vacation. But, too ashamed to tell her parents she had been kicked out, Kristin took her favorite brown leather jacket and ran away.

At noon, Constance Rossum and her youngest son Pierce arrived at the dorm and found no sign of Kristin. While they were searching her room to see if she had left a note, the phone rang. Constance answered and was horrified to hear her daughter's old Claremont drug dealer on the line, asking for Kristin.

"I said, 'I know who you are. I know what you have done. Now stop it!' " she would later testify.

The university was deserted, as students had left for vacation, so Constance and her young son got in their car and drove back to Claremont. Ralph Rossum was livid when he heard his daughter was missing and that her old drug connection was still in the picture. Over the next few hours, he frantically called Teddy Maya and his mother, knowing that Teddy had seen Kristin the night before.

"That was peculiar," remembered Karen Maya. "I had never spoken with him or Mrs. Rossum before, and he seemed rather put out. His tone of voice was belligerent. I had no idea where she was, and neither did Teddy."

Nine days later, on December 26, Kristin called Teddy, asking him to meet her at Redlands. He dropped everything and drove to the campus, where she fell into his arms and asked him to get them a hotel room for the night. He was shocked at her haggard appearance. She was running a temperature of 104 degrees and was "pale and clammy" from days of taking crystal meth.

"She must have been coming down from a long binge," he said. "She was obviously really messed up and she told me she hadn't slept for I don't know how long."

That night, as they made love, Kristin opened up to him as never before. She told him she had been staying in nearby Hemet with a boy she knew, but swore she had remained faithful. She had then gone to Newport Beach to spend Christmas with another male student from Redlands and his family. Then they had driven her back to Redlands.

But although Maya was suspicious that she had been playing around, he once again fell under her spell.

"She was telling me I was great and saying whatever I wanted to hear," he sadly remembered. "I mean, she was such a good liar that I think she basically believed her own lies."

While they were in bed, Kristin tearfully admitted that she had been expelled for drugs and was ashamed she had let her parents down again. She told Teddy about her problem with methamphetamine and how she had lied to him in the past. Now, she vowed, she would give up drugs once and for all so they could be together.

"I was so young and naïve," he would later admit. "I thought this person was the love of my life, and I wanted to get married. I told her she could come back to LA so we could be together. I had all these fantasies about how we can make things work and get an apartment. And she's just, 'Yeah, you're so great.' "

The next morning they got up and Kristin told Teddy to shower first. But when he came out of the bathroom, she had disappeared from the hotel room without a trace, stealing $200 out of his wallet.

Kristin's parents had been frantic when there was no word from their daughter. They initially filed a missing persons report with the Redlands Police Department but then, on Christmas Eve—seven days after her disappearance—they received a mysterious call from a stranger, claiming that their daughter was alive and well.

Two days later, when they discovered she had briefly resurfaced in Redlands with Maya before disappearing again, they called the Claremont Police Department and filed a second missing persons report. Professor Rossum told Officer George Dynes that his daughter was "depressed and suicidal," and that he had tried everything to locate her. The official report describes Kristin as 5'2" with blonde, chin-length hair, green eyes and wearing a waist-length brown leather jacket.

Constance Rossum would later say she feared that Kristin had been "harmed or kidnapped," and was back on drugs. Over Christmas week, the Rossums received a series of hang-up calls that they were convinced were from Kristin.

"I suspected because I heard mewing on the other end," said her mother. "It was a very sad month."

After she abandoned Teddy Maya in the Redlands hotel room, Kristin smoked some meth and went to the Amtrak Station, buying a one-way ticket to San Diego. When she arrived at Central Station, she took a trolley to Chula Vista, near the Mexican border, checking into a cheap, run-down hotel. That night she took the trolley four stops south on the Blue Line to the Mexican border and literally ran into Gregory de Villers.

Chapter 5

Greg

Gregory Tremolet de Villers was born in Chicago on November 12, 1973, the first of three sons. His parents Yves and Marie Tremolet de Villers were French and had emigrated a couple of years earlier, seeking a new life across the Atlantic.

Yves de Villers had always been ambitious. As a high school student in Montpellier he had passed his French baccalaureate in Mathematics and Philosophy before going to Montpellier University to study medicine and the sciences. After graduating, he served his internship working in hospitals around Montpellier.

In the early 1970s he fell in love with a beautiful young physical therapist named Marie. They married and then moved to America, which had better opportunities. They settled down in Chicago, where Dr. de Villers became a general surgeon at the Michael Resse Hospital and later an instructor of Surgery at the University of Illinois.

In early 1973, Marie became pregnant with Greg, who was personally delivered by his father on the living room couch. Exactly two years later, after the family had moved to Palm Springs, CA, their second son, Jerome, was born, followed by their youngest son, Bertrand, in 1979.

By the 1970s, Palm Springs was no longer the glamorous Hollywood playground it had once been, when it was a favorite of Frank Sinatra, Bob Hope and Bing Crosby.

Situated seventy-five miles east of Los Angeles, it had become run-down and would later be best known as the home of the Betty Ford Center.

The de Villers family thrived in Southern California, appearing to be living out the American dream. Dr. de Villers became a successful plastic surgeon with a thriving practice in Palm Springs, while his wife worked as a physical therapist. He was also appointed an assistant clinical professor of plastic surgery and teacher at the UCLA School of Medicine.

But in September 1981, one month before Greg's eighth birthday, his parents had an ugly divorce, which affected him deeply. In the divorce papers, Marie accused her husband of beating her with a closed fist until she was black-and-blue. In her signed divorce petition, she said she was afraid of her husband and that he had threatened to disfigure her face.

Twenty years later Marie would say she could not remember ever making these accusations.

She was granted custody of the three young boys, and Dr. de Villers moved to live in Monaco on the fashionable French Riviera. There he started a new life among the jet set, reportedly performing plastic surgery on Princess Grace before her tragic death in 1982.

Back in California, Marie de Villers struggled to bring up her three sons in a modest apartment, finding herself broke after legal fees for the divorce. She got a job as a physical therapist to make ends meet, always managing to feed and clothe her boys.

"My mom worked," said Jerome de Villers, "and my dad paid some child support."

Eventually, Dr. de Villers stopped supporting Marie and the children and they struggled to survive. But their many hardships only served to bring them far closer than most families. Years later, looking back at their childhood, Bertrand would acknowledge some resentment against their estranged father, but said that he and his brothers never stopped loving him.

As the oldest son, Greg became a surrogate father to his two young brothers, taking care of them and dispensing help and advice.

"He was special," said Laurie Shriber, a neighbor in Palm Springs, who was very close to the de Villers boys growing up. "We would do everything together on the weekends: hiking, movies, playing in the pool. We got a chance to watch those boys grow up."

Greg was a good student at Palm Springs High School and had many friends. His kind, good-natured attitude and positive outlook on life made him popular, and his younger brothers worshipped him.

"[We were] like normal brothers," Jerome would later testify. "But the fact that we didn't have any other family members in this country made us closer."

Bertrand said that Greg was like a father to him growing up, and always took care of the family.

"We'd run into hardships, but we'd always get through them," he remembered. "With my father gone, [Greg] was one of the providers for the household. He was very rational, calm and level-headed."

Christian Colantoni, who became good friends with Greg at Palm Springs High School, would later remember him as "happy, positive, outgoing." Over the years they became very close, often taking trips together to go skiing.

Another member of their close-knit high school group was Christian Maclean, who also stayed close friends with Greg after they graduated.

"[He was] a terrific friend," Maclean later remembered. "He was very outgoing, enjoyed his friends."

As a teenager, Greg wanted nothing to do with his father, blaming him for the divorce, which had taken a hard toll on his mother's health. A heavy smoker since her teens in France, Marie was rushed to the hospital several times with collapsed lungs. In those emergencies, Greg would always be there to raise everyone's spirits and nurse her back to health.

In 1991, 18-year-old Greg graduated Palm Springs High

School and spent two years at the College of the Desert (COD) in Palm Springs, building up enough credits to get into a better university. Founded in 1958 as a two-year junior college, COD had 3,000 students, of which only 500 were full-time.

To put himself through college and get extra money to help support his family, Greg found a part-time job filling shelves at Longs Drugs in Rancho Mirage. Once again, Greg's vibrant personality endeared him to everyone, and he made many lasting friendships at the store.

"I grew up playing tennis with Jerome, Bert and Greg," said fellow Longs employee William Leger. "We used to go hiking and skiing on the weekends."

Two years later, Greg was accepted into the prestigious University of California San Diego (UCSD) and moved out of the family home. Greg's relationship with his father became even more strained when Dr. de Villers reportedly refused to pay his tuition. Always independent, Greg decided to go it alone, getting a student loan and working for Rush Legal Services to pay for his education.

"I don't think Greg was bitter towards my father," Bertrand would later explain. "He decided that he was just fine on his own to succeed in life without help from my father."

By 20, Greg had blossomed into a handsome young man, standing 5'10" with curly brown hair. He had a ready smile that lit up his whole face and made people feel at ease. He had never had a long-term girlfriend and was somewhat inexperienced when it came to dating.

A year later, Jerome won a scholarship to UCSD and moved in with Greg and another student named Christopher Wren, whom they'd met at campus orientation. The three students signed a one-year lease on an inexpensive two-bedroom apartment on campus. Greg shared one bedroom with Wren, while Jerome slept in the other.

For a while, they lived the perfect student life, socializing together and hosting their many friends on weekends. But everything changed when the three de Villers brothers and their friend Aaron Waldo decided to have a fun night out in Tijuana.

The day after Christmas, Kristin Rossum was still coming down from crystal when she caught the trolley from Chula Vista to San Ysidro, by the Mexican border. It was early evening and the light was fading as she walked through the turnstile at the border crossing and dropped her brown leather jacket.

"I bent to pick it up and kind of bumped into Greg, literally," she would later remember. "We hit it off from there."

Greg gallantly introduced himself, his brothers and Aaron Waldo in French, and Kristin happily responded in her schoolgirl French. She told them she had just arrived in San Diego and was living in a motel until she could find a job, as she knew nobody in town. So Greg suggested she hang out with them that night, and Kristin readily agreed.

They all walked over the bridge into Mexico and hailed a taxi to Revolución Avenue, which Greg explained was the main drag for bars and clubs. From the moment they met, Greg seemed smitten with the beautiful blonde, giving her his full attention and hardly speaking to the rest of his party.

When they arrived at Revolución, they went straight to a bar, ordering a round of beer with tequila shots. It was obvious to everyone that Greg only had eyes for Kristin, so they left them alone.

As they moved from bar to bar, Jerome and Bertrand watched from the sidelines as Greg and Kristin got to know each other, discussing their lives. But, although Greg was very open about himself, Kristin was reticent, not mentioning at that point that she was a runaway.

"She had these eyes that would stare at you in a flirtatious manner," remembered Jerome. "[It was] mainly Greg, but if I tried to talk to her, she would give me similar eyes. I didn't know what was going on."

At one bar, Greg swept Kristin onto the dance floor and the others watched, as they passionately gyrated to the loud Mexican music.

It was the first time 14-year-old Bertrand had ever had alcohol, and he soon began to get drunk. At 2:00 a.m., they decided to go home. Greg asked Kristin where she was staying.

"I had only explained a little about my situation," Kristin would later testify. "I didn't tell him much."

She sadly explained that she was sleeping in a cheap hotel in Chula Vista until she could get on her feet. Greg said that it wasn't a safe neighborhood, suggesting she spend the night with him at his apartment. Kristin thanked him for his gallantry, saying she'd love to.

That night they had sex for the first time, and from that moment on, Kristin and Greg would be inseparable.

"My brother was pretty naïve when it comes to girls," Jerome would later say. "Kristin is an attractive girl and he was attracted to her. That's not love at first sight."

Chapter 6

San Diego

Kristin moved in with the brothers at La Jolla del Sol Apartments that night, changing the whole dynamic of their living situation. Jerome and Chris Wren were uneasy about having her live with them, but Greg insisted, saying he wanted to help her. So Wren moved out of Greg's room and into Jerome's—paying the same rent, as Kristin didn't have any money.

Within a week, Greg had declared his love for Kristin, asking her to be his live-in girlfriend. She eagerly agreed, saying that she felt the same way.

"He fell for her hard," said Jerome. "After they met, it was hard to see my brother without her."

A couple of weeks after she had moved in, Greg found a meth pipe in Kristin's jacket pocket. He was unsure what it was. Greg disliked all drugs, disdaining even his roommates' attempt to grow a pot plant. He asked them for their opinion.

"I knew it wasn't marijuana," Jerome would later remember. "It had a whitish-yellow substance in it."

When Greg confronted Kristin about smoking crystal methamphetamine in their apartment, she readily admitted a drug problem. She tearfully told him that she was now trying to quit, as she couldn't face her parents while she was tweaking. Greg was sympathetic and understanding, saying that he loved her and would help her give it up once and for all.

"I raised my concern," said Jerome. "I remember times when she was really twitchety[sic]. Really jerky."

Kristin also confessed her addiction to Chris Wren, saying she had run away from her family. She boasted of being at the top of her class, vowing to stay off drugs and straighten herself out.

By mid-January 1995, Kristin felt confident enough to write to her parents, asking to come home. In the letter, which bore a San Diego postmark, but no address, she promised to call soon. A few days later, she telephoned her mother in Claremont and they had a highly emotional fifteen-minute conversation.

"She wanted to come home and see us and see her brothers," Constance would later testify. "She reported that she had begun to get herself together and didn't want to come back until she could show us that she meant it this time. She said that she had met some nice people, and was staying with them."

She also telephoned Teddy Maya, claiming to have been kidnapped at gunpoint by white slavers and driven around Mexico in the trunk of a car before she escaped.

"She was obviously pretty messed up," he said. "That was not a rational story, and there were lots like that."

The following weekend, Greg lent Kristin his car while he and Jerome visited their mother in Palm Springs, and she drove up to Claremont to see her family for the first time in more than a month. Her anxious parents and brothers were waiting when Kristin arrived at the house for a tearful reunion. They all hugged and kissed, and Kristin said she had only run away to get off drugs and had now turned her life around. And she told them of Greg de Villers and how he had become her knight in shining armor, by helping her kick dope.

"Mom, I have three jobs," she declared enthusiastically. "I started at California Pizza Kitchen, I'm working at Monterey Pasta in La Jolla, and I'm teaching ballet to young children in the public school with a dance company called Twinkle Toes."

Her parents were delighted to have their wayward daughter back again, and instantly forgave her. They took her to church and then out for dinner, before buying her a California Pizza Kitchen uniform for her new job. As she was leaving, Kristin wrote down Greg's address and telephone number so they could contact her there. And she promised to stay in close touch.

"[There] were a lot of happy tears shed," Kristin later recalled. "Very hopeful."

Then Kristin went to the Claremont train station to meet Teddy Maya. Although she had driven up in Greg's car, she told him she had taken the train. They went to Nick's Café, their old dating spot, where she repeated the story of being kidnapped by white slavers.

"Kristin told me a lot of different stories about why she disappeared out of that hotel room," he remembered. "She said she had met Greg in San Diego and was staying with him.

"And I still wanted her back. After everything, I would have loved it to have worked out, to have it all turn around and be okay. I mean, I was young and in love. What did I know?"

During her first few months in San Diego, Kristin was a hive of activity. Every morning she left Greg's apartment early to go to work at one of her three jobs, returning late at night. But, before long, she found a new drug connection and began secretly using again. To pay for the drugs, she stole money by overcharging customers at the California Pizza Kitchen, and was subsequently fired. Years later she would maintain that she'd bought meth from her tips, and was dismissed for lateness and billing transaction errors.

Although Greg might have been besotted with her, there was great tension in the apartment as things started going missing. One day, Greg complained to Jerome that his treasured gold ring bearing the de Villers family crest had disappeared, along with an expensive gold necklace. Two of Chris Wren's bank checks also went missing while he was away on vacation.

When Greg accused some of Jerome's friends, his brother suggested that Kristin was responsible, leading to a big argument. Greg angrily insisted that that was impossible, but finally agreed to ask her.

To his surprise, Kristin immediately confessed and burst into tears, admitting her drug relapse. Initially Greg was furious, but soon forgave her, again vowing to help her beat her addiction. He even found her a new job with him at Rush Legal Services, so he could keep a closer eye on her.

"And then I realized how much I really did like Greg, and that he wanted to help me," she would explain. "I did end up giving him back the checks. Later he explained that to his roommate."

Whenever Chris and Jerome questioned Kristin's integrity, Greg would leap to her defense. He would become passionate, explaining how he was helping her beat drugs and that she was the love of his life.

"We didn't understand why Greg wouldn't realize and wake up that things were missing from the apartment," explained Wren. "She's stealing money trying to support the addiction. It was an admirable thing he was trying to do, but . . ."

Kristin soon became a divisive influence on the brothers. And Chris Wren found himself in a difficult position as Jerome and Greg constantly argued over Kristin, and whether she should stay.

"It was very apparent that she was separating the brothers," said Wren, who decided to look for a new apartment when their lease ran out that summer.

Over the next few months, Kristin's behavior became even more disturbing. Chris Wren thought her "bipolar," observing how her "quirkiness" came and went for no obvious reason. And he began to get suspicious that Kristin was cheating on Greg when he came home to find a strange man alone with her.

But her bizarre behavior at a small party in their apartment made him even more uncomfortable. As they were welcoming guests, Kristin seemed to be under the influence of something. She sat on Wren's lap and when somebody asked if they were a couple, she started to cry, saying she needed to talk to him outside on the balcony.

"[She was] in one of these emotional states," Wren remembered. "She felt I was meant to be with her and it wasn't Greg."

In February, Kristin invited her parents to San Diego to meet Greg over a long lunch. The Rossums drove down and met Kristin and Greg in the parking lot of Sfuzzi Restaurant in the historic Gaslamp Quarter. It was a weekday, and Greg, who was working part-time at Rush Legal Services, came on his lunch hour. He was dressed casually, wearing a suede jacket and sunglasses, which he later removed in the restaurant. Constance Rossum was instantly struck by his "very kind eyes."

Professor Rossum felt awkward meeting this new man in his daughter's life whom he had heard so much about. Besides, he was still smarting from how she had "thoroughly messed up" his Christmas season by running away.

But after a couple of hours with Greg, the professor was most impressed with his easy charm and good looks.

"I thought Kristin had met a really good person," he would later testify. "We liked him. We had a good time."

Kristin had carefully briefed Greg not to say they were living together, knowing that her parents would not approve of the arrangement. She had told them she was sharing an apartment with a female friend from Monterey Pasta Parlor.

The Rossums returned to Claremont relieved that their daughter was safe and in good hands. And a month later, Professor Rossum arranged to deliver her furniture and possessions to where she said she was living, in Point Loma, by the U.S. Naval Station.

Soon afterwards, her parents discovered she had been lying all along, when they kept calling and found her with Greg and never with her girlfriend. But they resigned themselves to the situation, considering it the lesser of two evils. At least she was not living in a crack house.

"I consider myself a devout Episcopalian," Professor Rossum would later explain. "I don't approve of premarital sex. Greg and the life they had together was much better than the life she had been going through before."

That April, Ralph and Constance Rossum summoned Kristin to dinner to discuss her future. The professor still had lofty academic ambitions for his daughter, and had decided she should return to the university to complete her education.

Kristin agreed to enroll at San Diego State University (SDSU) and her parents said they would pay her rent and tuition. They bought her a 1990 Toyota Cressida for $5,000, and her mother began looking for a new apartment for her. Constance called the superintendent at La Jolla del Sol Apartments, where Greg and Jerome were living, managing to secure an apartment for Kristin at a reasonable rent.

Constance next obtained the forms to enroll Kristin in SDSU and filled them in herself, omitting any reference to her daughter flunking out of Redlands University.

To ensure that Greg did not move into the new apartment with her daughter, Constance wrote to the complex's super, insisting Kristin have no visitors.

"I didn't want to support Greg de Villers and have him move in with Kristin, since I was paying the bills," she would later explain. "That changed when they said they were getting married, and we couldn't control it."

In June, Greg proposed marriage to Kristin and she accepted. He asked her to move to Monaco where his father had his plastic surgery practice, saying they could study in France.

Kristin's parents were less than enthusiastic.

"Ralph and I were very stern," said Constance. " 'We can't stop you from getting married. But we want you to go back to school, get a job and then get married.' I asked them to wait."

Professor Rossum also weighed in, emphasizing the importance of getting a first-rate education if they were to make something of themselves. He told them they were young and should get their degrees before thinking about getting married.

Greg and Kristin agreed to put their wedding plans on hold, but remained informally engaged.

That summer, Kristin stayed away from drugs, enjoying her new clean and sober life with Greg. In July they moved into Apartment 204 at the La Jolla del Sol complex on Regents Road, near Greg's old one on the UCSD campus. Jerome, who was "shocked" at hearing that his brother wanted to marry Kristin, had now transferred to the University of California in Santa Barbara to study economics. And Chris Wren found new roommates, relieved to be away from Kristin and the tension she had caused.

The small $700-a-month one-bedroom apartment was perfect for a young couple working for their degrees. It had a balcony overlooking quiet Regents Road and plenty of room for Kristin and Greg to study. Constance Rossum personally furnished the apartment, buying a dining room table, four chairs, a TV and VCR and some new kitchen equipment. And over the next four years, the Rossums would estimate, they gave the couple almost $75,000

Kristin started part-time at SDSU as a freshman, taking two courses in Biology. She still worked twenty hours a week at Rush Legal Services, serving subpoenas and copying documents. And Greg, who now worked full-time for the company, agreed to resume studies at UCSD, where he majored in Biology.

Although Greg's name was on the lease for the new apartment, Ralph Rossum paid the rent. He also gave Kristin spending money, paid for her tuition and books, and bought her clothes and gasoline and car insurance for her Toyota.

"We'd send checks to Kristin and she would give them to Greg or however they divvied it up," said her mother. "They would remind us if the rent check was late."

According to Constance, Greg now became part of their family, developing a very close relationship with her husband.

"Greg loved Ralph," she would later testify. "He looked at him as a surrogate father."

Over the next four-and-a-half years, the Rossums would see a lot of Greg. Once a month they would drive down to San Diego and take them to dinner, and Kristin and Greg would also regularly stop off in Claremont on their way to visit his mother in Palm Springs.

Since kicking drugs, Kristin had started referring to Greg as "my angel," and the Rossums were delighted that she was now studying hard and back on the straight-and-narrow.

"They seemed a perfect couple," Professor Rossum later remembered. "They seemed in love—very committed and concerned about each other. Greg was looking after a pretty girl."

Kristin later said that she and Greg became very close during this period, spending all their time together, apart from working.

"We got along wonderfully from the time we met," she would say. "He was basically my best friend. I really needed the steady support he was able to offer me."

That summer, Kristin's best friend at Claremont High School, Melissa Prager, tracked her down and they renewed their friendship. The two had lost touch after Kristin's disappearance. So when she telephoned, suggesting they meet for lunch in San Diego, Kristin was delighted. She invited Melissa to come over for dinner and spend the night.

But according to Prager, the evening was a disaster, as the usually genial Greg uncharacteristically showed little interest in getting to know her.

"[He didn't] seem to want me there," she would later say. "I was excited to finally share some time with Kristin, and he never left the room. I felt very uncomfortable."

In the summer of 1996, Kristin went to the south of France with her parents. It was the first time she had been apart from Greg since they had met eighteen months earlier. Although there was a nine-hour time difference between France and California, every day at a prearranged time, Greg dutifully called Kristin, who would be waiting by the phone.

"[It was] kind of giddy and childish," said her mother. "[Like] lovebirds."

That winter, Kristin switched her major to Chemistry and became a straight-A student. Studying under Professor Bill Tong, who would later call her one of the best undergraduate students he ever taught, she shone academically. Professor Tong was so impressed with his beautiful new student, he hand-picked her for his research group, where Kristin had to use lasers to study chemical reactions. Without the crippling distractions of crystal methamphetamine, Kristin was highly motivated and seemed capable of achieving anything she set her mind to.

"I observed her to be a team player," Tong would later remember. "She always [had a] positive attitude. She [had] all the qualities of a good research student."

Professor Tong actively encouraged Kristin to go to

graduate school, believing she had the right stuff to become a "leading scientist" one day.

Her parents were delighted when she was selected as the outstanding junior in the SDSU Chemistry Department that year. They closely monitored her academic progress, satisfying themselves that she could not be taking drugs, as her workload was so tough.

"We just thought the drug issue was permanently and completely behind her," said Professor Rossum.

On Friday, October 25, 1996, Kristin turned twenty and Greg drove her down the toll road to the Lobster Village in Puerto Nuevo, Mexico, to celebrate. When Kristin opened the glove compartment to put in the toll ticket, she glimpsed a jewelry box. After a romantic lobster dinner, they returned to the car, where Greg opened the glove box, gallantly bringing out an engagement ring and slipping it on her finger. Once again he asked Kristin to marry him and she gladly accepted.

The following day, Kristin drove to Claremont to show her mother her engagement ring. She happily described Greg's romantic Mexican proposal. But Constance Rossum told her she hoped it would be a long engagement.

A couple of days later, Kristin's Aunt Marge and her grandmother, who happened to be visiting from back East, came to San Diego with her parents for a small engagement party at a local restaurant. Kristin turned up late by herself, explaining that Greg couldn't make it as he was in bed not feeling well.

"We were very excited because we were going to meet him for the first time," said her aunt. "But we didn't get to meet him."

Chapter 7

The Medical Examiner's Office

By summer 1997 Kristin and Greg had been together two-and-a-half years, and against the odds, they seemed to be making it. Their friends thought them a perfect young couple that was going places, and Kristin's parents still considered Greg their daughter's savior from drugs.

On June 4, Kristin applied for one of two student intern positions at the San Diego Medical Examiner's Office. She was interviewed by Frank Barnhart, the ME's laboratory manager. He was impressed, and hired her on the spot. At the time, Kristin was reading Patricia Cornwall novels, and identified with Cornwall's forensic pathologist heroine, Dr. Kay Scarpella.

Now in addition to her studies at SDSU, Kristin spent a couple of days a week at the ME's office, seven miles west of her apartment. As a lowly student intern among the fifty employees, she worked in the toxicology section, doing menial lab work, like keeping the glass equipment clean, logging in specimens and later preparing them. But within a few months, she was given the additional responsibilities of drug screening, sending drugs out for analysis and sample preparation. She worked with five pathologists and two other student workers, and she loved the informal atmosphere of the office. Kristin decided that her future lay in forensic pathology.

"She was an excellent student worker," remembered toxicologist Catherine Hamm, who had worked at the ME's office for twelve years.

Kristin's early reviews from laboratory manager Dwight Reed were enthusiastic. She was seen as a very bright, hard worker who learned fast and was dependable. But as there had been no background checks when she applied for the job, no one at the ME's office knew of her former drug addiction. She was given free access to the samples of hard drugs, including methamphetamine and heroin, often found at scenes of accidental death. For a while she was content to do her job and merely log the drugs into her computer. But that would soon change.

The same month, Greg graduated from UCSD and began looking for work. Kristin attended his graduation ceremony, and a few days later, the Rossums came to San Diego for a celebratory dinner. Greg had recently been offered the position of manager at Rush Legal Services, but was also interested in a career in fish farming, as he liked the outdoors. Professor Rossum took his future son-in-law in hand, counseling him to aim far higher and utilize his Biology major.

"I told him, 'Look,' " Professor Rossum would later testify, " 'you are not taking advantage of your educational experience.' "

So the Rossums introduced Greg to a friend who had good contacts in the gaming industry. The friend arranged for Greg to take a basic examination with the Department of Fish and Game. But just two days after Kristin started at the ME's office, Greg heard he had failed the exam. He was crestfallen.

Over the July Fourth weekend, Kristin joined Greg and his youngest brother on the first of three family backpacking trips to Mammoth Lake. She and Greg drove four hundred miles to the popular Northern California ski resort to meet Bertrand, who had just been accepted into UCLA.

"I considered Kristin a sister," Bertrand would later remember. "She was part of the group."

Greg and his two brothers had been hiking in Mammoth for years and knew the trails well. They immediately headed to Duck Lake, where they made camp, before setting off on a six-mile hike up the mountain. Kristin was out of condition, finding the hike difficult, but Greg, a seasoned hiker, soon came to her rescue.

"Greg had to pay a lot of attention to her," said Bertrand. "I remember it was quite a struggle for her."

Bertrand observed the couple's interaction for the first time since they had met in Tijuana. He thought they seemed devoted to each other, and was happy the relationship appeared to be going so well.

Over the long weekend, the brothers also made a point of spending quality time together. They discussed their mother Marie, who had been ill lately, and who was moving to Thousand Oaks in the fall. Jerome, who would soon graduate from the University of Santa Barbara, planned to move there too, so he could be near her. Their father was also back in the picture: having launched a successful plastic surgery and liposuction practice in Thousand Oaks, he was now splitting his time between Southern California and Monaco.

Toward the end of 1997 Greg interviewed for a job at an up-and-coming San Diego biotech company called Pharmagen, and was hired. The company's vice president of research and development, Dr. Stefan Gruenwald, made him his assistant and office manager. The German-born doctor liked Greg from the beginning, taking him under his wing and becoming his mentor.

Apart from assisting Dr. Gruenwald, Greg did general office work, including filing and preparing computer databases. And over the next few months, Greg worked hard to prove himself, developing a sterling reputation as a reliable and tenacious worker. He was soon promoted to licensing manager, but Dr. Gruenwald had his eye on Greg for much bigger things.

• • •

On October 3, 1997, Kristin Rossum logged in a vial of ten milligrams of fentanyl citrate, a toxic poison almost a hundred times more powerful than morphine. It was the first time she had ever come into contact with the drug, which is highly restricted.

Later, during the course of her work, she would learn how fentanyl was first introduced in 1968 by a Belgian pharmaceutical company as an anesthetic in surgery because of its minimal effects on the heart. Later, doctors found it useful in treating chronic pain.

But in the 1980s, illegal laboratories began producing fentanyl derivatives, which produced similar effects to heroin and morphine. They were soon sold on the streets of Los Angeles under the names of "China White," "Goodfellow," and "Tango & Cash."

At one time, the San Diego ME's Office had routinely tested bodies for fentanyl, but that had stopped in the early 1990s. Not only was it was too expensive, finding instances of the drug was almost unheard of, as pharmaceutical fentanyl was only available in hospitals and in the offices of medical examiners.

Throughout 1998, Kristin and Greg worked long hours at their various jobs and studies. They settled into a routine, with Kristin playing the part of the dutiful wife while she studied hard at SDSU and made her mark at the medical examiner's office. She appeared to be content with her busy life in San Diego, telling old friends how happy she was to have found Greg, and how he'd saved her in her time of need.

But secretly she was growing restless with her new stability, looking for adventure outside the relationship. Since her drug days had ended, her natural beauty had reappeared, and she turned heads wherever she went.

That winter, Kristin embarked on a passionate affair with

a fellow worker at the ME's office named Dick Henderson (not his real name). They started taking long lunches together and began a physical relationship, meeting wherever and whenever they could. It would be the first of several secret love affairs over the next couple of years of which her fiancé would know nothing.

At Thanksgiving, Ralph and Constance Rossum invited the de Villers family to Claremont to discuss arrangements for Kristin and Greg's upcoming nuptials. Her parents had finally given their blessing—Greg was now working and their daughter was one semester away from graduating—and a wedding date had been set for June 5, 1999.

"We were perfectly happy," said Professor Rossum, "delighted to give our blessing to their future marriage."

Greg, his mother Marie, and two brothers, Jerome and Bertrand, sat around the Rossums' dinner table to finalize details for the wedding. Constance Rossum was making all the arrangements, and had already booked Claremont College's prestigious Padua Hills Theater for the private ceremony and reception.

Marie de Villers said she wished to be listed on the official wedding invitation as "Dr. and Mrs. Yves R. Tremolet–de Villers. But Greg became furious to find his estranged father's name on the invitation list.

"Greg started shouting at us," Constance would later testify. "He didn't want his father at the wedding. He wanted nothing to do with him."

Constance told her future son-in-law to be "civil," and that it was his mother's decision. Greg then grudgingly backed down, but stayed unusually silent for the rest of the meal.

Things were working out well for Greg in his new job at Pharmagen. By Christmas, he had been promoted, and invited Kristin to the staff Christmas party. Kristin looked radiant, as her proud fiancé introduced her to his boss, Dr. Gruenwald, and the rest of his new colleagues.

At the party, Greg and Kristin happily discussed their impending marriage with everyone. They seemed the perfect young San Diego couple who both seemed destined for success. And although Greg didn't know it yet, Dr. Gruenwald had already hatched a plan to start a new company with his ambitious young assistant playing a key role.

In early January 1999, Kristin went with Greg to his dentist, Dr. Milder, for treatment for a painful wisdom tooth. In his office, she heard the doctor tell Greg he would have to remove the tooth, and would use a powerful painkiller called fentanyl to dull the pain. On January 8, Dr. Milder sedated Greg with fentanyl via an IV for the successful procedure. Then Kristin took him home.

A month later, a middle-aged investigator at the county medical examiner's office, Stan Berdan, suddenly died. His untimely death caused a stir at the ME's office and was the topic of much discussion.

To avoid any possible conflicts of interest, and in line with the ME's policy, Berdan's body was sent to the UCSD for autopsy, but all the toxicology work stayed in-house at the ME's office.

As a student intern, Kristin had occasionally rubbed shoulders with Berdan and was aware of the ME's policy of dealing with deaths of staff members or their close families. She would eventually utilize this knowledge, prosecutors would later contend, with fatal consequences.

Since the Rossum and de Villers family meeting at Thanksgiving, Kristin and her mother spoke almost daily, fine-tuning the wedding arrangements. Together they contacted caterers, worked on the invitation list, and began looking for wedding dresses so Kristin could look her best on her wedding day. Constance Rossum planned the day with almost military precision, hoping it would be the Claremont society wedding of the year.

In April, two months before the wedding, Constance organized a secret lunch in Claremont to meet Greg's father for the first time. Dr. de Villers, who was in California on business, attended with his ex-wife Marie, but Greg was not told, as they feared he would cause a scene.

"It was a very nice lunch," Constance would later remember. "Yves is very charming and learned. He's very formal and flowery."

Dr. de Villers asked Professor Rossum to mediate a reconciliation with Greg. But when he tried to do so, Greg was adamant that his father not attend the wedding.

"It was the one issue [where] I really saw passion and flaring anger," said Professor Rossum. "Real passion."

A few weeks later, Greg discovered that his father had secretly met his future in-laws.

"He was irate," Kristin would later testify. "He did not want me to have any contact with his father whatsoever. But I wanted to make sure I know both in-laws before proceeding with the wedding."

Two years later, Kristin would tell police that she had wanted Greg to be a "bigger man" and reconcile with his father.

"He had no desire whatsoever," she said. "He said 'No, my life is better off without him.' "

Even while finalizing her wedding plans, Kristin was carrying on her affair with Dick Henderson, and exchanging passionate e-mails. In April 1999, Henderson left San Diego for a law job in New York and e-mailed Kristin at her SDSU address, saying, "Hey, Gorgeous. Miss Me?"

A month later, he e-mailed again, asking: "Hey, how are you? I was a little worried about the last time we spoke."

Now, a few weeks away from graduation and marriage, Kristin began to have second thoughts, suddenly realizing that her life would change forever. And as she had always done, she looked to her parents for support and advice.

Professor Rossum was supportive when he received an

emotional phone call from his daughter, saying that she was seriously considering cancelling the wedding, even though the invitations had all gone out.

Said Professor Rossum: "I told her, 'Look, if you want out, it's going to be complicated to tell Greg that you don't want to marry him when you are actually already living with him.' "

He even offered to hire a truck and drive to San Diego to help her move out of the apartment and come back to Claremont. Kristin refused, saying she would come and see them soon to talk it out.

Later she would claim to have been having "doubts and reservations" about marrying Greg for months.

"I was getting very nervous about the wedding," she said.

When she went to see her parents to talk out her "wedding jitters," Greg insisted on coming too. Constance took her daughter to a nearby park so they could be alone while Professor Rossum had a heart-to-heart talk with Greg in the front room.

Breaking down in tears, Kristin told her mother she was "really scared." Although she loved Greg, she explained, she wasn't sure that she was *in love* with him.

"I was afraid," Kristin would explain. "I didn't know if I was doing the right thing."

Constance Rossum questioned the wisdom of cancelling the wedding at the last minute.

"We decided the wedding should go on," Kristin said. "I decided that day that it must be cold feet."

On May 20, 1999, Kristin was inducted into the Phi Beta Kappa honor society, joining the likes of Presidents Bill Clinton, George H. W. Bush and six current Supreme Court justices, including Professor Rossum's friend Antonin Scalia. Founded a few months after the Revolutionary War, Phi Beta Kappa is the nation's oldest honor society and the most prestigious. Its SDSU chapter was established in 1974 for the most distinguished students in the arts and sciences.

Professor Rossum was there for her initiation, especially proud after all the troubles she had put the family through. Drugs now seemed to belong to Kristin's past, and he looked forward to her following in his footsteps and making her mark on the academic world.

A few days later, Kristin attended her first professional toxicology conference, a sign that the young intern was a shoo-in for a permanent job at the ME's office. That year the California Association of Toxicologists (CAT) held their annual conference in San Diego and Kristin was one of several ME's office employees selected to go.

She was introduced to some of the leading forensic toxicologists, and her flirtatious smile and good looks impressed many. Brimming with confidence, Kristin made easy conversation with the other delegates, telling them how she longed for a career in toxicology.

"She was still an intern at that time," remembered Dr. Daniel Anderson, a supervising toxicologist with the Los Angeles County Coroner's Office, who said she was overly friendly with the delegates, both male and female. "Obviously she's striking in her appearance, and I got to know her a little bit. I remember she flirted with everyone . . . kisse[d] the women also.

"She's a manipulator, and knew just how to get what she wants in life."

Chapter 8

A Blushing June Bride

On Saturday, June 5, 1999, Kristin and Greg were married in a beautiful outdoor ceremony on the grounds of the Colleges of Claremont. It was a perfect sunny day and more than one hundred family and friends were there to help them celebrate. But few guests knew that the wedding had almost been cancelled the night before.

As the wedding party gathered at the Rossum house prior to the rehearsal dinner, the twenty-five-year-old groom was furious, discovering that his father had been invited to the wedding.

According to the Rossums, Greg flew into "a rage," and started shouting about calling off the wedding. Constance Rossum apologized for not telling him that Dr. de Villers had been invited, saying she should have been more sensitive. Then her husband took Greg to one side for a man-to-man talk.

"Look, if you don't want to marry Kristin," Ralph told him, "don't marry Kristin because you don't want to marry Kristin. Not because your father is in town."

Finally Greg calmed down and went back to his motel before joining the wedding party at a local restaurant for the rehearsal dinner, which went off without a hitch. Kristin left to spend the night at her parents' home, while Greg and his brothers went back to his motel for a few drinks, celebrating his last night as a bachelor. Back in their motel room, somebody rolled a marijuana joint and passed it around. Greg took a hit, surprising his brothers and their friend William Leger.

"He acted like he was high on marijuana," remembered his brother Bertrand. "I think he felt like he shouldn't have done that. He didn't really like it."

The next morning, Greg was nervous when he arrived for the 11:00 a.m. outdoor ceremony at Mount Baldy, with his best man, Jerome. Immaculately dressed in his morning coat, his spiky dark hair brushed back neatly, he seemed awkward and uncomfortable.

After the scene the night before, Professor Rossum had asked Dr. de Villers not to show up at the wedding to save further embarrassment. Rossum even warned the priest, caterer and few select family friends to expect trouble if Greg's father came.

"We wanted people to be on guard in case that happened," explained Professor Rossum. Dr. de Villers diplomatically did not attend after being warned there might be a scene, although he had contributed $1,500 for the liquor.

Constance Rossum supervised her daughter's wedding preparations at the house, where a hairdresser and florist were making sure she looked her best.

"She seemed happy," remembered her mother. "She had decided to marry Greg."

Greg's childhood friend Laurie Shriber remembers the groom being "delighted" and "very much in love."

By 10:30 p.m. the one hundred invited guests started arriving for the wedding, which had a rustic theme. Many of Greg's high school and college friends turned up; Jerome de Villers was surprised that none of Kristin's were there and that there were no bridesmaids to attend her. But whatever she lacked in friends, she made up for in family. For the Rossums far outnumbered the de Villerses, who all lived in France. And many of Professor Rossum's Claremont academic colleagues had been invited to the prestigious social event.

To capture the joyous day, the Rossums had hired a

video production company as well as a still photographer.

Just after 11:00 a.m., to the strains of Johann Sebastian Bach, Professor Rossum escorted his daughter down the white satin aisle. Kristin looked beautiful, in a lacy white gown with a décolletage. Her long blonde hair was braided above her head, held in place by a matching white headband, and she wore a single string of pearls. She was also holding a bouquet of a dozen white roses, her favorite flower.

Greg turned to look at his bride for the first time in her wedding dress, and a smile lit up his face. Then the music stopped as the priest began the ceremony to join Greg and Kristin together for life in holy matrimony.

After a moving liturgy, the priest asked Greg if he took Kristin to be his wife until death they did part. He smiled at her nervously, before replying, "I do."

"Kristin," continued the priest, "will you have this man to be your husband?"

"I will," she declared as the priest placed her gold wedding band on her finger.

It was all over in twenty-five minutes, and now Kristin and Greg were man and wife, after a four-year engagement.

"It was a perfect wedding," Professor Rossum would later say. "The weather cooperated. The liturgy was beautiful. The music was sublime."

The Rossums' official wedding photographer, Christopher Michael, thought it a really classy affair.

"It was a gorgeous wedding," he remembered. "Kristin was beautiful and very pleasant and quite shy."

Then, after taking the official photographs of the bride and groom, everyone adjourned to the Padua Hills Theater for the formal sit-down luncheon. After the lunch was served, best man Jerome de Villers stood up to launch the official round of toasts. Although Jerome did not particularly like Kristin or approve of the wedding, he said how happy he was for his brother as he raised his glass for a champagne toast.

Then the emotional bridegroom stood up to address the wedding guests.

"Kristin is the most wonderful person I've ever met," he said, looking at his new bride with love in his eyes. "[She's] incredible in so many ways . . . so intelligent, kind and caring . . . I can't wait to spend the rest of my life with her."

The newlyweds flew off that night to honeymoon in Whistler, British Columbia. They had a marvelous time hiking and snowboarding, before returning to San Diego to start married life.

Less than two weeks after the wedding, Kristin e-mailed her secret boyfriend Dick Henderson, saying that she still loved him although she had married Greg.

"Congratulations," Henderson e-mailed back from New Jersey on June 19. "I really can't wait to see you, too . . . I was really worried that you didn't love me anymore."

Henderson then told Kristin that he was due in San Diego in August, and would call her when he arrived.

That summer, Kristin took classes at SDSU to complete credits for her Bachelor of Science degree. She was still interning at the medical examiner's office, where she had been given additional responsibilities for analytical work.

Soon after the marriage, Greg told Kristin that he wanted a baby girl, and even went as far as naming this imagined first addition to their family Isabelle. But Kristin had no intention of becoming a mother, trading her studies and future career in forensic toxicology to be a stay-at-home mom. And that soon became a major issue between the newlyweds.

"[I was] developing more confidence," she would later explain. "I was thinking a lot about who I was and what was important to me in life. I think that Greg felt very threatened by that."

In early September, Kristin saw the Kevin Spacey movie *American Beauty* and adored it. The film, which would go on to win five Academy Awards the following year, tells of the obsessive crush an older married man (Spacey) has on his daughter's best friend (Mena Suvari), and his fantasies of her lying naked covered in red rose petals. It struck a real chord in Kristin, who would see it again and again, telling friends it was her favorite movie.

That fall, Greg helped organize a fishing trip off the coast of Mexico for six employees at Pharmagen.

"Greg said the fishing is better when the water is cold," said his boss, Dr. Gruenwald, who went along. "It was quite a long trip. We left at midnight and went all day and came back in the morning."

Kristin and the other spouses were all invited, but none attended.

While Greg was away, Kristin met up with Dick Henderson when he visited San Diego. Later, on October 25, he e-mailed her to thank her for the wonderful time they had spent together.

"Hey, sweetness," he wrote. "It was great to see you, although I wish we had more time together."

The previous March, Frank Barnhart, who had brought Kristin into the ME's office two years earlier, left after twenty-nine years to start working for the San Diego County Sheriff's Department's Regional Crime Laboratory. He had become good friends with Kristin, watching her excel as an intern. And in September he suggested his "Li'l Bandit," as he had affectionately nicknamed her, apply for a full-time job at the sheriff's department, promising to give her a good recommendation.

With her graduation in sight, Kristin eagerly filled in the official job application form on September 13, but this time her mother was not there to help her. And when she filled it out, she admitted to having been arrested and jailed for possession and being under the influence of a controlled substance. She also admitted using methamphetamine between thirty and forty times between September 1993 and May 1995, snorting cocaine twice between September and

November 1993, and smoking marijuana twice between September 1993 and June 1994. And she further owned up to having been fired from the California Pizza Kitchen "because of bill discrepancies and mistakes," explaining that drugs had "influenced my performance."

"She went overboard in her honesty," her mother, who had lectured on ethics, would later contend. "She had filled it out before talking to us."

Not surprisingly, Kristin was rejected by the sheriff's department as unsuitable, but though she had signed an authorization to release her personal information, word of her past criminal history never got back to the ME's office.

That Thanksgiving, Greg and Kristin went to Claremont to celebrate the holiday with the Rossum family. After only five months of marriage, Constance detected subtle strains in the relationship.

"He was obviously very much in love with her," she remembered, "but it wasn't as happy as it appeared to be earlier."

And Kristin's 14-year-old brother Pierce also complained that Greg had changed, no longer wanting to play games and watch movies with him.

"He stopped playing video games," Pierce would later testify. "Stopped talking with the family. [He] just became overprotective of Kristin and very clingy. He followed her from room to room."

At Thanksgiving dinner, Constance asked her new son-in-law what he wanted for Christmas. He told her he wanted framed baby pictures of Kristin as a 3-year-old, including one special one. After dinner, Constance took out the family album so Greg could select some.

"He had [a] special request, but I couldn't find that photo," she remembered. "I gave him the promise that he'd get it a little later."

Greg then selected a composite of Kristin's modeling pictures, as well as a few others.

If Greg ever suspected Kristin's affair with Dick Henderson, he never confronted her about it. And by December, when she finished her classes at SDSU, things had definitely cooled down between them.

"Merry Christmas," Henderson e-mailed her on December 17. "I miss you terribly and think about you all the time. I'm truly sorry we have grown apart."

But unknown to Henderson, Kristin had now embarked on a passionate new adulterous affair to provide the excitement fix she was craving. Although she dutifully sent out wedding pictures to all their friends and family as Christmas cards, Kristin had moved on from her marriage.

Later, Kristin Rossum would claim that it was at this point that she and Greg started drifting apart. And although she had been unfaithful with two ardent admirers whom she'd actively encouraged, she appeared to blame Greg for all their problems. At the beginning of January, Kristin had her first serious conversation with Greg about the state of their relationship.

"I told him that I was concerned . . . with how I was feeling about the marriage," she would later say. "Like I was not having enough personal space and not enough room to develop on my own."

And when her mother remarked how exciting it must be "to be newlyweds facing the new Millennium," Kristin came right out and told her they had "no future" together.

By mid-January, Kristin had embarked on a new affair with a student named Jack Hawkins (not his real name), with whom she had taken a class at SDSU. On Wednesday, January 26, 2000, Hawkins e-mailed Kristin.

"I like you a lot. [I want to leave] you with a burning desire to see me again as soon as possible. I promise that the next time you tell me you are tired, I will slow the pace and hold you awhile so you can rest."

Two days later, Hawkins e-mailed Kristin to fix up a

rendezvous, saying the following Monday would be good, as his girlfriend would be working.

On Monday, January 31, Hawkins wrote: "Let's meet in the park, 12:10. I'm about to leave the house, so I'll see you there."

But a couple of days later, Kristin was back in touch with Dick Henderson.

"Hello," she e-mailed. "Is anybody home? Missing you."

Henderson, now working for a New Jersey law firm, replied immediately, saying he missed her "terribly" and thought about her whenever he heard "Iris" by the Goo Goo Dolls.

A few days later, he followed up with an e-mail beginning: "Hello Gorgeous."

"I miss you, too," he wrote. "I'll be in San Diego in either June or July. We'll definitely get together. . . . How is married life? School? The M.E.'s Office? . . ."

In early February, Kristin submitted her official application to become a full-time toxicologist at the San Diego ME's Office. There was one available toxicologist position and Kristin had no doubt she would be accepted. In the formal application, she was never asked if she had a prior criminal history or whether she had ever been involved with drugs. And unlike the police department and other government organizations, the ME's office did not conduct background checks.

In her new job, Kristin would have easy access to many dangerous narcotics and stimulants, and temptation would always be there.

"I fell in love with the job," she would later tell Homicide detectives. "It was something I really loved, because it was something I was really close to. Close, probably too close."

On March 1, Kristin Rossum was formally offered the position of Toxicologist 1 by the ME's operations administrator, Lloyd Amborn. The new job paid $23,448 a year, with an increase of 3 percent on July 1. Kristin was jubilant that she would now have a career in forensic toxicology, and she called her parents immediately.

Later that day, Amborn sent her written confirmation of the job, and she began working full-time at the ME's office on March 10. Among her new responsibilities was to maintain the drug log, recording and managing samples of every illegal narcotic that came into the ME's office. She was also given a key to the office and could now come and go as she pleased, 24/7. Later, some would liken it to giving an alcoholic the keys to a brewery.

Things were also looking up for Greg de Villers. On February 16, Dr. Stefan Gruenwald left Pharmagen to start up a new biotech company he christened Orbigen. It was an ambitious endeavor with its stated mission of "Enabling the Proteomics Revolution," initially only employing a handful of people. But Dr. Gruenwald had given Greg the heads-up that if all went well, he would soon be hired.

With their demanding jobs, Kristin and Greg saw less of each other than ever. They both worked long hours, and by the time they got home, they were tired, speaking little about their deteriorating relationship.

On Monday, March 27, a couple of weeks after Kristin started full-time at the ME's office, Dick Henderson e-mailed her, asking, "Hey Stranger, is there anybody out there?"

Kristin immediately replied: "I have been thinking about you so much lately. I graduated in December am now a fully fledged TOXICOLOGIST here!!! . . . I miss you terribly."

The following day Henderson invited Kristin to fly to New York and spend a romantic weekend with him.

Kristin e-mailed back that it sounded like "great fun," and she would give it serious consideration. Henderson promised to take care of everything, if she could get away from Greg.

"Don't I wish that was possible," she replied a few

minutes later. "That might be a bit difficult to explain . . . But hey—a girl can dream can't she."

Henderson then e-mailed Kristin: "I am getting excited just thinking about it . . . My heart is racing and my palms are sweating."

But Kristin had no intention of flying to New York to see Henderson. For she was more interested in a tall, handsome 30-year-old Australian doctor named Michael Robertson, who had just been hired at the ME's office as chief toxicologist. She was attracted to her new boss from the moment they met, and before long, sparks would fly.

Chapter 9
Dr. Michael Robertson

Dr. Michael Robertson was *the* "golden boy" of international forensic science, and looked set to go right to the top. After graduating from Australia's Monash University with a Ph.D., Dr. Robertson worked at the coroner's office in Melbourne, where he was soon on the fast-track to success. He was viewed as a highly gifted toxicologist whose easy charm and unlimited confidence won him respect wherever he went. But there were others who thought him arrogant and self-serving.

Dr. Robertson had a major flaw: he loved to play the field. He had several affairs at the coroner's office before and after he met his wife, Nicole.

"Michael Robertson is a player of women's emotions," said a friend who knew him in Australia. "He has been since a young age. I think he is driven by the need for everyone to like him, and will compromise everything and everyone to achieve this."

Before meeting Nicole, he reportedly had "multiple" girlfriends, often beginning new relationships before ending old ones. He soon won a reputation at the coroner's office as a sexual adventurer. But he was hard-working and serious about his career in forensics, and his superiors turned a blind eye to his extra-curricular activities.

In April 1996, Dr. Robertson's old teacher at Monash, Dr. Olaf Drummer, recommended him for a forensic toxicologist position at National Medical Services (NMS) in Willow Grove, Pennsylvania, the world's leading independent toxicology laboratory. He was interviewed and then hired by NMS founder Dr. Frederic Rieders, and he and Nicole emigrated to America to start a new life.

"He wanted to come here for a residency," remembered Dr. Rieders, "in order to qualify for board certification in forensic toxicology."

Starting as a junior resident, Dr. Robertson learned and performed forensic toxicology, preparing reports and giving testimony in court as an expert witness. His attractive young wife also found a job with a pharmaceutical company near Philadelphia, doing research work.

Dr. Reiders, who viewed Nicole as a daughter, fondly remembered her as a "very bright and charming woman." He knew nothing about Dr. Robertson's extra-marital affairs, during the four years he worked there.

His Australian friend claimed that within a few months of moving to America, Dr. Robertson had started sleeping with one of Nicole's friends, as well as with another female NMS employee.

"He looks for women that are needy, and then is very supportive and friendly," said the friend. "They all fall for him."

Later, San Diego police would interview Mary Wright (not her real name), one of Michael and Nicole's closest friends, whom he had had an affair with. After it burned itself out, Wright had gotten married, but stayed in close touch with Robertson via e-mails for the next few years.

Most of Robertson's friends knew of his womanizing and never condoned his behavior. They found it easier to ignore it, puzzled as to why he would cheat on his beautiful young wife.

But Robertson was also highly ambitious, joining the Society of Forensic Toxicologists (SOFT), and becoming a regular presenter at their annual meetings. Over the next few years, he chaired SOFT meetings, covering everything from date rape to rave drugs, befriending some of the nation's most distinguished toxicologists.

Dr. Daniel Anderson, of the LA Coroner's Office, first met Robertson at a SOFT conference in Denver soon after he had arrived from Australia. It was the first SOFT meeting for both of them, and they became good friends, discovering much in common professionally.

"He was charismatic, young and energetic," remembered Dr. Anderson. "He had it all going for him. He was an up-and-coming star."

From then on, Dr. Robertson would be a major presence at annual SOFT conferences, holding forensic toxicology workshops and presenting papers. The other toxicologists all liked him, agreeing that he was the life and soul of the party during the conferences' many social events.

In early 2000, Dr. Robertson accepted the position of forensic laboratory manager at the San Diego County Medical Examiner's Office and he and Nicole moved to La Jolla, just a few blocks away from Kristin Rossum.

When Dr. Robertson arrived at the San Diego ME's Office, he was still awaiting a work visa, so he spent the first two months as an unpaid visitor, learning the ropes. But it was common knowledge among the other employees that he would take over as forensic laboratory manager as soon as the Immigration and Naturalization Service rubber-stamped his papers.

Although still not an official employee, Dr. Robertson soon became a major presence in the ME's office, dispensing advice and helping with analytical procedures. He made no secret of the fact that he wanted to revamp the ME's toxicology section, which he felt was old-fashioned and sloppy.

"He wasn't actually our boss yet, but he was going to be," said toxicologist Catherine Hamm. "I think we all treated him that way."

Within a few days of his arrival, Kristin Rossum was going out of her way to be friendly, spending as much time with her future boss as she could. And there appeared to be an instant attraction between the two.

"They seemed to hit it off, really, right from the beginning," said Hamm. "It seemed pretty quick."

Dr. Robertson loved the perfect year-round San Diego climate, which resembled his native Australia, and soon found a new set of friends. He became a regular at several Australian bars, joining the San Diego Lions Australian football team as a backliner. Most weekends he would play league games, before joining the other players at the bar for a celebratory night out.

When his visa finally came through at the beginning of March, he officially became forensic laboratory manager, taking over the everyday running of the toxicology lab.

His new office had a perfect view of Kristin Rossum's desk, and over the next few weeks, Kristin seemed to be in there incessantly, which did not go unnoticed by their fellow workers.

"We hit it off right off the bat," Kristin would later testify. "We were both in marriages we weren't happy with. We gravitated toward one another."

In early April, they both attended a going-away party for a toxicologist named Nadia Giorgi at the 94th Aero Squadron Restaurant in San Diego. It was the first time that Kristin and Robertson had met socially outside work, and he invited her out.

The following week they secretly sneaked off for lunch together, and soon they started meeting up after work and whenever they could. But their unusually close employee–boss relationship created resentment among the other toxicologists, who felt that Kristin was getting preferential treatment.

"There was a lot of discussion," said Cathy Hamm. "I think people, myself definitely, were unhappy. We felt that most of his attention was directed towards her and whatever projects she was doing."

One night James Fogacci, a toxicologist who had been at the ME's office for twenty-five years, was closing up the office when he discovered Dr. Robertson and Rossum in a romantic clinch at the back of the laboratory. As soon as they saw him, they moved away from one another, looking embarrassed.

"I had the feeling that I surprised them," remembered Fogacci, now retired. "[Later] I mentioned to him that it was not a good idea to have an association with another employee."

When Fogacci warned Robertson that previous secret affairs in the ME's office had led to written warnings, the forensic laboratory manager looked blank and walked out without saying a word.

Around that time, Melissa Prager lunched with Kristin in San Diego, gettting the impression that her friend's marriage was under strain. Prager, now living in San Francisco, had agreed to meet Kristin at the Miracles Café in North County, and was surprised when Greg turned up, as it was just supposed to be the two of them.

"I was eager to see [Kristin] and spend some time with her alone," said Prager. "I wondered why Greg came along."

Since their strained first meeting a few years earlier, Prager had concluded that Greg might be shy, and decided to give him the benefit of the doubt. During lunch, the women discussed taking a trip together to New York later that year, but Prager sensed that Greg did not approve.

"[He was] hinting at the fact she needed to check with him first," Prager said, adding that he appeared overprotective.

Throughout April, Kristin and Dr. Robertson spent more and more time together. They appeared infatuated with each other, discussing the most intimate parts of their lives and a possible future together.

One day Kristin confessed that she had been addicted to crystal methamphetamine, swearing it was all in the past. Her boss was understanding, saying he did not approve of drugs and that he did not want her to have anything to do with them.

So far the relationship had not been consummated. So Dr. Robertson invited Kristin to accompany him to the May conference of the California Association of Toxicologists (CAT) in Anaheim, which was being organized by his friend Dr. Daniel Anderson. She agreed to come with him. But when she told Greg she was going, he was most upset.

A couple of weeks later, Kristin and Greg went on a hiking trip to the Grand Canyon with her youngest brother Pierce. During the drive up there, they argued about her attending the weekend conference.

"Greg said, 'I don't leave you, don't leave me,' " Pierce would later testify. "They got into an argument. She wanted to go to the conference."

Later, Kristin would admit that Greg "gave me a lot of problems" about it, explaining that she went anyway as "I thought it was important."

On Friday, May 5, Dr. Robertson led a group of his toxicologists, including Kristin, Cathy Hamm and Donald Lowe, to the CAT conference. Kristin wanted to make a good impression, but she was also careful to keep her distance from her boss to avoid any further office gossip.

Kristin watched proudly as Robertson addressed the Saturday afternoon conference with a paper entitled: "Why All the Rave? Basic Pharmacology of Rave Drugs."

Later that night, Doctors Robertson and Anderson took Kristin and a group of toxicologists out drinking. Afterwards, back at their hotel, Kristin Rossum and Michael Robertson made love for the first time, and decided that they had a future together. They were each other's destiny.

Chapter 10

Destiny

After the Anaheim CAT conference, Rossum and Robertson's relationship moved fast, going from a fling into a passionate love affair within days. On May 12, Kristin gave Robertson an assortment of romantic gifts, declaring her love for him. It included a picture of her as a 13-year-old dancing *The Nutcracker* and five books of her favorite poems, including the "Desiderata."

"Michael, this is a beautiful little book I was given as a little girl," she wrote on the fly-cover. "It brought me comfort during difficult times. I love you with all my heart and all that I hope to be."

On another book of poems, Kristin toasted the beginning of their new life together, and she dedicated a third to "My love, with heartfelt adoration."

Being in love had apparently also inspired Kristin to sign up for ballet lessons at a local school. Already the lovers planned to attend the upcoming Milwaukee SOFT conference in October, where they would co-present a paper called "Death by Strychnine."

Most mornings, Dr. Robertson would arrive at work with a single rose and present it to Kristin, who would place it in her desk. At noon they would furtively sneak out for lunches together, causing even more gossip and giggles when they returned to the office within minutes of each other, freshly showered.

On May 15 came the first in a long series of passionate e-mails between the two.

"Hi there," wrote Kristin. "Thinking of you . . . Love You. . . . K."

The following morning, from her desk just a few feet away from Dr. Robertson's office, Kristin wrote: "The deepest love is being able to let down all barriers and give yourself to another who has done the same. This is what I feel for you."

An hour later, her boss replied, writing: "You're a beay-tiful [sic] person and an inspiration to me. I want nothing more than to give my all to you. My life, my love, my world . . ."

Two days later, Robertson e-mailed Kristin at lunch time, saying he loved her and that was all he wanted to say. Kristin immediately replied that those were "the most precious three words" he could ever say to her. Later that afternoon she wished him a "lovely evening of sailing," adding: "I'll be thinking of you and all the future has to offer. I can't wait for it to begin."

But Kristin, the masterful dissembler, was simultane-ously sending e-mails to Greg. In one she declared that she loved him "more than anything in the world," asking why he didn't e-mail her more often. Twenty minutes later, she e-mailed Dr. Robertson to tell him she wanted to spend the rest of her life with him.

On Thursday morning, Kristin e-mailed her brother Brent at their parents' house, saying she needed to talk to him, as she was so unhappy with Greg. She wrote of the deep misgivings she'd had before they got married eleven months earlier, saying she now needed a true life compan-ion.

She accused her parents of pushing her into the mar-riage, because she hadn't wanted to let them down after they had invested so much "time and money."

"Well here I am a year later," she wrote. "And looking back I wish I hadn't gone through with it. I just haven't been happy."

She went on to call Greg unsupportive, saying she did not want to spend the rest of her life with the wrong person. The "most significant reason" to remain in the marriage, she told her brother, was not to disappoint their parents.

"Yuck," she ended. "I feel so torn apart inside."

That evening, Dr. Robertson was Kristin's date for her pre-graduation SDSU Chemistry Department picnic, where they danced together. At 7:52 a.m. the next morning, he told her about his sweet dreams, featuring her "smiles," "dancing" and "laughing." "Maybe soon I can put on a too-too [sic] and show you how it should be done," he joked. "Can't wait for lunch."

And there was also a concerned reply from her brother Brent, saying he'd had no idea her marriage was so rocky, promising to support her 100 percent in whatever she decided to do.

Then, just before leaving for the weekend, Kristin e-mailed Robertson.

"You mean so much to me," she told him, promising that she'd be thinking about him over the weekend.

But early Sunday morning, he e-mailed her again from a supermarket on the way to an Australian football game.

"As of 9:00 a.m.," he wrote, "my missing you has been officially upgraded to 'intensely,' soon to move to 'unbearably.' "

The following week Robertson and Rossum threw caution to the wind, as their affair became increasingly obvious to everyone at the ME's office. Acting like two teenagers in the first throes of love, they became fodder for even more gossip at the water cooler.

Oblivious to how much attention they were creating, they spent much of their working days writing ever more passionate e-mails to one another. Kristin said she wanted to leave Greg and move to Australia to marry Robertson. And Robertson sought advice from friends about whether to leave Nicole for Kristin.

"I along with everyone have spent some time now getting used to the concept of 'Michael and Nicole,' " replied his friend Nick, in an e-mail which Robertson immediately forwarded to Kristin. Expressing doubts about the prospects for a stable future for Michael and Kristin, Nick observed: "It's sort of harsh, but being divorced from Nicole would already suggest that your perception on marriage and relationships is somewhat unreliable and this of course would also apply to Kristin, as it seems that she is currently also married."

On Tuesday morning, Kristin visited her boss's apartment. Back at the office, Robertson thanked her for helping him experience "some of the most wonderful and intense feelings" of his life. He signed off with some "cyber-hugs 'n kisses."

Kristin replied that "this morning was just a little peek into what we have to look forward to," thanking him for the "incredible feelings" he'd stirred up in her. She then said she was certain she wanted to spend the rest of her life by his side.

By Thursday the rampant rumors of their affair had reached the ears of Robertson's immediate boss, Lloyd Amborn, who had retired from the U.S. Navy after thirty years' service and was now the Operations Administrator for the ME's office. Concerned, Amborn summoned his forensic laboratory manager into his office.

"I spoke to him about reports that were reaching me that there might be an improper relationship between him and Kristin Rossum," Amborn would later testify. "I told him we could not have such a relationship in the senior–subordinate chain of command, and it would be deleterious to the morale of that division."

Dr. Robertson absolutely denied there was anything between him and Kristin, and with no proof, there was little Amborn could do.

Straight after leaving Amborn's office, Robertson warned Kristin in an e-mail entitled, "Read Now Babe."

"Hey it's a little after noon and Lloyd just got hold of me re- 'our conduct.' '

He warned her to expect to be called in to explain that

afternoon, saying Amborn had no definite proof beyond rumors.

"He sounds like he can be quite stern," warned Dr. Robertson. "Will fill you in on my conversation later."

Then he told Kristin to delete all his e-mails after she read them, warning "any snoop" can check her in-box and it would "not be well-received."

Later that afternoon, Robertson was there in Lloyd Amborn's office when Rossum was summoned. Carefully choosing his words, Amborn counseled her not to be in "such close physical proximity" to her boss, as it made other workers uncomfortable. He never directly asked her if they were having an illicit relationship, and she never volunteered it.

Just before leaving work that day, Dr. Robertson wrote Kristin that "meeting and falling in love with you" was the high point of his life, and was something he would "cherish" forever.

On Sunday, May 28, 2000, Kristin officially graduated summa cum laude, and was awarded the honor of Outstanding Graduate in the 120-strong Chemistry Department. Her distinction meant that she had at least a 3.8 average on a 4.0 scale.

A month earlier, SDSU had written Kristin to invite her to the special ceremony they would be holding for a select number of *the* best honors graduates.

"Dear Kristin Margrethe," it began. "San Diego State University has arranged a special recognition at commencement for students who had tentatively been identified as eligible for Summa Cum Laude designation."

A few days before graduation she was presented with a gold honors cord to be worn over her gown and asked to lead the commencement procession.

"The University hopes that this token of recognition for your outstanding academic performance will signify its pride in your accomplishment."

Kristin's proud parents and husband were all there to see her graduate at SDSU's 101st commencement ceremony, which was followed by a special prize-giving at the College of Sciences in the Cox Arena.

The beautiful 22-year-old graduate shone in her black gown and gold cord, as she mounted the stage of the university's white-and-pink Chemistry Sciences Laboratory to graduate in Chemistry (Biochemistry).

At the exact moment Kristin was graduating, Dr. Robertson sent her an e-mail with the subject: "Rad Grad Chick."

"Dear Adrenalin," he wrote, explaining that this was his new name for her, as, at just the thought of her, "my heart starts pounding, my blood rushing and my head spinning."

Bemoaning the fact that he couldn't be at her graduation to cheer from the back row, he was cheering her on the inside and loving her "like crazy."

There is a bitter irony that at the moment of Kristin Rossum's greatest academic triumph, she should start smoking crystal methamphetamine again. For soon after she began full-time as a toxicologist, Kristin started stealing a variety of drugs from the ME's balance room, where they were stored before being disposed of by the sheriff's office.

Part of her job included logging into her computer illicit drugs found at death scenes, as well as the ones used as standards in toxicology analysis. She had full access to all areas where the drugs were stored and, during an eight-month period in 2000, Kristin took varying quantities of illegal methamphetamine and amphetamine that had been impounded at death scenes in no fewer than seven different cases. Later, a full audit of the lab would also reveal that numerous vials of professionally manufactured methamphetamine were missing.

While Rossum worked at the ME's office, security was lax. All drugs found by investigators at death scenes were routinely taken to the ME's office, placed in brown envelopes, and then dropped in a locked box in the investigators' office. But when the box filled up, it was easy to pull the envelopes out of the slot.

Eventually, when the drop box was full, it would be emptied and the evidence envelopes moved to the toxicology lab. There they were often left out on a desk or work bench, until they could be stored in a locked cabinet in a hallway. However, the key was kept in an unlocked desk drawer, easily accessible to all toxicologists.

After stealing the methamphetamine, Rossum would smoke it in the comparative safety of the High-Pressure Liquid Chromatography (HPLC) room, which was only used by her. She knew that the strong smell would be dissipated by the vented machine, which removes fumes from chemicals being evaporated.

Even Michael Robertson would later agree that the ME's system for drug storage was woefully inadequate, but it would be another six months before he discovered how Kristin was fully exploiting the weaknesses to get high.

Chapter 11

Betrayal

On Monday, June 5, 2000, Greg and Kristin celebrated their first wedding anniversary. That same day, Greg started a new job at Orbigen. True to his word, Dr. Gruenwald had hired him for his small start-up biotech company. He was appointed business development manager with a brief to acquire hot new technology. As part of his new job package, Greg was also given shares in the company to provide an added incentive.

Greg was still convinced that everything was going well in the marriage, blissfully unaware that Kristin was in love with another man and planning to walk out. As they still had sex occasionally, Greg had no idea his wife was also sleeping with someone else.

That night, Kristin prepared a special candle-lit dinner to celebrate their first year of marriage. But before leaving for work, she e-mailed Michael Robertson, telling him she loved him and couldn't wait to see him Tuesday morning.

Two days later, in an e-mail to her brother Brent, Rossum said she was "hanging in there," and that the anniversary had been "all right." But she complained that although she had bought Greg a picture frame with her picture for his new desk, some silk boxer shorts and a cookbook, he didn't even get her a card.

Lloyd Amborn's caution had done nothing to dampen her affair with Robertson. Within hours of their warning,

Kristin told him he was *the* most important person in her life and meant the world to her.

Despite Amborn's concerns about improper behavior, the following week, Dr. Robertson was promoted to the position of chief toxicologist. He would now be in charge of all toxicology work at the San Diego County ME's Office. Kristin was delighted, even hiding a congratulations card in his desk.

Robertson then told her to go into his office while he was at his morning planning meeting. There, in a box under his desk, he had left her some roses with a love letter. After finding his gift, a delighted Kristin wrote him an impassioned e-mail, gushing over his "simple gesture of love" and declaring that her life finally made sense.

"I love you Michael! Everything I ever imagined wanting in a lifelong companion, husband, best friend, is present in you. When I see you . . . I see my future . . ."

Some months later she would discover that Dr. Robertson had been two-timing her, sleeping with other women as he proclaimed his everlasting love for her.

After Robertson was appointed chief toxicologist, his cavalier attitude knew no bounds. He viewed the upcoming SOFT conference in Milwaukee, which he was helping to organize, as the perfect excuse for a long, passionate weekend with Kristin. Even better, the ME's office would be paying for it. But in order to qualify for her flight and hotel expenses, Kristin would have to deliver a paper at the conference. Dr. Robertson offered to help her, writing up an abstract for the paper they had discussed delivering jointly, called "Death by Strychnine."

On Monday, June 19, with the deadline approaching, he e-mailed the co-chairman of the conference, Dr. Steve Wong.

"Just a quick 'am I too late to submit an abstract' question."

A week later, Dr. Wong replied in an e-mail, inviting

Robertson to submit the strychnine abstract as soon as possible. Delighted, Robertson forwarded it to Kristin, asking: "What do you think? Are you up for it?"

For ambitious Kristin a chance to address SOFT delegates would provide her with an official entrée into the world of forensic toxicology. It also wouldn't hurt that she was being groomed by one of the best known toxicologists in America.

In late June, the San Diego County Medical Examiner, Dr. Brian Blackbourne, summoned his new chief toxicologist to a meeting in his office. When he arrived, he found Dr. Blackbourne with San Diego Homicide Detective Terry Torgersen, who explained that he was re-opening a case of a woman whose death had been ruled a drug overdose five years earlier. Now the detective had new information that she had really died of fentanyl poisoning, not routinely tested for at the San Diego ME's Office.

Dr. Robertson then arranged for the dead woman's blood work to be sent to his old employer, National Medical Services, who later discovered that she had died from fentanyl.

It would later be claimed that Kristin and Dr. Robertson made good use of the knowledge that their office did not screen for fentanyl.

That spring, Kristin and Greg regularly visited Claremont on weekends. And while Greg played golf with Professor Rossum and his sons, Kristin would discuss her troubled marriage with her mother. But she never mentioned her affair with Dr. Robertson.

"I felt I was in love," Rossum would later testify. "I loved him very much. It was very romantic, very exciting, very passionate."

Right from the beginning of their affair, Kristin and Robertson exchanged different colored roses, which they saw as a symbol of their love. On one occasion Kristin gave him a red, a pink, a yellow and a white rose and handwrote notes with each explaining what each color represented to her. Roses would become a special language of love between them, each color signifying a different emotion.

She would later complain to Homicide detectives that her husband was unromantic, never buying her roses because they were too expensive.

"I really like romance," she said. "I told Greg that I always wished that he was more romantic. How much is it just to [buy me] a flower now and again?"

By the beginning of July, the lovers were sending each other ever more passionate e-mails and love notes, several times a day. They were also arranging secret trysts, either at Robertson's apartment or in a quiet park near hers that they affectionately termed "the Willows."

Now under the influence of methamphetamine, Kristin secretly met her lover after work at the same time as she was preparing to go with Greg on their annual July Fourth trip to Mammoth Mountain.

On the afternoon of June 20, she e-mailed Greg saying she would be late getting home as she was meeting her friend Rena at a Starbucks in La Jolla.

A week later, after an extended coffee break with Robertson, she e-mailed Greg, saying she had won a spare ticket to a Natalie Merchant concert at SDSU in an office raffle, and asking permission to go with with Dr. Robertson. Ironically, although he had told Kristin that his wife Nicole had dropped out, he had initially bought the ticket for another girlfriend who had stood him up.

"Would you mind if I went?" she asked her husband. "Let me know what you think so he can give it to the runner-up if you don't want me to go."

Ultimately Kristin didn't go to the concert—Greg didn't want her to—and Robertson took someone else. Later, she would say she deliberately mentioned Dr. Robertson by name, wanting Greg to know exactly who she would be going with.

On Thursday, June 29, Kristin and Greg drove to Mammoth for their annual trip, where they met up with Jerome and Bertrand and their girlfriends. They set up camp together and Greg appeared in good spirits and getting on well with Kristin.

During the trip, they all climbed the mountain, which was 10,000 feet above sea level, and Greg reached the summit first.

"We'd go pretty fast," remembered Jerome. "He beat me to the top."

Another time the three brothers went fishing at their favorite spot on the deepest part of the lake, a place they called "the rock." Over the years, they had discovered that this was the place to catch the biggest fish.

On their return to camp a couple of hours later, Kristin was in tears, upset that Greg had been away so long.

"Kristin was almost yelling at him," Jerome would later testify. "I was kind of surprised."

But the couple soon made up, later spending the night together in their tent.

While Kristin was away in Mammoth, Michael Robertson sent her a series of passionate e-mails he entitled, "Missing a Girl," lamenting that she was with her husband and not him.

"Hi beautiful," he wrote on Friday evening. "I gather about now you're all hot 'n' sweaty finishing up your hike . . . Only problem is we're way too far apart, but I am thinking of you and missing you like crazy."

He wrote of smelling her perfume every time he entered the office.

"Well cutie . . . only four days to go," he signed off.

By Sunday afternoon he sent another e-mail with a love poem, calling Kristin his "life's partner and my destiny." Saying he couldn't wait to see her face again, he waxed lyrically that: "To have lived but not loved would be my greatest regret. Your beauty is unparalleled and my heart beats your beat for you."

The following afternoon he sent her an e-mail from his office, entitled, "4 down and 2 to go."

"Today wasn't too bad here at work," he wrote, "but it's the nights I struggle with. I miss you so much and at night I wonder what you are doing . . . I smell you in the pages and just cling to your words. . . ."

On July 5, her first day back, Kristin sent him a passionate e-mail, saying she couldn't believe how her "heart continues to swell and my feelings for you continue to deepen with each passing day."

It was signed with their new secret code word, "ELE," an acronym for "Eye Love Ewe." And increasingly they would boldly use this signoff in professional e-mails to other colleagues in displays of bravado.

When Dr. Robertson received her message, he immediately replied that there was more than his heart "throbbing" with feelings for her, crudely noting that he had a "rudey."

"Oh behave you bad boy!" came Kristin's reply. "Or I will have to give you a spanking."

They were also busy that day working on Kristin's upcoming SOFT presentation, which Robertson appeared to be writing.

"Have a read and let me know of any changes," he e-mailed her. "We should try and get it out today."

She sent it back, saying it was ready for printing on the submission form. Then Robertson e-mailed it to SOFT chairman, Dr. Steven Wong, with a c.c. to Kristin Rossum, saying he would send on three hard copies and a disk as required. He signed it "Michael (ELE)," and forwarded it to Kristin, knowing she would appreciate his inside joke.

Then everything changed. Greg found one of Robertson's love letters the weekend after they returned from Mammoth. He was furious, forcing Kristin to admit that she had "developed very strong feelings" for her boss, who Greg had briefly met a few weeks earlier at a social function. Greg made her give him Robertson's phone number and called, warning him not to have "inappropriate contact" with his wife.

He also threatened to call the medical examiner and reveal the affair, but, to Kristin's relief, he never did. Later she would claim that she only told Greg about the relationship to spur him into marriage counseling, saying she wanted him to realize why she was seeking "an emotional attachment" outside the marriage.

"He said, 'I can't live without you,'" she would later claim.

Traumatized that Greg had found out about her affair, Kristin sought solace in her lover's arms. Robertson seemed unfazed, offering her his support as a friend in whatever she decided to do in her marriage.

"As you begin to head down the slippery slope," he wrote the day after Greg had confronted him, "remember I will always be there for you . . ."

Now the only obstacles standing in the way of their being together and fulfilling their "destiny" were Gregory de Villers and Robertson's wife, Nicole.

For the rest of the summer, Kristin began looking for a new apartment, without telling Greg. Encouraged by Michael Robertson, who told her that once they put their "troubled times" behind them, they would be *the* "happiest couple in town," Kristin signed up with an apartment rental service.

She also confided in Tom Horn, a young student worker at the ME's office whom she had trained. She told him in confidence that she and Dr. Robertson were having an affair, asking if he knew of available apartments in the Mission Hills area, where he lived.

"She wasn't happy in her marriage," Horn remembered. "[She] was looking to move out of her current residence."

And Kristin also told Melissa Prager, her old high school friend, about Dr. Robertson one afternoon. They were walking in La Jolla after lunch and Prager had complimented Kristin on looking great and less stressed than usual. Suddenly Kristin announced that she had found a new love and wanted to leave Greg, telling her friend how she had finally found someone who respected her mind and appreciated her beauty.

"She said it was Michael Robertson," said Prager. "The man she was working with."

Kristin explained how she had told Greg about the affair and it had led to bitter arguments.

"She wanted to somehow fix the arguing, either by moving out or by counseling. [She] asked if maybe I would consider moving down to San Diego and finding an apartment together."

But even if Kristin was telling friends and family she wanted out of the marriage, Greg was too proud to tell anyone that he was being cuckolded. He never mentioned a word about Kristin's affair to his brothers or any of his friends. After his parents' divorce, he was determined to make a success of his marriage, always believing that they could resolve their differences.

During a day out at the San Diego Zoo with his old friend Bill Leger, he and Kristin acted like nothing was wrong.

"We had a lovely time," remembered Leger. "It was a lot of fun. I still have pictures on my fridge from that day."

During the rest of July and into August, Rossum and Robertson were planning for their future. Robertson again suggested they start a new life in Australia, and Kristin enthusiastically looked it up on the Internet to find out everything she could.

On nights when Kristin couldn't find an excuse to meet Robertson, he would send flowery e-mails lamenting how much he craved her body.

"Oh, so we didn't get to have caddles [sic] last night," he wrote on July 19. "Nor were we able to make dinner, take a bath and make love while staring into each other's eyes. . . . I love you Kristin!! I hope you have a wonderful day and I can't wait for tonight, when I do get to cuddle you."

The following day, Kristin sent him an e-mail informing him, "My cheeks hurt!!!!"

• • •

Although Kristin had squelched Greg's dream of starting a family with her, she now talked of having Robertson's children. On July 23, sitting in his desk at the ME's office, the chief toxicologist wrote that she was his "perfect match," and he could see her beside him "at the alter, at home, holding my children."

They were now sneaking off to make love at "the Willows" several times a week, scheduling their rendezvous by e-mail.

"So at what time will you be visiting the Willows? ELE," asked Kristin at 3:00 p.m. on Friday, August 4.

"OK how does 4 sound," was Robertson's reply.

The following week, they secretly met at the Willows three times for what they termed "quickie breaks."

And the lovesick couple were now living in the future when they could be together without their spouses.

"Better to create a future we love than to endure one we don't," Robertson would tell her.

One morning in August, Dr. Michael Robertson asked his intern Tom Horn to go into the balance room and retrieve a manila envelope containing some fentanyl patches, which had been impounded some months earlier. Robertson gave him his key to the room, and Horn went in, finally finding the envelope, which was case #1591, and handing it to his boss.

A few days later another member of the ME's staff asked Horn to find Case #1591 and he went back into the balance room, but couldn't find it. Suddenly remembering that he had earlier given it to Dr. Robertson, Horn went into his office and found the envelope containing the fentanyl lying on a small round table by Robertson's desk.

A blood sample from the envelope was then sent out for testing, but the fentanyl was left there. Three months later, during an audit, all the fentanyl patches from Case #1591 were missing and have never been recovered.

Chapter 12

Disintegration

By the fall, Kristin Rossum and Dr. Michael Robertson were becoming increasingly frustrated in their respective relationships. Feeling trapped in an unhappy marriage with Greg, Kristin was taking more and more drugs to self-medicate. But she still managed to fool everybody around her, and her work performance never suffered, although she was now regularly smoking crystal methamphetamine at the ME's office and at home.

Kristin would later complain that Greg refused to discuss their disintegrating marriage, channeling all his energies into Orbigen. As licensing manager for the eight-employee company, Greg was now responsible for locating cutting-edge new biotechnologies being developed at universities, and then persuading those universities to grant Orbigen licenses. It was a highly demanding job with long hours, but Greg enjoyed it, viewing it as a great opportunity. He dreamed of Orbigen one day going public and making him rich.

Every morning Greg would make the short drive to the company offices on Nancy Ridge Drive, Mira Mesa. There he spent nearly all his time on his computer, or phoning people on his huge, 2000-name database, working 500 active leads at any one time. He impressed Dr. Gruenwald and his partner, Dr. Terry Huang, another former Pharmagen employee, with his tenacity and dedication.

"He was excellent," remembered Dr. Gruenwald. "He was very meticulous and very hard-working. A problem solver. A team player."

Greg never brought his marital problems into the office, where he was viewed as Orbigen's most positive employee. He was usually the first to arrive in the morning and the last to leave, and Dr. Huang even gave him an iMac computer and a high speed cable modem, so he could work at home.

"We were a very small company," explained Dr. Huang. "Sometimes we worried about whether we can make it or not. [Greg was] usually very optimistic about what we [were] doing."

Every Friday, Greg was the driving force behind Orbigen's morale-boosting T.G.I.F. afternoon get-togethers. He was also organizing a fishing trip to Mexico for staff, like the one at Pharmagen, several years earlier.

Later, Kristin would portray her husband as dark and moody after he found out about Michael Robertson. But none of his colleagues ever saw that side of him.

"There was a period where he basically went to bed for a couple of days and wouldn't talk to me or anyone," Kristin would later claim. "I was devastated, too. It was pretty painful to see someone you love hurt so much."

In mid-August, Greg and Kristin drove to Claremont for her parents' twenty-eighth wedding anniversary. Kristin's Aunt Marge had flown in from Indiana for a small family party, and it was the first time she'd seen the young married couple since the wedding.

Her aunt had never approved of Greg, thinking him "wimpy" and "immature," complaining that he "didn't act like a man" after he once lost a shooting contest with Kristin's brothers. At one point, she would later testify, she ended up alone with Greg in the kitchen and he asked her for a video of Kristin dancing *The Nutcracker Suite* at school. Then he went off to play it by himself in the living room.

When Kristin's youngest brother Pierce came in after

washing his car, he was surprised to see Greg sitting on a couch, watching the ten-minute videotape, over and over again.

"I said, 'Come on, Greg, let's play,' " Pierce remembered. "He said, 'Come on. Let me watch this.' "

A couple of weeks later, Kristin and Greg cancelled a long-planned camping trip with Jerome and Bertrand at the last minute, saying they couldn't afford to go. But on September 2, they drove to Thousand Oaks for Greg's mother's birthday, and after going out for dinner, they stayed the night.

Although the three de Villers brothers were now spread across California, they kept in close touch via telephone and e-mail. Greg talked to Jerome and Bertrand once or twice a week, always appearing positive about his marriage. He still talked enthusiastically of having kids with Kristin and moving to a large house one day. And they never realized his problems with Kristin until it was too late.

Greg's main topic of conversation was his new job at Orbigen and how well it was all going.

"He was real excited about it," said Jerome. "I kind of got the impression he thought he had a good chance to get in, start with a small company, and make it big."

On Saturday, September 9, Kristin began writing a personal journal, trying to make sense of her convoluted life by examining her innermost feelings. She described it as "a journey of self-discovery," although it never once mentioned her affair with Robertson or her relapse into drugs. Later, prosecutors would claim the cliché-ridden journal was written solely for Greg's benefit, as the beginning of an elaborate cover-up for the perfect murder.

"I want to learn about myself," she began in her neat, precise handwriting. "A deeper understanding of who I am . . ."

Her life, she wrote, had been a "roller-coaster of highs and lows." And now that she had come to rest in a "stable,

secure" relationship, she questioned why she was still un-
fulfilled and feeling like a prisoner.

"Why do I yearn for more?" she asked. "Am I seeking
out a fairytale existence that just doesn't happen in real
life?" She mourned the loss of her carefree life and wondered how she had come, one year into her marriage, to
such an unsettling turning point. Was she wrong to still be
looking for the perfect "soul mate" who would offer pure
romance and overwhelming passion?

Voicing her regrets about ever marrying Greg, she
blamed her mother for not taking her pre-wedding panic
seriously and for failing to stop the wedding. Convinced
that it was too late to break off the engagement, she had
given up her dream of escape, ignoring her "inner voice."
She had yearned to hear her mother tell her not to marry
Greg if she didn't want to.

"The wedding is about the bride and groom and not the
efforts of the mother who planned the event. If I had been
given the family support that I so desperately needed . . . I
wouldn't be a wife. I wouldn't have Greg in my life. I
wouldn't be struggling like I am now."

Fueled by crystal methamphetamine, Kristin Rossum spent
much of September preparing for the upcoming SOFT conference and her long-anticipated weekend with Michael
Robertson. But more importantly, she was determined to
make a memorable debut in the world of international forensic toxicology, and practiced delivering her strychnine
paper again and again.

In the second week of September, Kristin submitted her
travel request for flight and hotel reimbursement after it was
approved by Dr. Robertson. Under the "Comments" section, her boss gave the official reasons why Kristin should
attend the week-long Milwaukee conference with him.

"As a forensic toxicologist, this is one of the most important conferences she can attend," he wrote. "It will improve her knowledge and experience."

On September 12, Kristin and Michael bought two round-trip tickets to Milwaukee on TWA and made a reservation for a single room at the Inn Towne Hotel, a few miles away from the Hyatt Regency, the official conference hotel, as they didn't want to be seen together by the other delegates. Later they would alter hotel receipts and be reimbursed for two rooms out of the ME's budget.

Dr. Robertson's superior, Lloyd Amborn, had heard more gossip about an "improper relationship," so once again he summoned the chief toxicologist into his office, asking if there was anything unprofessional going on.

"He denied it," said Amborn. "He felt the rumors were being caused by the fact that he was mentoring Kristin more closely than the other toxicologists because she was more professionally interested."

As the conference drew nearer, Greg de Villers became increasingly uncomfortable about his wife going, suspecting that Michael Robertson would be there. Again, Kristin assured him it was just an "emotional attachment," and nothing for him to worry about.

"He told me I was not to go," Rossum would later testify. "He voiced repeated concern about it for several months."

But Kristin paid little heed to Greg's wishes, sometimes accusing him of trying to control her. On September 20, in preparation for the conference, she visited Planned Parenthood. She also gave her boss a book on sexual positions, entitled, *52 Invitations to Grrreat Sex*, to make their love life a little more adventurous.

"Well Sweetheart," she wrote on the inside cover, "together we will enjoy a lifetime of passion. This is just the beginning. I love you, Kristin."

The following day, she made the first of many trips to Tijuana to buy an assortment of drugs at a pharmacy, including Soma and an amphetamine substitute called Asenlix. A doctor at the pharmacy wrote her a prescription for the drugs, no questions asked, citing "obesity," although Kristin was underweight.

Soon afterwards, Kristin pondered in her journal why she needed amphetamines to control her body, noting her ongoing inner conflict between logic and unattainable ideals. "I guess that my belief is that it is within *my power* to control the shape of my body," she wrote.

Unhappy about her physical appearance, she went on to complain that her "bottom" was a little rounder than it once had been, and that her inner thighs "jiggle a bit too much," her stomach could be flatter and her arms better toned. She concluded that she was unhappy with her body because it wasn't perfect, even though she knew that perfection was "imaginary." She felt that she would be more empowered if she were taller and also wanted "big, full pouty lips."

Straining to conform to the feminine ideal, Kristin believed that she would finally attain "inner-peace" only after she repaired all her physical flaws to achieve the "perfect body."

In mid-September, Professor Ralph Rossum conducted a judicial seminar in San Diego, and his wife, Constance, and son, Pierce, rode down with him. While Pierce went off to play a round of golf with Greg, Constance met her daughter for lunch in downtown La Jolla, before they went shopping in a nearby mall.

"She wanted to talk about Greg," her mother later testified. "She was definitely leaving."

According to her mother, Kristin wanted Greg to suffer as little pain as possible, as his mother was sick. But Constance told her that she couldn't stay with Greg just to spare his mother's feelings.

"I wanted her to leave him," she said. "[I] said, 'We can move you out today.' "

"Mom, I'm his whole life," Kristin told her. "I've been with him for five years. I can't say, 'Goodbye, have a nice life.' "

Kristin said that she had already started looking for an

affordable apartment, and planned to leave in early November, in time for the holidays.

The following night, Kristin pondered the "very emotional" lunch in her journal, saying that she had made an effort to connect with her mother and that they had engaged in a little mother–daughter bonding.

"I have never felt particularly close to my mom," she wrote. "It always seemed to me that she rarely was able to just be herself."

Accusing her mother of always carefully presenting the image of "the perpetual hostess," Kristin observed that she seldom revealed the "real person beneath the façade."

Kristin was also engrossed in Mitch Albom's heart-tugging bestseller *Tuesdays With Morrie*, about the life lessons he learned from his dying professor. Apparently it had prompted her to think about life, death and the bigger picture. But she also wrote passages about her marriage, apparently designed to be read by Greg sometime in the future.

"I feel for Greg and what my doubts are doing to him," she wrote. And she now admitted that it was unfair of her to have committed to a marriage without first dealing with her issues.

A few days later she questioned why she was not in love with Greg, although he tried so hard to please her.

"He must be frustrated," she concluded. "It's difficult when one person loves the other more, when it's uneven."

A day later, she became nostalgic for her old boyfriend, Teddy Maya, whom she'd abandoned and robbed six years earlier.

Kristin admitted she had treated him "horribly," writing that he was her "first real love." Now she wanted to write him a letter of apology. She felt the need to own up to her past because she was tired of running away.

But although she obtained Maya's address from Melissa Prager, she would never put pen to paper.

Chapter 13

The SOFT Conference

On Tuesday, September 26, three days before the SOFT conference, the lovers' eight-page conference application landed on Lloyd Amborn's desk, and he immediately called his chief toxicologist into his office for the third time to explain himself.

"It was for the two of them to attend the conference," he remembered. "I wanted to talk to him about it."

Once again, Dr. Robertson denied that his relationship with Kristin was anything but professional, insisting that the strychnine paper she would present at the conference would be a vital part of her toxicologist training. Without proof that Robertson was lying, Amborn had little choice but to reluctantly sign the application.

In the days leading up to the Milwaukee conference, Greg de Villers began exploring job opportunities for Kristin at Orbigen, to get her away from Michael Robertson. He told Dr. Gruenwald that his wife was unhappy at the ME's office and wanted to switch jobs. But although Orbigen had a vacancy, the biotech company did not employ chemists. So Greg asked him to let him know if he heard of any suitable new jobs for Kristin through his network of contacts.

Most nights, Kristin wrote in her journal, which she would then casually leave lying around in the kitchen, sending Greg a clear message about how she felt about him trying to prevent her going to Milwaukee.

Although she was nervous about delivering her fifteen-minute talk, she wrote, her main problem was Greg's attitude, as he was "obsessed" about whether Dr. Robertson would be there. Then she laid a red herring for her husband, writing that her boss was probably not attending anyway, although she knew he would definitely be there.

She then accused him of not understanding her, asking what they had together if he didn't trust her, and questioning if their relationship was beyond repair.

By Friday, September 29, three days before the start of the conference, Greg de Villers had resigned himself to Kristin attending. He wrote her an e-mail giving an 800 number where she could call him during her week away.

"Good luck again on your practice talk," he said. "Give me a call to let me know how it went. Love you, Greg."

On Saturday morning, Greg drove Kristin to San Diego International Airport and left her at the terminal. She removed her wedding ring before meeting up with Dr. Robertson by the gate. The two lovers then boarded the airplane, sitting next to each other for the six-hour flight. It was late afternoon when they arrived and caught a taxi to the Inn Towne Hotel, where they spent the rest of the evening.

On Sunday they had a free day and officially checked in at the Hyatt Regency Hotel, where they were given a registration package. Among the materials it contained was an eight-page article on fentanyl, written by Robertson's friend, Dr. Daniel Anderson, entitled, "25 Deaths on Fentanyl." A few days later, Dr. Robertson and Kristin would attend a presentation at the conference on fentanyl overdoses resulting in unintentional death or suicide.

On Monday—the first day of the conference—Dr. Robertson chaired a four-hour afternoon workshop titled, "Benzodiazepines: Pharmacology and Analytical Challenges," while Kristin attended another workshop. Later, they left the conference to spend the evening together.

At 7:00 the next morning, Kristin took part in a Six Kilometer Fun Run and, after finishing, she and Robertson saw her old friend, Frank Barnhart, who had initially hired her at the San Diego ME's office and had unsuccessfully tried to get her a job at the San Diego Sheriff's Department, where he now worked. He chatted briefly to his "Li'l Bandit," and they would bump into each other frequently over the course of the conference.

That night, at a welcoming reception at the Milwaukee County Museum, Dr. Robertson introduced Kristin to all his colleagues, but they were both careful not to appear as a couple. Dressed in a sexy but tasteful dress, Kristin flirted with all the male toxicologists and made quite an impression.

"Obviously the older men were taken with her," said Dr. Anderson. "[Kristin's] a cute little thing, and she has the body and she has the looks. She was looking up to all these people and basically brown-nosing them all. But a lot of people were pretty upset because of the way she acted."

The LA toxicologist saw her as ambitious and manipulative, desperately trying to establish herself among the "inner-circle" without paying her dues.

While Robertson and Rossum were sipping cocktails at the reception, Frank Barnhart came over and grabbed her left hand, showing a colleague that she was not wearing a wedding ring.

Later, while they were milling around at the buffet dinner, Dr. Robertson and Kristin suddenly announced to Dr. Anderson and a couple of other friends that they were now a couple. Apparently seeking acceptance, they explained that they were in love, but both in unhappy marriages.

"I'd heard the rumors, so I wasn't totally surprised," said Anderson. "But I certainly didn't give them my blessing, because I knew Michael's wife and I liked her a lot. I thought he was crazy for getting involved at all, because Nicole would divorce him."

Anderson told them straight off that he didn't approve of their relationship, as it was unfair to their respective spouses. He then walked to another part of the reception hall, but Kristin followed him.

"She started tearing up," he said. "I remember saying, 'Don't do this to me.'"

Then Kristin burst into tears, telling Anderson how much she and Michael valued him as a friend and respected him as a toxicologist.

"She's crying, but I didn't want to make a scene," he said. "I basically wanted to end the conversation there. I wasn't going to condone it, so there was nothing really left to talk about."

Out of loyalty to Nicole, he tried to avoid them for the rest of the conference.

But a couple of days later, Dr. Anderson saw Kristin deliver her talk on "Death by Strychnine—A Case for Postmortem Redistribution."

"Strychnine, a potent and naturally occurring alkaloid, has been attributed to many cases of death due to toxicity," she began nervously. "Strychnine is a very lipophilic and rapidly acting toxin producing post-synaptic inhibition of the central inhibitory neurotransmitter glycine, resulting in central nervous system stimulation, convulsions, and death."

Her presentation was not received well by her audience, and at one point, one of SOFT's most senior members stood up and challenged her, which was unprecedented in conference history.

"He basically ripped her a new one," said Dr. Anderson. "I mean, she presented the paper, but it sounded like Michael's words coming out of her mouth."

Humiliated, Kristin left the stage and burst into tears, as Dr. Robertson tried to comfort her. But Dr. Anderson and many of his other colleagues laughed, feeling she had gotten her just rewards.

"It served her right," he said, "because she was riding on the coattails of somebody that had a name so she would be introduced to all the bigwigs, while the rest of us actually had to create our own names. I mean, there's no such thing as an easy in, and all of a sudden she has one because of him. I don't think so."

Kristin and Dr. Robertson returned to San Diego on Saturday, going off to their respective homes. After spending a full week together, they were more in love than ever, and Kristin now resolved to separate herself from Greg—by whatever means necessary, prosecutors would later argue.

During the week Kristin was away in Milwaukee, Greg de Villers worked late every night at Orbigen, so he wouldn't have to return to an empty apartment. Tortured by suspicions that his wife was with Dr. Robertson, he put in such long hours that Dr. Gruenwald asked him if there was anything wrong.

"He said his wife was at a conference," remembered Dr. Gruenwald, "so he has some time and he doesn't want to go home."

Greg was also looking to his future, asking Dr. Gruenwald if Orbigen would sponsor him through law school to become a patent lawyer. Gruenwald told him to wait a year or two until the new company was more established, and then they would happily do so.

From the minute Greg collected Kristin from San Diego Airport, the arguments started. Kristin was more in love than ever with Robertson, and no longer bothered to put up a false front with her anxious husband. So, on her mother's advice, she asked him for a trial separation, maintaining that Robertson was not a factor in her wanting out of the marriage.

"He was very upset, as anyone would be," Kristin would later testify. "I had been trying throughout the year to help him understand that this wasn't just about Michael Robertson. I wanted him to realize that it would be best for us long-term."

As they prepared for work on Monday morning, they

had another bitter argument. And, suspicious that his wife had relapsed into drugs, Greg searched Kristin's purse and found three different types of pills.

On her arrival at the medical examiner's office at 8:51 a.m., she wrote Greg an angry e-mail, defending herself against his accusations that she was using again. Knowing that Greg knew nothing about drugs, she lied about the ones he'd found and why she was taking them, claiming that they had been provided by a friend at the conference.

"Flat yellow (Diazepam), muscle relaxant given to me by Julia for cramps," it began. She also claimed that a yellow pill found by Greg was an antidepressant sample obtained from a doctor because of the "severe anxiety I've been experiencing as a result of our relationship."

Kristin also claimed that her doctor had recommended she see a psychologist to help her work through her marital issues.

Later she would accuse Greg of violating her trust by searching her purse, admitting that she had deliberately led him on "a wild goose chase" to make a point.

A week after he'd returned from the SOFT conference, Michael Robertson separated from his wife Nicole and moved out to a new apartment in Hillcrest. They agreed to go into marriage counseling, and for the next few months they would unsuccessfully attempt to repair their marriage while he continued his affair with Kristin.

On Saturday, October 14, 2000, Greg drove Kristin to Cathedral City to attend the wedding of his old friend, Aaron Waldo, who had been in Tijuana the night they'd met.

Jerome de Villers was also there and was placed at Greg and Kristin's table for the wedding dinner, after the ceremony. And despite the problems in their marriage, neither gave any indication that there was anything wrong. Kristin looked radiant in a simple black dress with a string of pearls, and Greg appeared upbeat and happy throughout the weekend.

During dinner, Greg invited his brother to go golfing the next day and suggested they go snowboarding at Mammoth later in the year. Then Greg surprised him by suddenly announcing that he wanted to buy a house and have children with Kristin.

"I was like, 'Wow,'" said Jerome. "It took me by surprise."

Kristin then turned around to her brother-in-law, declaring that she was not ready to have kids, but they wanted a large house as she wanted to get a dog.

After the wedding, the three drove back to a friend's house, where they were spending the night. Their host, Christian Colantoni, had invited some mutual friends of theirs over for a reunion, and after a few drinks they watched the movie *Office Space*, the directorial debut of *Beavis and Butt-head* creator Mike Judge.

During the video there was a scene where one of the office employees is terminated, and then attempts suicide by running his car engine in a closed garage.

One of their friends, Jason Bacarella, an emergency medical technician, remarked that this was probably the best way of committing suicide.

Suddenly Kristin turned around and contradicted him, explaining that she was a toxicologist and reeling off a specific combination of poisons which were painless and undetectable.

"This is what I do," Kristin told them, adding that she'd just given a talk about strychnine at a major toxicologists' conference. "And this is why I know this."

Bacarella disagreed, but didn't press the point. Then they all went back to watching the movie.

On Sunday morning, Greg took Kristin shopping in Palm Springs, buying her a pair of sunglasses and some perfume. Then they met up with their friends to play eighteen holes of golf, with Kristin sharing Greg's golf cart.

Colantoni, who had finished law school and was awaiting the results of his bar exam, mentioned that if he passed, he was going to Las Vegas to celebrate the following weekend. Greg and Kristin immediately agreed to join him and his girlfriend.

Then, after nine holes, Greg and Kristin left for the long, tense drive back to San Diego.

Chapter 14

The Devil's Drug

On Wednesday, October 25, Kristin Rossum celebrated her 24th birthday. The night before, Dr. Robertson had thoughtfully hidden roses and a box of truffle chocolates in her desk, as a present. She also received two dozen red roses and a birthday e-mail from Greg, wishing her much happiness and a successful year.

Kristin was now high on crystal methamphetamine all the time. Later, her neighbors would remember how she always seemed in a hurry, dashing from her car into her apartment for no apparent reason. Her appearance also changed. She lost weight, developed acne and was "geeking,"—picking at her fingernails as she had done when she was strung out at Redlands, before Greg helped her clean up. To Greg's consternation, she had also started smoking cigarettes.

On Thursday, Kristin was working on a case involving fentanyl, which she was supposed to log into the ME's drug room. But the Duragesic fentanyl patches didn't end up in the standards locker, and prosecutors believe she stole them, as they have never been recovered.

She had now exhausted the supply of methamphetamine she had stolen from the ME's office, and was looking for alternative supplies of the drug she so craved.

That afternoon, before leaving for work, she began searching Web sites on her office computer to discover how to synthesize methamphetamine. She logged onto one of the reference sites for methamphetamine that describes how to manufacture "the Devil's Drug."

Then, back at home, she logged onto Greg's iMac computer and typed "making crystal meth easy" into a search engine, punching up dozens of different hits on synthesizing methamphetamine.

Greg had recently renewed his California driver's license with the Department of Motor Vehicles, and that night a blank organ donor's card arrived at their apartment. Greg filled it in, saying that in the event of an accident he wished to donate his entire body to help others. He and Kristin co-signed it, mailing it off the next day.

A few miles away at his new Hillcrest apartment, Robertson watched the Yankees beat the New York Mets in the World Series. After it finished, he sat down and wrote Kristin a passionate two-and-a-half-page love letter, urging her to make a life-long commitment to him, and hinting that he would leave her if she didn't act now.

"Hi Gorgeous," began the letter, later found in his office desk. Robertson proclaimed that he was "madly in love" with Kristin and eagerly waiting for the day when he could express his feelings in public as well as private. He told her that, in falling in love, they were playing out their "destiny" and that he had finally learned "to let myself go completely."

He then wrote of his frustration that she had celebrated her birthday and other family holidays with her husband and not him.

On Friday, Kristin felt overpowered by everything that was happening, and plunged back into crystal methamphetamine with a vengeance. She felt guilty for letting everyone down, but she desperately needed the drug to numb her troubled mind and do what she had to do.

Crystal changes the chemical composition of the brain, and studies have proved it does irreparable damage. If taken regularly, it can lead to paranoid psychosis, depression and memory lapses. Addicts with the biggest behavioral problems to begin with usually suffer the most damage.

That day, she was obsessed with getting high from crystal meth. At 8:48 a.m., as soon as she arrived at her desk, she began searching Web sites for synthesizing the drug.

Then, during an extended lunch break, Kristin went to Tijuana, where she met, a local taxi driver, Armando, who also facilitated drug buys.

"I had [read] a newspaper article a couple of years before," she would later testify, "that if you ever wanted to find anything in Tijuana, all you had to do was ask a taxi driver."

When Kristin got into his yellow cab, Armando asked her if she wanted pharmacy drugs or something else, mentioning "Christina." She said yes, giving him a hundred dollars, and he drove her to a dealer. There, he bought her a bindle of meth for seventy dollars, pocketing the rest of the money as commission.

Back at the border, Armando gave her his business card so she could call him next time from San Diego, to arrange things ahead of time. When Kristin returned to the ME's office, she carefully hid his card in her desk and then went to the HPLC room to chase her dragons.

On Sunday, Kristin wrote in her personal journal for the first time in a few weeks. Once again, she was apparently weighing up the pros and cons of her marriage to Greg, debating on how she was going to leave him.

"This is not going to go away on its own," she concluded. "I hope Greg realizes that it is what is best for the marriage."

But her affair with Dr. Robertson, and the escalating amounts of drugs she was taking, remained unmentioned.

On Monday, October 30, Kristin purchased a cell phone and a crack pipe, from Woody's Smoke Shop. But it would be another week before she used the phone.

The next day, Halloween, she bought a second pipe and

went on-line scouring the methamphetamine sites once
again.

That night, Greg and Kristin had planned to go to a
fancy-dress Halloween party at the home of their friends,
Jen and Ronnie Flores. A few nights earlier, Greg had made
a rare visit to the ME's office to pick up Kristin so they
could buy their costumes at a Party City store.

On Tuesday, Greg seemed worried when he arrived at
work. At lunchtime he asked Dr. Gruenwald for the afternoon off, saying he had to deal with an urgent family matter. Dr. Gruenwald, who had never seen Greg take any time
off, suspected he was going home to talk to Kristin about
something.

That night they put on their costumes and went to the
party and enjoyed themselves, posing together for photographs.

On Wednesday morning, Greg was back at work and
seemed in his usual good spirits. That week he was involved in trying to organize a new Orbigen business plan
with his old high school friend Christian Maclean, a financial advisor at Merrill Lynch.

"He worked at a new company," said Maclean. "[It was]
trying to get some funding."

In a telephone conversation to discuss the plan, Greg
seemed "excited" and "optimistic" about his future at Orbigen and happy to be part of the team. Maclean said he
would come to San Diego soon to see Greg and talk over
the business plan in person.

"I was looking forward to just spending time down there
with Greg," he said. "An opportunity to hang out with my
buddy."

That night Greg called his brother Jerome for a chat.
Jerome was engrossed in a DVD about Alaska and wasn't
in the mood to talk.

"I kind of put him off," he would later remember. "We
had both had long days. I remember telling him that I felt
tired and I was going to bed soon."

Greg said he was also tired because he was working so

hard. The brothers agreed to talk again soon.

But it would be the last conversation they would ever have.

On Thursday, November 2, Kristin got up early and smoked some crystal at a ladies' restroom on the way to work. During the morning, she and Greg exchanged e-mails to arrange to meet for lunch. They discussed different restaurants in Little Italy, but finally decided to meet back at their apartment.

Before leaving for lunch, Kristin hid her pipe in a drawer at the HPLC room and took a one-page love letter she had received from Dr. Robertson in July, putting it in her purse. The letter, which had been written on stationery from the Westin Rio Mar Beach Hotel, where the 1999 SOFT conference had been held, was addressed, "To a beautiful girl."

"When I think of the future," it said, "I smile and think of the future and you. And we'll come together. And it makes me so excited."

She was re-reading the letter in the living room when Greg suddenly came home and caught her. According to Kristin, she didn't have enough time to hide it, and Greg saw her putting it into her back pocket. He then accused Kristin of being on drugs, and searched her purse, looking for evidence.

As she vehemently denied taking anything, and protested her innocence, Greg found Dr. Robertson's love letter.

"He basically wrestled me to the ground to get the letter," she would testify. "He almost struck me. He read the letter and was infuriated by it, and was storming around."

Then Kristin grabbed the note from Greg's hand and pushed it into a shredding machine. Greg snatched the pieces and, according to Kristin, spent hours trying to put them back together with Scotch tape over the next couple of days.

They spent the entire afternoon arguing. Kristin demanded a trial separation, saying she was already looking for a new apartment. They both called work, saying they would not be in the rest of the day for personal reasons.

At one point that afternoon, Greg became so incensed that he threatened to take the letter to the medical examiner and reveal her affair with her boss if she didn't stop using drugs and end her affair. For once, Kristin was terrified that he might go through with his threats.

That night they had a takeout dinner and then slept in the same bed.

"It was an emotionally draining day," remembered Kristin. "We were both tired from arguing."

Later, prosecutors would contend that Kristin had lied about Greg finding the note and trying to repair it, as part of her elaborate preparations for murder. And it would take a computer expert six weeks working around the clock to finally reconstitute it.

On Friday morning they both went to work as usual. Greg seemed particularly worried and preoccupied that day, obsessing about a high school friend whom he thought had cheated Orbigen on a project on which he had been hired as a consultant. Greg spent the morning trying to track him, calling pizza places all over San Diego, hoping one of them would have his address.

"I will nail him now," Greg excitedly told Dr. Gruenwald once he had the information. "I got him. I will visit him tonight."

Kristin also went to work that morning shaken about Greg's ultimatum to tell the medical examiner about her affair and drug use. She even stopped smoking meth after the argument, in case Greg went through with his threat and she was drug-tested.

Soon after she arrived, she went into Dr. Robertson's office and told him about Greg's ultimatum.

"He was concerned," she would later explain. "I had taken off a half-day on Thursday and he wondered what it was all about."

Dr. Robertson would later tell Homicide detectives that Kristin had told him that Greg suspected she was using drugs again, although she denied it. But Robertson already had his suspicions, he said.

"She was not doing her routine as far as work was concerned. She would take breaks and things like that. I started to wonder whether or not she was maybe re-using again."

That evening, Kristin and Greg left work early to go grocery shopping. Greg would turn 27 in a week and a half, and her parents were coming to San Diego to celebrate both their birthdays. It was the first time they had seen the Rossums in almost a month.

They went to a Vons supermarket and bought ingredients to make gin martinis, thinking that would be a suitable summer drink. And according to Kristin, they had agreed to be on their best behavior, so her parents wouldn't be uncomfortable.

Greg had made reservations for four at the Prado Italian restaurant in Balboa Park for 8:00 p.m., but Ralph and Constance Rossum got caught in traffic on I-5 and didn't arrive at their apartment until almost 7:30.

When they walked in, Greg welcomed them, offering them gin martinis.

"I didn't really want one," Constance would later remember. "But I didn't want to hurt his feelings."

As the Rossums shared a drink, Constance remarked that a single red rose in a vase in the kitchen looked "exquisite." Greg explained that he had bought Kristin two dozen roses for her birthday, and this was the only remaining one.

Constance would later claim that Greg scared her, by suddenly saying dramatically, "Of all the roses, that single one survived."

"Ralph and I looked at each other," she later testified. "We thought, 'Wow, you are waxing poetic there.'"

Kristin got her camera and they took photographs of each other, smiling at the dining room table. Then Greg drove them all to the Prado, where they were seated for dinner. They ordered drinks and then had a bottle of wine with their meal.

Professor Rossum would later accuse his son-in-law of

twice making a scene at dinner, and having to be told to keep it down.

"Greg seemed very agitated about a number of matters," Constance would remember. "Very strange table conversation."

The Rossums claim that Greg seemed upset that his mother had still not received her wedding album, seventeen months after the event. Constance assured him she had already spoken to the photographer, and it was being taken care of.

Later in the meal, Greg brought up his former friend whom he suspected of taking financial advantage of Orbigen.

"He said, 'I'm going to ruin his life forever,' " said Professor Rossum. "That was not at all characteristic of Greg."

At one point Constance kicked her daughter under the table to signal that they should go to the ladies' room for a private talk. According to her mother, Kristin told her things were "really bad" between her and Greg, and that she was leaving him next week.

"I said, 'You can leave with us now, Kristin. Please let us be there when you leave.' "

Then Constance asked if she minded if they looked for a condominium in San Diego that she would be able to rent from them. Kristin had no objection.

However uncomfortable the Rossums remembered the meal being, the photographs show Kristin nestling her head on Greg's shoulder, looking every bit the devoted wife.

It was a clear, beautiful November night, so after the meal, they went walking in Balboa Park, and then Greg took them on a tour of the historic Gaslight District in Downtown San Diego.

After picking up their car at La Jolla del Sol Apartments, the Rossums drove to the Marriott in Solana Beach, where they were staying overnight. During the short drive to the hotel, Constance told her husband that Kristin was leaving

Greg the following week and had accepted their offer to buy a condo she could rent.

The next morning after breakfast, the Rossums went to two realtors to look for condos. Constance asked for something reasonable, in the $200,000 range, that they could buy as an investment, explaining that they wanted to rent to their daughter and son-in-law.

"I didn't want to divulge anything," she later explained.

They then spent three hours driving around the Solano Beach and Encinitas areas, looking at a number of available properties in the half-million-dollar range, before returning to Claremont.

While her parents were looking at condominiums for her to move into, Kristin started researching methamphetamine, opium and heroin production on Greg's new iMac. The twenty-five different Web sites she hit included, "Secrets of Methamphetamine Manufacture," "Making Crystal Meth Easy," and "Opium Preparations."

Kristin would later claim that she spent much of Saturday arguing with Greg, after telling him she was leaving within the week.

"He was not in a state to talk about it all," Kristin would later tell Homicide detectives. "He was never able to handle things in a very logical way."

She would later tell police that they had started drinking some wine in the afternoon and then Greg downed a couple of beers before she made him a gin and tonic. Finally they decided to change the subject to relieve the tension. Greg barbecued some steaks that her brother Brent had sent them as birthday presents, while Kristin made pasta.

After eating, they put in a DVD of *Fiddler on the Roof*, and during the first half of the movie, Greg, who wasn't used to drinking gin, became sick.

"He had drank too much," Kristin said. "[He] went to the bathroom."

Then they stopped the movie and went to bed together.

• • •

On Sunday, November 5, Kristin got up early and went to the medical examiner's office, spending three hours updating her résumé. Greg's threat to expose her affair with Dr. Robertson had scared her, and she wanted to be prepared to find a new job if he went through with it.

"He wanted me to quit my job there," she would later testify. "And if I didn't, he was going to bring in the evidence of *that* letter, plus the accusation that I had begun using drugs again."

At 9:23 a.m., she called Greg and had a one-minute conversation. Six minutes later she telephoned the smoke shop where she had previously bought a meth pipe. Half an hour later she called home again to ask Greg a question.

After transferring her résumé to a floppy disk, she had a dark epiphany. There and then, it is believed, she decided she was not going to sit by and let Greg carry out his threat to expose her affair and drug use to the medical examiner. She loved her job and Dr. Robertson, and besides, she was addicted to methamphetamine. There was no way Greg was going to come between her and her present life.

Soon after she left the ME's office, Dr. Robertson walked in, looking uncharacteristically disheveled, as if he hadn't shaved in a couple of days. Since Thursday he had been suspicious that Kristin was back on meth, and went straight to the HPLC room, where she spent most of her time.

While he was going through cabinets, he was disturbed by toxicologist Cathy Hamm, who was preparing equipment for a presentation. She asked him what he was doing, and he was abrupt with her, saying he was just cleaning and throwing junk away.

Then he offered to help her set up her equipment, asking sarcastically if she was happy now.

"He was real short," she said. "I thought that was very unusual."

After Hamm left, Dr. Robertson resumed his search, finding a bindle of methamphetamine in Kristin's desk drawer.

"Being the scientist that I am, I ran a quick little spot test," he would tell police. "It was consistent with a stimulant. A methamphetamine compound."

Greg got up late that Sunday, nursing a hangover after the gin the night before. At 3:37 p.m., his brother Bertrand called him from Thousand Oaks for advice on setting up their mother's new America Online account on her laptop.

After Greg talked him through the installation process, Bertrand asked why he sounded so tired.

"He told me that Kristin had made him a couple of drinks and it surprised him how much he felt the effects of alcohol," said Bertrand. "They were kind of celebrating, [but] Greg wasn't a big drinker."

The brothers discussed snowboarding on his upcoming November 12 birthday, and Bertrand told him he was short of funds and couldn't afford the trip. Greg understood, saying it was a luxury they didn't need right now. Instead, Greg suggested he and Kristin come to Thousand Oaks the following weekend and have a birthday dinner with his family.

At the end of the four-minute conversation, Greg promised to call during the week to finalize arrangements. Bertrand would be the last person, apart from Kristin Rossum, whom Greg would ever talk to.

Kristin later told police that, after leaving the ME's office, she had run errands and gone shopping for Greg's birthday present.

"I was trying to get out," she said, "because I couldn't be there."

She would later claim that at 5:00 p.m., she and Greg had another argument about her leaving, lasting until he went to bed at 8:30.

"I started pushing the issue again," she explained. "He cried just a little bit. He told me to go away. He went to bed."

Kristin shut the bedroom door and saw the love letter that Greg had been trying to piece together on the kitchen table. She cleared it off as it was making a mess, leaving it on another table nearby.

At around 9:00 p.m. she left the apartment to call Michael Robertson, because she was "frustrated," and needed to hear a "comforting voice." It would be the very first call she made on her new phone which she had bought six days earlier. The call lasted just two minutes, but prosecutors believe it would seal Greg de Villers' fate.

After her short conversation with Dr. Robertson, Kristin claims she returned to the apartment and watched television until about 10:45 p.m.

"I was getting ready for bed," she would say, "when he emerged from the room, saying he was tossing and turning, couldn't sleep."

Greg then got some water and went back to bed at 11:00, with Kristin following shortly after. She would later complain that he had kept her up most of the night breathing hard and snoring.

"I would kind of elbow him," she said, "and he would stop for a little bit."

But Homicide detectives believe that Kristin had already given her husband a cocktail of drugs, which would be found in his body later.

Greg de Villers was already dying.

Chapter 15

"My Husband Is Not Breathing!"

When Kristin Rossum awoke at around 7:00 a.m. on Monday, November 6, Greg was almost certainly unconscious, fast lapsing into a coma. Forensic experts later speculated that she had first sedated Greg the night before with clonazepam, a date-rape drug, and oxycodone, a powerful painkiller known on the streets as "hillbilly heroin." Then, said the experts, as Greg lay unconscious in his bed that morning, Kristin began methodically administering fentanyl, either as a liquid, or through patches similar to ones smokers use to quit.

Fentanyl is a lethal drug many times stronger than morphine, but it takes time to work its way into the bloodstream. Greg was in good physical shape and his body valiantly fought off the effects for many hours. According to prosecutors, Kristin would spend the day shuttling between work and her apartment, administering more and more doses, until her husband was finally dead.

At 7:16 a.m., telephone records show, Kristin called her Mexican drug dealer Armando from her home phone, something she had never done before. When there was no answer, she called his cell phone three times in rapid succession. She was clearly desperate to buy drugs, as her methamphetamine stash at home was almost exhausted. Her desperation was understandable, prosecutors would later argue: she knew she needed to numb herself with dope to get through her ordeal.

At 7:42, Kristin called Greg's personal voicemail extension at Orbigen, leaving a message that her husband would not be in that day. Later it was noted that she called his personal extension instead of Orbigen's main number, which was readily available in the phone book.

"This is Kristin, Greg's wife calling," said her message. "He's not feeling well at all today. So he's most likely going to be taking the whole day off. Hopefully someone else will get this message and that it will not be a problem. Okay. Bye. Thank you."

Shortly after making the call, she went to work. Forensic investigators would later conclude that she left her dying husband on their bed, his lungs filling up with fluid from bronchopneumonia and his bladder no longer functioning.

She arrived at the medical examiner's office at 8:00 a.m., more than an hour later than usual. Her fellow toxicologists recall her looking distressed and near tears. At 9:30, when Dr. Robertson returned from his regular morning meeting, she rushed straight into his office, closing the door behind her.

"They seemed to be having a very serious discussion," said Cathy Hamm, who could see them clearly through his glass door, from her desk. "She was crying at one point. She was very upset."

Kristin would later claim that her boss had then angrily challenged her about the methamphetamine he had found in her drawer, but prosecutors believe that that was a red herring and they were actually discussing Greg's deteriorating condition.

After about half an hour, Kristin left Robertson's office, walking out past the other toxicologists without saying a word. Then she jumped in her car and drove home. During the ten minutes she was there, Kristin claims she washed her face and looked in on Greg. But it also would have given her adequate time to give him more fentanyl, say prosecutors.

At 10:11 a.m., as Kristin was preparing to return to the ME's office, the phone next to Greg's bed rang, but he couldn't answer. The caller was his boss, Stefan Gruenwald, concerned that Greg hadn't turned up for work without reporting in sick. In all the years he had worked with Greg at Pharmagen and Orbigen, Dr. Gruenwald had never known him to take a sick day.

"I was actually very worried," said Dr. Gruenwald, who didn't leave a message. "I thought something strange was going on."

Dr. Gruenwald voiced his concerns to Orbigen's general manager Terry Huang, who agreed, saying he would also try to contact Greg. Huang called at 10:17 a.m., and when there was no answer, decided to try again later.

After leaving her apartment, Kristin returned to the medical examiner's office, spending the next hour working in the HPLC room, where she kept her stash of crystal meth and pipes. She tried to distract herself with work, but just before midday she went home again. Kristin later claimed that she was concerned about Greg and wanted to check on him. But the evidence would tell a different story: That she knew Greg was dying and wanted to see if he was still alive.

Kristin was probably high on meth and not thinking straight. At 12:10 p.m. the La Jolla del Sol's regional service manager, Herman Schledwitz, was walking to his office when he saw Kristin's Toyota Cressida careen into the parking lot, parking at a 45-degree angle. He watched in astonishment as she got out of the car and ran into her building.

Ten minutes later, after looking in on her dying husband, she called Michael Robertson on her new cell phone. It was during that conversation, prosecutors would argue at trial, that the couple finalized plans to stage Greg's death as a suicide. Then Kristin drove straight to Vons, purchasing soup, cold medicine and a single rose. As she was paying the cashier, she handed the clerk her Vons discount card to save a few cents, and it recorded the transaction at 12:41

p.m. This would be her single biggest mistake.

She returned home yet again to see whether Greg had died. According to the forensic evidence, he would have by now been in a deep coma, his crippled body bravely struggling against the lethal drugs overpowering him. But he was still alive, and it was at this point, perhaps, that Kristin gave him another dose of fentanyl.

Back at Orbigen, Dr. Gruenwald was getting increasingly concerned about Greg, who still hadn't called in. At lunchtime, he went into Terry Huang's office and they decided to try his home again. But the phone next to Greg's bed kept ringing and the answering machine didn't pick up. Huang would try yet again at 2:24 p.m. with similar results.

"I was worried," said Dr. Gruenwald. "I thought that there was something going on at home. An emergency in the family, maybe someone in the hospital."

Dr. Gruenwald even considered driving to Greg's apartment to check on him, but he was too busy to make the short trip.

By 1:30 p.m., Kristin was back in the medical examiner's office, appearing "frazzled."

"She still looked upset to me," remembered Cathy Hamm. "She was cleaning up. It seemed like she was maybe wrapping things up in the lab."

An hour later, she left the ME's office and made the fifteen-minute drive back to her apartment. Donna Tabor, the La Jolla del Sol marketing director, later remembered seeing Rossum's car parked askew next to hers when she left for lunch at 2:45.

Just after 3:00, Dr. Michael Robertson suddenly left work to meet Kristin near her home. For the next few hours they would be together, later providing each other with alibis.

"These two meet," Deputy DA Dan Goldstein would later tell a jury. "That reason is to finish Greg off."

According to Goldstein, Kristin and Dr. Robertson went back to her apartment and injected a massive dose of fentanyl into Greg's left arm, as he wasn't dying fast enough.

Later, experts would testify that it was enough to kill him many times over. In fact, they had never seen a body with so much of the drug in it. Paramedics would also find a needle puncture mark on his arm that could not be accounted for.

At 5:40 p.m. the phone rang in Kristin's apartment and this time she answered. It was Terry Huang from Orbigen.

"I asked for Greg," remembered Huang, "and she said he was sleeping. I said I was concerned that everything was okay [because] he was not in the office."

Kristin calmly explained that she had called in sick for him that morning, leaving a message on his answerphone. She assured him that her husband was all right and had had some soup at lunchtime and would be back at his desk tomorrow. But she would not let him talk to Greg, saying he was sleeping. Huang felt as though Kristin was being unresponsive and trying to rush him off the line.

"I did feel some uneasiness there," he said later. "But I was not certain."

At 6:30 p.m., Kristin drove to the ME's office one last time that day. Later, she would claim she went to turn off the HPLC machine, but it is believed she was dumping evidence.

When Kristin returned to her apartment ninety minutes later, Greg was almost certainly dead. It was then, prosecutors say, that she began carefully setting the scene for his "suicide," knowing that she had to get away with murder. Here is how investigators reconstructed Kristin's actions over the next hour and a half:

Inspired by American Beauty, *she took the red rose she had bought in Vons and scattered the fresh petals around Greg's body dressed only in his pajama bottoms and lying on the bed. Then she took their favorite framed wedding photo, placed it by his head and carefully left her journal open on a nearby table.*

She also wrote a note to Greg, which she placed near the bed.

"Hi Sleepy," it read. "I'm going to go shopping to get

a wedding gift for Barb. Leftovers in the fridge for you. I hope you feel better and I'll see you later."

At about 9:00 p.m., satisfied that everything was in place, she took a quick shower and put on her pajamas. She then smoked some crystal methamphetamine before taking one final look at her carefully orchestrated suicide scene.

Then she dialed 911 from the cordless phone in the kitchen.

Kristin Rossum's hysterical 911 call came in to the UCSD emergency dispatcher at 9:22 p.m. as a "code blue," meaning that the patient has no pulse and is apneic.

"My husband is not breathing," sobbed Kristin hysterically.

The dispatcher transferred her to the fire medical dispatcher, who asked Greg's age and where he was.

"Okay, stay on the line with me," said the dispatcher, "because I need to give you some instructions."

"He's cold," Kristin screamed, as the dispatcher assured her that paramedics were on the way.

Through sobs, Rossum explained that her 26-year-old husband had stopped breathing, adding that he hadn't been feeling well the previous day and had slept a lot.

"I came home a little while ago to check on him," she said. "And then I took my bath and . . ."

The dispatcher told her to listen carefully as he guided her through cardiopulmonary resuscitation, to try to revive Greg. But when the dispatcher ordered her to put Greg on the floor, she would have had to think fast—if, as investigators believe, her staged suicide scene was by now fast falling apart.

"And is he in bed?" asked the dispatcher.

"What?" asked Kristin, evidently taken by surprise.

"Is he in bed?" repeated the dispatcher.

"Yes."

"Then take him off the bed and put him on the floor. Are you able to do that?"

"Uh . . . Maybe," she replied, adding that she was by herself and there was no one to help her.

Then, while speaking to the dispatcher on the cordless Princess phone, she apparently pulled Greg's 153-pound body off the bed. According to prosecutors, she began quickly re-staging the death scene before the paramedics arrived.

"Is he on the floor now?" asked the dispatcher.

"Yes," said Kristin. At this point, to maintain the "suicide" staging, she would have had to sweep the rose petals off the bed and begin re-scattering them around Greg's body. The stem of the rose ended up on the floor next to a pair of shoes.

After confirming that Greg was flat on his back without any pillows under his head, the dispatcher walked her through CPR.

"What I want you to do is put your hand on his forehead," he instructed. "Are you listening? Okay. Place your other hand under his neck and tilt his head back. I want you to put your ear next to his mouth and see if [you can] feel or hear any breathing, or if you can see his chest rise. Do that now."

Once again, Kristin broke down in tears, sobbing that Greg was not breathing. Meanwhile, prosecutors would later explain, she was carefully placing the deep red rose petals around Greg's body, from head to toe and re-positioning the wedding picture by his head.

"I'm going to tell you how to give mouth-to-mouth, okay?" said the dispatcher. "Are you listening?"

"I am," Kristin replied, as she apparently walked away out of the bedroom and into the kitchen.

The dispatcher then instructed her to pinch Greg's nose closed and cover his mouth with hers.

"I want you to force two deep breaths of air into his lungs like you're blowing up a balloon, okay? Do that now!"

Then, according to investigators, Kristin began to blow into the phone, pretending she was administering CPR to Greg. This was later considered to be her big mistake, as it is impossible to give CPR while talking on a cordless phone.

"Okay, I did it," said a tearful Kristin.

"Did you give him two breaths?"

"Yes."

"Did you see his chest rise?"

"Yes."

"Did you feel the air going in?"

"Yes."

The dispatcher then told Kristin to check Greg's pulse, by sliding her index or middle fingers into the grooves next to his Adam's apple. Kristin told the dispatcher she couldn't feel a pulse. He then told her to put the heel of her hand on Greg's breastbone in the center of his chest and put her other hand on top, between his nipples, and push down firmly two inches to begin CPR.

"And do it fifteen times," ordered the dispatcher, "like you're pumping his chest. Go ahead and start counting."

Kristin slowly counted up to fifteen, but prosecutors believe she was only pretending to pump Greg's chest. The dispatcher then told her to put her hand back under his neck and pinch his nose closed with the other, tilt his head back and give him two further deep breaths.

So Kristin simply blew into the telephone twice, prosecutors say, as she walked over and unlocked the front door, leaving it ajar for the paramedics. Then she was told to pump Greg's chest another fifteen times, and keep repeating the sequence, until help arrived.

Kristin was standing in the kitchen/living room area talking to the dispatcher on the cordless phone when the paramedics rushed through the front door, just three minutes after her initial 911 call.

"They're here!" she sobbed. "They're inside! They're setting up."

• • •

At 9:23 p.m., veteran Firefighter Paramedic Sean Jordan and his EMT assistant April Butler were working an overtime shift in Torrey Pines, when they received the emergency call from the police dispatcher. They were ordered to #204, 8150 Regents Road on the UCSD campus, for a "non-breather." Butler immediately turned on the ambulance's flashing red lights and siren, driving straight to La Jolla del Sol, where they arrived three minutes later.

Butler parked the ambulance on the red-brick driveway outside the complex, where a security guard let them in. Then Jordan grabbed the heart monitor and drug box, while Butler took the defibrillator and suction device. Then they rushed up one flight of stairs, where they saw Kristin wearing pajamas in the living room, talking on the phone.

"I saw the wife," Jordan would later testify. "She was crying."

When he asked where Greg was, Kristin pointed toward the bedroom, saying he had overdosed. Then, to their astonishment, Jordan and Butler walked into the bedroom, where they saw the eerie tableau of Greg's body naked to the waist, lying to the right of the bed by a dresser, surrounded by red rose petals. He and Kristin's wedding photo was lying on the floor by the dresser, as if Greg were looking at it. By the head of the bed lay a yellow cup, a blue one on the right side of the bed on the dresser and another blue cup in the bedroom. None of them would ever be examined later.

Both paramedics would later testify that there were no red marks on Greg's chest, which would have been inevitable if Kristin had been giving him CPR. They also noted there were no rose petals underneath Greg. There were none on top of him either, as would have been expected when she had pulled him onto the floor.

"He was pale and cyanotic. Blue around his lips. He looked dead," said Butler, who remembers that the bed looked freshly made, as if no one had slept in it.

Still sobbing, Kristin remained in the living room talking on the phone, as Jordan walked up to Greg's head to check his vital signs.

"He still felt warm," he said. "Still felt like he had recently taken his last breath. Like he was newly deceased. He didn't have any rigor mortis."

Then Jordan went into action, sticking a tube down Greg's throat so he could breathe for him. As he furiously worked on Greg, Butler began setting up a cardiac monitor and an IV bag. But it was already too late. Greg's pupils were fixed and dilated and a heart monitor showed he was flatlining.

While Jordan was trying to resuscitate Greg, a "hysterical" Kristin came into the bedroom in tears. The paramedic asked her what had happened, trying to ascertain why an apparently healthy 26-year-old man would be in this condition: he was far too young to die from heart disease.

"We tried to find out some information," he would testify. "Does he do drugs? Does he have some medical history we need to know about?"

Kristin broke down, saying Greg had overdosed on medication that she believed he had been taking for a while. Then she went back into the living room and resumed talking on the phone.

"We thought [it] was kind of weird," Butler would later testify. "As we were working on her husband, she was more outside and in the kitchen and living room on the phone. Most family members want to be near us and helping us out."

Then their superior officer, Captain James Barnett, arrived and began questioning Kristin. She explained that she had found Greg in bed and thought he was breathing funny. She believed he might have taken some oxycodone and clonazepam, which he had had for several years, but she thought he had thrown away.

Hearing this, Jordan and Butler searched unsuccessfully for any sign of drugs in the apartment that might explain Greg's cardiac arrest.

"He's twenty-something years old," said Jordan. "It's just not normal for somebody that age to be down. It's usually a drug-related thing."

Then Jordan began intubating Greg's body, trying to establish an airway to help him breathe, and looking for a suitable vein to start setting up an IV, so he could try to insert a catheter to revive Greg with cardiac medications. As he was doing this, another team of four firefighter engineer paramedics from the San Diego Fire Department arrived, led by Joseph Preciado and Paramedic Engineer Kevin Carter.

"I saw the dark blotches," remembered Preciado, who would later testify that he thought Kristin looked as if she were under the influence of a stimulant. "I thought it was blood that was all over the room. When I knelt down, I saw them move [and] realized it wasn't blood. It was rose petals."

Immediately, Preciado asked if there was anything that he needed to do, and Jordan asked him to help start up an intravenous line, which he did. Butler kneeled down behind Greg's head, placing a mask over his mouth and squeezing an ambu bag to help him breathe.

An agitated Kristin came into the bedroom again, repeating that her husband had overdosed on pills. Then she walked into the bathroom, looked through some drawers and produced a vicodin pill bottle, which she handed to Jordan, who put it on the dresser.

Jordan worked on finding a good vein in Greg's left arm above the elbow, while Preciado tried the right one. Preciado was unsuccessful, but on Jordan's second attempt, he got a flash of blood from a vein, meaning it was suitable. He stuck in a needle and hooked up a catheter, dispatching the cardiac drugs atropine and epinephrine through a saline solution on the IV. He then administered two milligrams of narcan, which would neutralize any opiates present in Greg's body. He also gave Greg D-50, pure sugar, through the IV, as his blood sugar was low.

"At that point we were pretty much throwing in our drug

box," said Jordan. "We were trying to do everything we could do to get him back."

As the paramedics desperately fought to revive Greg, UCSD uniformed police officers Edward Garcia, Scofield and Bill MacIntyre arrived at 9:27 p.m., and immediately began interviewing Kristin in the kitchen. Leaning against a counter, she tearfully repeated her story of how Greg had been ill the previous day and had overdosed on medicine.

Officer Garcia started searching the apartment for any signs of drugs or a suicide note, but found nothing except a bottle of cough syrup and a Ziploc bag on the dining room table. When he asked about the bag, she explained it was a note from an old boyfriend that she had shredded after her husband had found it. She said he had spent much of the weekend trying to tape it back together.

"I asked her what happened to him today," said Officer Garcia. "She said that in the morning she left for work, and she came back to check on him, and he was asleep. She came back home from lunch to check on him, and he was still asleep."

At about 9:30 p.m., as the paramedics were trying to resuscitate Greg, Dr. Gruenwald called again and Kristin picked up on the first ring.

"She was very agitated," remembered Dr. Gruenwald. "She said, 'Oh, Stefan, I can't talk, the ambulance is here right now.' "

Dr. Gruenwald asked her what was going on and Kristin said that Greg wasn't feeling well and that she really couldn't talk, as the ambulance was there. Then she promised to call him back. He waited anxiously by the phone until 1:00 a.m., but she never called.

By this time, Greg had turned blue from lack of oxygen and Jordan and Preciado log-rolled him onto a backboard, strapping him down to move him out of the apartment. Jordan noticed that there was already some lividity in Greg's body, as his blood began to pool in his back and buttocks, where he had been lying. They also noticed there were no red rose petals under his body.

"[There] was pretty much no chance of bringing him back," said Jordan.

At 10:03 p.m.—thirty-seven minutes after the first paramedics had arrived—EMT April Butler began bagging Greg's body to transport it to Scripps La Jolla Hospital for the official death pronouncement. Kristin was still talking on the cordless phone as her husband's body was carried out of the apartment, down a flight of stairs and into the waiting ambulance outside.

Chapter 16

"The Patient Can Give No History Due to His Condition"

At 10:07 p.m. Paramedics Jordan and Preciado wheeled Greg into the ER at Scripps Memorial Hospital in La Jolla. A minute later, Kristin Rossum arrived, still in her pajamas, having been driven there by Officer Garcia. As emergency room doctors spent another ten minutes desperately trying to revive Greg, Kristin called Dr. Robertson on her cell phone, asking him to meet her at the hospital.

Gregory Tremolet de Villers was pronounced dead at 10:19 p.m. by Dr. Monte Mellon. As his body was being transported to the morgue, ER supervisor Nurse Diane Bartlett found Kristin and Dr. Robertson sitting together in the registration area in front of the ER. Kristin explained that Robertson was a co-worker who had come to help her.

As Kristin was given the news that Greg had been officially pronounced dead, Dr. Robertson stood by her side, holding her hand.

"I asked her if she knew what had happened to him," remembered Nurse Bartlett. "She told me that there was a possibility that he had taken an overdose."

Rossum explained that she thought he might have taken some oxycodone that that she had bought in Tijuana some five years earlier, as she was trying to kick crystal meth. She also told the nurse that she had taken the day off from work to care for Greg, and that they had been arguing all day. She said she had left the apartment in the afternoon to take a break from the fighting.

"I said, 'Why didn't you call the paramedics long before now?' " said Bartlett. "She goes, 'Well, I've been watching him.' "

The nurse asked Kristin and Robertson if she wanted to go and view her husband's body in the privacy of the orthopedic room. Kristin said she did. Then Robertson kissed her on the mouth and they embraced, surprising Bartlett that she would be so "intimate" with a co-worker, so soon after her husband's death.

Dr. Robertson did not want to see the body, so Bartlett led Kristin to where Greg was laid out, thinking it unusual that her friend did not want to come and support her. She was also surprised at how calm and collected the new widow appeared to be.

"I was a bit taken aback that she was not as emotional as I thought she might be," Bartlett later testified. "I did not see tears. I think I would have been devastated."

But when social worker Bethany Warren took Kristin to see her husband's body, she broke down as she identified him.

"She was kind of wailing as she was in there," Warren would remember. "She touched him on the chest, laid her head down on his chest."

When they left the orthopedic room and returned to where Dr. Robertson was waiting at the registration desk, Kristin gave his cell phone number to Nurse Bartlett, saying she should contact her through him. Then Warren interviewed Kristin, telling her and Robertson that an investigator from the medical examiner's office would be arriving soon, as the cause of death was unknown.

Kristin explained that she and Robertson both worked for the ME's office, appearing embarrassed.

"I know these people," she told Warren. "I don't want to be around when they are here. Let's go!"

But Michael Robertson calmed her down, saying he would take care of the matter. At 11:00 p.m. he put in a call to the ME's on-duty death investigator, Angie Wagner, alerting her to Greg's death. Wagner had already received a call from the hospital a few minutes earlier and knew the brief facts. Dr. Robertson informed her that the dead man was Kristin Rossum's husband, and Wagner made the case a priority, as it was the spouse of an office employee. Soon after talking to Dr. Robertson, she left for the Scripps Hospital to begin her investigation.

ER Physician Dr. Monte Mellon, who had led the unsuccessful hospital battle to save Greg, also spoke to Kristin. He later wrote a report.

"The patient can give no history due to his condition," he wrote. "Further history was obtained from the female accompanying him, who admitted she had an addiction problem with crystal meth and obtained some oxycodone from Mexico to help her calm down during these periods.

"The patient and her had gotten into some sort of disagreement this weekend. He had taken some of the oxycodone and had been sleeping much the last several hours. She claimed she had seen him just an hour and a half before, woke him up. He seemed to be okay. He went back to sleep. Then when she went to check on him again . . . she found the patient pulseless and apneic."

As Kristin and Robertson were preparing to leave the hospital, they were intercepted by Operations Supervisor Michelle La Fontaine, who helped Kristin fill out the necessary paperwork. La Fontaine took Kristin and Dr. Robertson into the triage room for privacy, while they discussed donating Greg's organs.

Within one hour of Greg being pronounced dead, Kristin, as next of kin, gave her permission for all of his organs to be removed and given to the tissue donation center. At 11:30 p.m. she quickly read the consent forms, allowing doctors to remove whatever body parts were needed, and then signed "K. Rossum–de Villers."

Ten minutes later, Kristin and Dr. Robertson left the hospital and drove straight back to her apartment.

• • •

By this time Professor Ralph Rossum was heading toward San Diego, after receiving a frantic phone call from his daughter at the hospital.

"Daddy, Greg stopped breathing," Kristin had tearfully declared. "I'm so scared."

He told his daughter he was driving straight there, and she gave him directions to the hospital. Then he gave his wife Constance the phone and left.

"Mom, I'm at the hospital with Greg," Kristin told her mother. "He's in intensive care."

Constance Rossum assured Kristin that her father was on his way to help her and put the phone down.

A few minutes later, Dr. Robertson called Constance Rossum from his cell phone. It was the first time they had ever spoken.

"He identified himself," Constance would later remember. "We had never met him or heard of him. I thanked him for being with her and asked him to please drive her home, because she was in her pajamas and [had] told me she was cold and wearing a sweatshirt."

After putting the phone down, Constance immediately called Greg's mother, Marie, saying that Greg was in the hospital after having a bad reaction to some medication. Then a startled Marie telephoned Jerome in his apartment a few miles away in Thousand Oaks.

"I immediately called the hospital to find out what was going on," remembered Jerome. "I spoke to a nurse who scared me and asked if I was alone. I told her I was and she said she would call back."

But she never did.

Then Jerome drove straight to his mother's house and called Constance Rossum, who told him she had spoken to Kristin, who said Greg had had an allergic reaction to cough syrup. Jerome called the hospital again, eventually being put through to a nurse who told her that his brother had "expired."

At that moment a sheriff's car pulled up in the driveway to give them the terrible news. Jerome tried to compose himself and then called his younger brother Bertrand in Westwood to tell him.

"I was shocked," Bertrand would later testify. "I started crying."

Jerome said he would drive straight over to Thousand Oaks, twenty-five minutes away, but he was in such shock that his roommate Adam insisted on taking him.

Greg's mother was inconsolable, crying uncontrollably. Jerome was very scared for her, as he knew she had serious lung problems.

"I was just trying to comfort her," he said. "She was crying so hard that she was having a hard time breathing."

Bertrand remembers the three of them being very confused that night about what had happened to Greg. Jerome called his father in Monaco to tell him the tragic news, and Dr. de Villers said he would be on the next plane out to San Diego.

They also kept calling Constance Rossum for updates, and she promised that her husband would call when he arrived in San Diego. They waited all night by the phone for his call, but it never came.

Detective Sergeant Robert Jones of the University of California Police Department was in Escondido, home in bed, when he received a call from one of his patrol officers at the hospital, saying that there had been a suspicious death. He was told that although the deceased, Greg de Villers, had died of an apparent suicide, there were questions.

"Some of the goings-on that morning just didn't ring true to them," the veteran detective would recall. "Call it sixth sense. Call it intuition. It didn't feel right."

Detective Sergeant Jones immediately dressed in a tee-shirt and jeans and drove to the de Villerses' apartment in La Jolla, arriving at 11:25 p.m. Waiting for him were Officers Edward Garcia, Scofield and Bill MacIntyre, who had just returned from the hospital.

They quickly walked him through the death scene, briefing him on what little Kristin had told them.

"And they showed me the bedroom," he said. "They showed me the thirty rose petals on the floor, the wedding photograph. They showed me what they had found on the coffee table—the journal."

Det Sergeant Jones thumbed through Kristin's journal, looking at highlights his officers pointed out. He carefully noted the passages where she had expressed discomfort in her marriage and that she had made a mistake. He then viewed the shredded note in the plastic Ziploc bag and the "Hi Sleepy" note. He was also shown newspaper clippings where Kristin had circled rental apartments.

"So we took a look at it and tried to connect the dots," said the detective, "to see if the story she was telling us was consistent to what we were seeing there on the scene."

During his thirty years as a police officer, the last twenty with the campus police, Det Jones had visited scores of death scenes. He knew there were just four ways a person can die—homicide, suicide, accidental and natural.

"He was a young man with no indications of health problems," said Det Jones. "No indication that it would be a natural death. Intuitively you can eliminate that. He didn't fall off a ladder. A truck didn't crash through the building and run him over. So you can pretty well eliminate the fact that it was an accident."

Det Sergeant Jones was then left with the only two alternatives, homicide or suicide.

About twenty-five minutes after he arrived at the death scene, Kristin and Dr. Robertson turned up at the apartment. Jones met them in the outside hallway leading to the apartment. Kristin then entered, leaving Robertson outside in the hall. He remained there for the next two hours.

Det Jones sat Kristin down in the living room and interviewed her. He noted that the Kristin before him looked totally different from the beautiful healthy-looking bride he had seen in the numerous wedding pictures all over the apartment walls.

"She was in tears," he remembered. "She looked disheveled. She looked haggard. She looked unhealthy. Very thin. She was a completely different-looking woman and was not what I expected to see."

Tearfully, Kristin recounted her version of the weekend's events. She told how her parents had taken her and Greg out to dinner the previous Friday night, and how earlier that week he had given her some long-stemmed roses for her birthday. She admitted they had had marital differences, and that when she told Greg she was leaving, he had become very depressed. He had apparently taken some clonazepam and oxycodone, which, she thought, had long been thrown away.

That morning, Kristin sobbed, Greg hadn't been feeling well, so she had called in sick for him and then gone to work. After calling him a couple of times and not getting an answer, she came home at about 10:00 a.m. to check up on him. She claimed he was "fine" and "breathing," so she had gone back to the ME's office.

At noon she returned home for lunch and he had some soup. She said he told her he had taken the pills. She went back to work thinking he was okay, and checking up on him once more in the middle of the afternoon.

"She came home after work and found him breathing and sleeping," said Det Sergeant Jones. "Then she gave him a kiss and wrote the 'Hi Sleepy' note and she left."

Kristin said that she came home again about 8:00 p.m. and found Greg sleeping and breathing normally. She had then taken a long bath and shower and come out of the bathroom an hour later to go to bed.

"That's when she discovered him not breathing," said Jones. "That's when she dialed 911. That was *her* story."

Jones then began searching the apartment for evidence to verify Kristin's account. Kristin watched him like a hawk, concerned that he might discover her stash of crystal methamphetamine, hidden in a drawer in the kitchen, under some towels. Det Jones and the other investigators would never find it. Instead he found an empty soup can, consistent with her story of Greg's having had soup at lunchtime.

Jones went into the bathroom and noticed that the bath/ shower stopper was unscrewed and on the shelf. He immediately wondered why anyone would go to the trouble of unscrewing the water stopper after taking a bath.

"Well, that was *the* Columbo clue for me," Jones would explain. "An indicator. Something that didn't make sense."

Although the rose petals on the floor were "bizarre," the detective didn't discount that as beyond the realms of possibility. He noted the other evidence of suicide—the journal, the "Hi Sleepy" note and the shredded love letter from her boyfriend.

"Yes, he had reason to be depressed and upset and despondent, maybe to the degree that he would commit suicide," Jones reasoned. "On the other hand, it could clearly be the way you stage a suicide."

Soon after Jones completed his initial interview with Kristin at about midnight, Professor Rossum arrived from Claremont. He had first gone to Scripps Memorial Hospital, where he was told by a social worker that Greg had just died. Then he had driven to Kristin's apartment to take her back to Claremont.

"He was shocked," said Det Jones, "but he was supportive and he was helpful."

A few minutes after her father arrived, the ME's death investigator, Angie Wagner, walked in from the hospital. There she had viewed Greg's body, ninety minutes after he had been certified dead. He was still lying on a plastic backboard on a gurney, a sheet covering him from the neck down.

"Removal of the sheet revealed a well-developed, well-nourished body that was cooling to the touch," she would later write in her official report. "[It] was enveloped in early rigor mortis with incomplete dorsal lividity."

She noted that the body was clothed in pajama bottoms, which had been cut by doctors. An endotracheal tube was protruding from Greg's mouth, with a pink-tinged frothy liquid on his chin, and an IV of saline solution still hooked up to his arm.

She also noted a needle puncture wound on each arm, the right one still exuding blood onto the bedding.

"No obvious trauma was noted," she wrote, "or foul play suspected."

Wagner saw Kristin and Dr. Robertson almost daily in the ME's office, but knew nothing of their relationship.

At five minutes past midnight on Tuesday morning, Greg's body was bagged to be transported to the medical examiner's office.

At 1:00 a.m., Investigator Wagner climbed the flight of stairs at 8150 Regents Road, where she was met by Dr. Robertson, still waiting in the hallway outside the apartment. She walked in and introduced herself to Det Jones, showing her identification badge. And then, with the detective and Professor Rossum present, interviewed Kristin Rossum.

When Wagner asked her about the rose petals, Kristin said she did not know where they had come from, as there were no fresh roses in the house.

"Her response was that she hadn't had roses in the house for some time," the investigator duly noted. "All the roses that Greg had given her recently she had either thrown away or they were dried by now."

Wagner then investigated the bedroom, taking pictures of the death scene. She viewed the "numerous fresh rose petals" on the carpet to the right of the bed, along with the stem and sepals. On a nightstand by the bed there was an opened aspirin bottle, with about fifty tablets still in it, and a plastic cup containing "a clear odorless liquid consistent with water," which she sniffed. In the bathroom she discovered a near-empty bottle of prescribed Histinex cough syrup, dated 2/6/1999, which she put into an evidence envelope for later testing by the ME's office.

In the midst of her 2002 murder trial, Kristin Rossum takes a lunch recess with her mother, Constance. (AP Photo/Denis Poroy)

Greg de Villers—son, husband, murder victim. (Yves T. de Villers)

Kristin's Australian lover, Michael Robertson, who was also her boss and chief toxicologist at the San Diego Medical Examiner's Office. The San Diego Police murder investigation into Robertson remains ongoing. (*Melbourne Herald Sun*)

The Mexican border, which Kristin Rossum would regularly cross to score methamphetamine from her dealer. (John Glatt)

The turnstiles at the San Ysidro border crossing, where Kristin first bumped into Greg de Villers. (John Glatt)

Tijuana's La Revoluciòn main drag, where Kristin and Greg went drinking and dancing the night they met. (John Glatt)

The prestigious San Diego State University, where Kristin was viewed as one of the best students. (John Glatt)

The Chemistry Science Lab at SDSU, where Kristin studied to become one of the university's top students in her chosen subject. (John Glatt)

The apartment complex where Kristin lived with Greg for more than five years. (John Glatt)

The top floor balcony of the La Jolla Del Sol apartment where Greg died of a massive Fentanyl overdose on November 6, 2000. (John Glatt)

USCD Campus Detective Robert Jones, the first policeman on the scene to investigate Greg de Villers' death. (John Glatt)

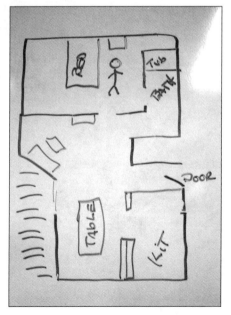

Detective Jones' drawing of the murder scene at La Jolla Del Sol.

The San Diego County Courthouse became a media circus during Kristin's high-profile murder trial in late 2002. (John Glatt)

Deputy District Attorney Dave Hendren, who helped prosecute Kristin Rossum for the murder of her husband. (John Glatt)

Attorney Alex Loebig, who defended Kristin Rossum at her murder trial. (John Glatt)

Greg's mother, Marie de Villers, flanked by her sons Jerome (*left*) and Bertrand (*right*), leaves the courthouse on October 31, 2002. (AP Photo/ Lenny Ignelzi)

Kristin's heartbroken parents, Constance and Ralph Rossum, leave the courthouse after their daughter was sentenced to life without parole on December 12, 2002. (AP Photo/ Denis Poroy)

Beautiful convicted killer Kristin Rossum.
(AP Photo/ Denis Poroy)

"No additional prescription medications, illicit drugs or suicide note was located at the residence," she wrote.

At 1:40 a.m., Det Jones and Angela Wagner left the apartment, leaving Kristin, her father and Dr. Robertson there alone. But as Jones drove home to Escondido, he felt that there were many unanswered questions surrounding Greg's death. He decided to return the following morning to continue his investigation.

"I left there that morning not being completely satisfied that it was suicide," he remembered. "Nor did I leave there thinking it was a homicide. There were questions. It was an equivocal death, and that means we're uncertain."

At 2:30 a.m., Professor Rossum drove Kristin back to Claremont, after telling her she couldn't stay the night in the apartment. Throughout the two-hour journey, he tried to console her as she kept bursting into tears, sobbing: "I have lost my Greggy. I have lost my best friend."

She also told him what had happened that evening, saying that the petals were on Greg's chest under the cover, and he was "clutching" the wedding photo in his hands.

Later he would describe her as looking "terrible," saying her face was "puffy" and her eyes "swollen."

They arrived back in Claremont at 4:15 and went straight to bed. At this point Kristin had every reason to feel confident that the police and medical investigators had accepted Greg's death as a suicide. It would now be only a matter of days until she and Dr. Robertson could finally be together and fulfill their destiny.

Chapter 17

Autopsy

At 6:15 a.m. Tuesday morning, Robert Sutton, the San Diego Medical Examiner's autopsy room supervisor, arrived at work. Every morning his first task was to take the bodies that had come in overnight out of the refrigerator and prepare them for processing. Greg de Villers' body was lying on a rolling table in the refrigerator, and Sutton weighed it before leaving it in the examining room.

An hour later, Detective Bob Jones called Professor Rossum in Claremont for permission to revisit the apartment and take photographs and videos of the death scene. He had also made notes from his interviews the previous night and listened to the 911 tape.

"I started thinking about what I had seen," he would testify. "I had some unanswered questions."

Prof. Rossum was already up, after just two hours' sleep, preparing his son Pierce for school, when Constance handed him the telephone, saying, "Darling, it's Bob Jones from the San Diego Police Department."

Then, after getting permission to tape the call, Det Sergeant Jones asked if the professor had learned anything new from his daughter that might assist his inquiries, adding that he was mainly calling to see how Kristin was doing.

The detective then asked about the previous Friday night, when they had taken Greg and Kristin out for their birthday dinner.

Rossum said they had "a very pleasant evening" and "a nice meal," never mentioning Greg's alleged outbursts that night. Det Jones asked him about his remarking on the remaining rose Greg had bought for Kristin's birthday, and Rossum told him how his wife had commented on how beautiful it was. He made no mention of Greg "waxing poetically" about the rose and becoming emotional. Then Kristin came on the line, giving permission for police to gain access to the apartment to gather evidence.

At 8:30 a.m., Jones and two of his detectives returned to the La Jolla del Sol apartment, borrowing a key from the manager. Det Jones was concerned that during the seven hours since he had been there, evidence might have been removed and the death scene tampered with. But on a cursory look, he decided that everything seemed to be as he had left it, except that Kristin's journal had been removed and there was a new glass of water on the kitchen counter.

He and his officers then spent two-and-a-quarter hours taking photographs and videotaping the death scene. They measured the red streaks on the bed and made careful notes, taking the "Hi Sleepy" note and shredded love letter in the Ziploc bag. But they never removed any of the cups or the trash from the apartment for further analysis.

After the three officers left, Kristin Rossum was free to return to the apartment to resume her life.

Dr. Michael Robertson also rose early that Tuesday morning. He arrived at the ME's office at 7:00 a.m. and called toxicologists Donald Lowe and Ray Gary into his office. There he informed them that Greg de Villers had committed suicide the previous evening, by taking an overdose of drugs. Lowe was immediately suspicious, knowing the rumors that the chief toxicologist was having an affair with Kristin. But he kept quiet and let Robertson do the talking.

Later that morning, Robertson would summon all the toxicologists into his office to tell them the sad news. He appeared uncharacteristically emotional as he asked them to support Kristin in her hour of need.

Then the chief toxicologist went to his morning meeting to discuss the new cases that had been brought into the ME's office and whether cases they should be autopsied or not. One of the first on the agenda was Greg de Villers'. Also at the meeting was Chief Deputy Medical Examiner Dr. Harry Bonnell, Chief Investigator Cal Vine and Autopsy Room Supervisor Robert Sutton.

Dr. Robertson chaired the meeting, summarizing Angie Wagner's official report on Greg de Villers' death, which she had written up the night before.

"He appeared a little uneasy," Sutton would later testify. "More uneasy than normal."

Dr. Robertson told the meeting he had been in the emergency room with Kristin, and it was agreed that Greg's body would be autopsied that afternoon at UCSD Medical Center in Hillcrest, in line with office policy involving the death of an employee family member.

At 8:15 a.m., Lloyd Amborn, who oversaw the day-to-day administrative running of the San Diego Medical Examiners' Office, heard of Greg de Villers' death when he arrived at work. Remembering the persistent rumors of an improper relationship between Kristin and Dr. Robertson, Amborn decided to take special measures.

He immediately arranged to use the UCSD morgue facility for the autopsy and, for the first time ever in office history, he would send all Greg's toxicology work to an outside agency, to avoid any appearance of a conflict of interest. Then he called Dr. Robertson into his office to inform him of that decision.

"[He] expressed real surprise," remembered Amborn. "Shock, I would say. I emphasized to him that because of this decision, neither the tox lab or anyone in it, including him, was to have anything to do with the toxicology in this case."

Amborn then called Kristin's friend Frank Barnhart, the former employee of the ME's office who was now with the sheriff's department crime lab, and he agreed to store Greg's toxicology until it could be sent out for analysis.

Then he made one final call to San Diego County Medical Examiner Brian Blackbourne at his home, informing him of Greg's demise.

"He told me that Kristin Rossum had made a request that I perform the autopsy," said Dr. Blackbourne, who was taking the day off. "I was happy to do that."

At 8:15 a.m., after Professor Rossum had left to take Pierce to school, Kristin remembered that she had forgotten to tell Greg's boss, Dr. Gruenwald, about the tragedy. Her mother immediately volunteered to call.

As Kristin had done the previous day, Constance called Greg's personal voicemail and immediately hung up. She tried the same number again, this time asking for Dr. Gruenwald's son, Chris, who shared the same line as Greg, and left a message. Then she called 411 and got Orbigen's main switchboard number.

Kristin then called Michael Robertson at the ME's office and he agreed to call Dr. Gruenwald and give him their number.

It was just after 9:00 a.m. when Gruenwald drove into the Orbigen parking lot, hoping to see Greg's car in its spot. When he didn't see it, he walked into the building, planning to make another round of calls to find Greg. As he was putting down his briefcase, his assistant, Esme Nguyen, told him there was a phone call for him from a Michael Robertson, whom he had never heard of.

Dr. Robertson introduced himself, saying, "Don't ask me any questions. This is regarding Gregory de Villers, and something's happened to him."

Robertson then gave him Kristin's parents' phone number in Claremont, telling him to call immediately. When Dr. Gruenwald asked what had happened to Greg, Robertson told him to call the Rossums and hung up.

When Dr. Gruenwald called the number, Constance Rossum answered, introducing herself as Kristin's mom. He told her he was very concerned about Greg and asked what had happened.

"Oh, he passed away yesterday," Constance told him. "Well, he took some drugs and it was an allergic reaction."

Totally shocked by the news, Dr. Gruenwald asked her what drugs, as he knew Greg hated them. Constance said that her son-in-law had taken cough medicine over the weekend with some other drugs, as he was not feeling well. The drug combination must have produced an allergic reaction, she told him.

As a medical doctor, Dr. Gruenwald asked exactly what drugs he had taken, and Constance told him that Greg had not felt well on Saturday, and had continued taking medicine through Sunday. Then, when she told him Greg's allergic reaction had happened Monday night just before he died, Dr. Gruenwald became suspicious.

"This is totally unusual," he said. "When you have an allergic reaction, like a bee sting, it comes right away, not after two days. It was the first thing that made me a little suspicious there's something maybe going on."

Throughout Monday morning, Kristin made calls to friends from her parents' house in Claremont, informing them of Greg's death. She also received a call from Greg's childhood friend and neighbor Laurie Shriber, who had heard the sad news from Bertrand de Villers.

"I was truly beside myself," said Shriber. "I wanted to hear from Kristin what had happened. I took the liberty of calling her at her father's home."

When she asked how Greg had died, Kristin said he had taken an overdose of over-the-counter sleeping pills.

"Well, she was not crying," Shriber remembered. "She was not hysterical. She was sorry. Gregory would be missed. I was uncomfortable with the conversation."

Late that morning, Greg's mother, Marie, and brothers, Jerome and Bertrand, drove from Thousand Oaks to Claremont for a family meeting to decide funeral arrangements. They arrived at lunch time, and as they drew up to the house, Kristin was standing in the courtyard by herself crying.

Jerome started to talk to her and was shocked by her drug-ravaged appearance.

"She was skinnier than I had ever seen her," he remembered. "She had scabs on her head, face, all over."

Jerome asked her what had happened to his brother, and she replied that he had taken her old medication. Then she broke down, sobbing that she didn't mean to hurt him.

Then, between long pauses of hysterical crying, Kristin said that Greg had taken all of her oxycodone and clonazepam.

She also told Jerome that Greg had been upset as she had refused to stop seeing an old boyfriend and he did not like her working in the ME's office.

"I just had no idea what was going on," he said. "She never clarified anything."

Bertrand was also startled by his sister-in-law's appearance when he went to hug her.

"She kind of felt bony," he said. "She was very skinny, especially in her face."

He was also appalled to see the scabs on her face and hands, and her chapped lips.

Then Constance Rossum sat the de Villers family around the kitchen table, alongside Kristin, Professor Rossum, Brent and Pierce.

"Marie asked that he be cremated because of the ashes going to heaven," recalled Constance Rossum.

It was finally decided that Greg's remains would be cremated the following Sunday, which would have been his 27th birthday. The memorial service would just be for the family, and a celebration of his short life.

Professor Rossum had reservations about the funeral taking place on Greg's birthday, although he went along with the consensus choice.

Then Kristin announced that she was going back to

San Diego that afternoon to personally take care of the funeral arrangements, saying she only had three working days to pull everything together. She wanted to feel closer to Greg in their apartment, saying it would help her deal with his passing better.

"[That] was pretty strange to all of us," said Bertrand. "We were worried about her going back to the apartment where Greg had died."

Bertrand offered to drive her back, but she refused. She also turned down offers from Marie de Villers and her mother, who pleaded with her to let them accompany her. Finally she announced that her brother Brent would take her.

After the meeting, Bertrand, who used to play soccer with Brent years earlier, pulled him aside, saying that he shouldn't let his sister stay alone in the apartment.

"Yeah, you are probably right," said Brent. "Maybe we can stay with Mike."

On hearing that, Kristin looked visibly shaken, rushing over to explain.

"No, no," she cried. "That would be inappropriate. He's my supervisor."

Suddenly a light went on over Bertrand's head, and he began wondering who "Mike" was and why Kristin was so shaken up by what her brother had said.

"Her reaction was alarming to me," he said. "She made it seem like her brother said something he shouldn't have."

It was mid-afternoon when the de Villers family left to return to Thousand Oaks with more questions than answers about Greg's death. Jerome did not believe that his brother would ever kill himself with drugs. He was highly suspicious of Kristin's story, well aware of her past drug problems.

"Her emotions seemed fake to me," he would later explain. "Greg was anti-drugs. He wouldn't take drugs. I was being told this by someone who looked like she was on drugs."

• • •

While the two families were discussing arrangements for his cremation, Greg's body was wheeled to the UCSD Medical Center Tissue Bank, housed at the south side of the ME's office. There, in accordance with Kristin's wishes, doctors removed her husband's corneas, heart valve, femurs, knees, hip joints and even the skin off his back. His remains were then driven to the UCSD facility in Hillcrest to await autopsy.

Dr. Brian Blackbourne, the San Diego County Medical Examiner since 1990, began the autopsy at 3:30 p.m., assisted by Dan Schaff. But the prior removal of Greg's organs for tissue donation meant that the medical examiner could not conduct a complete examination of the body.

"At the time, we didn't think it was going to be an issue," Dr. Blackbourne said. "So our office did give permission for that to occur."

The autopsy began by documenting what was left of Greg's body from head to toe. There was an incision in the middle of his chest where his heart valve had been removed, and incisions over the hips and down each leg, where bones had been taken. There were also several five-inch-square fleshy areas on his back where his skin had been removed by a microtome machine, to help burn victims.

During the internal examination, Dr. Blackbourne removed Greg's lungs and weighed them. They were almost three times heavier than normal, indicating there was congestion and that Greg had been unconscious for six to twelve hours before death. The pathologist also found signs of early pneumonia, meaning that Greg had been unable to breathe properly and clear his lungs.

Greg's bladder was almost bursting with 550 milliliters of urine, and Dr. Blackbourne deduced from his body weight that he had not been able to relieve himself for at least ten hours.

"The books say 150 milliliters, you want to go and

empty your bladder," said the medical examiner. "400 milliliters of urine, it's rather urgent. At 550, it would be very uncomfortable."

Factoring in the condition of the lungs and bladder together, Dr. Blackbourne would later testify that Greg had probably been lying in bed unconscious from 7:30 Monday morning until 9:30 that night.

He also noted that there were three needle puncture marks on his left arm, although paramedic Sean Jordan had only made two when he was trying to find a vein to insert a catheter.

Dr. Blackbourne also removed specimens of tissue and blood for further laboratory analysis during the eighty-minute autopsy. These were taken back to the ME's office by Dan Schaff and transported to Frank Barnhart at the sheriff's office a couple of days later. He also wrote Barnhart a one-page note requesting that Greg's samples be sent out and tested for alcohol, drugs of abuse and a urine drug screen.

But he never asked for fentanyl testing, which was not routinely tested for by the ME's office.

"That was a drug we occasionally found," he explained. "But we hadn't found enough of it to make it economical to screen everybody for it."

That Tuesday, a brown box of Dr. Robertson's love notes to Kristin was removed from a shelf above her desk at work. The typed notes—including one reading "I.O.U. A night of love-making"—had been read by fellow toxicologist Ray Gary a week earlier, when he had examined her desk for proof of her relationship with Robertson.

"The box was there on [November] seventh," he would testify, "and was not there on the eighth."

Chapter 18

"Suicide Is Not an Option"

On Tuesday afternoon, Brent Rossum drove his sister back to her apartment in La Jolla, staying the night for emotional support. It was in a mess after the police and paramedics had left, but as soon as she walked in, Kristin started making phone calls.

"She called all of Greg's friends and let them know [he] had died," said Brent. "I was on the couch and heard every phone call. It was awful."

One of the first people she called was Bill Leger, who had first met Greg when they worked at Longs Drugs ten years earlier. Leger was stunned when she told him that Greg had died, saying he'd get the first plane out from his home in Lake Tahoe.

"I wanted to be with the grieving widow of one of my closest friends," he would later say.

But he found Kristin's tearful story of Greg overdosing on pills somewhat suspect.

"I had a really difficult time believing it," he later told CBS's *48 Hours*. "Him laying in bed all weekend popping pills. No. No, I don't see it."

Jerome de Villers was also having a tough time reconciling Kristin's version of events with the drug-hating brother he knew. During the drive back to Thousand Oaks, Bertrand had told him about his conversation with Brent and the mysterious "Mike."

Jerome knew that once Greg's body was cremated on Sunday, it might be too late to discover how he had really died. So he decided to go to San Diego and carry out his own investigation into their brother's death.

"I wanted to find out what killed my brother," said Jerome. "I was going to try and contact as many people as I could to see if they knew anything."

Late Tuesday night, after her brother Brent had gone to bed, Kristin Rossum sat down in her kitchen to write eight pages in her journal, apparently trying to come to terms with Greg's death. Whether she was high on crystal and rambling, or trying to lend support to the suicide story is a matter of conjecture. Over the next few months, she would voice her helpless plight in her journal, often blaming Greg for the suspicion she would increasingly find herself under.

"My dearest Gregie," she began. "Last night I lost you, your precious life so unfairly cut short. I can't believe you are truly gone from this world."

Writing that everything he had given her would be "etched into my soul," she claimed that she could still hear his voice, still see him gazing at her lovingly, still feel his embrace.

The grieving widow described her unbearable heartbreak at losing her best friend, lover, and "future father of my kids" and lamented that she had ever doubted the truth and purity of their love and marriage.

Then Kristin self-pityingly asked how she would ever move on and regain her life and rebuild her spirit.

"I have to take it hour by hour," she concluded. "Day by day. Only time will tell."

She ended on a euphoric note, writing that Greg's death had given her a new perspective on life. Underlining the Latin expression "*Carpe diem!*" ("Seize the day"), Kristin reasoned that ultimately she only wanted to be a "good wife" and a "good mother."

. . .

On Wednesday morning, Jerome de Villers drove from Thousand Oaks to San Diego, calling Greg's friends on his cell phone during the long drive. Chris Wren, who lived in Huntington, immediately volunteered to meet up and help.

He made another call to the San Diego Police Department, which was referred to an on-duty Homicide detective named Laurie Agnew. In her twenty-three years with the department, Det Agnew had worked narcotics, undercover and domestic violence, as well as spent eight years on special investigations.

She carefully listened to Jerome's concerns that his brother's death was being labeled suicide, noting that his body would soon be cremated.

"He wanted an independent autopsy," she would remember. "He wanted to talk to police about the circumstances of his brother's death. I agreed to meet him."

Half an hour later Jerome walked into Homicide and told Agnew what he knew so far. The detective took notes, promising to look into it and get back to him.

He then met up with Chris Wren and they went to UCSD Hospital, as he had been told Greg's autopsy had been performed there. When he was informed that it hadn't been, he thought it strange. They then drove to the medical examiner's office, where he met Dr. Brian Blackbourne, who had performed the autopsy.

During their fifteen-minute meeting, Dr. Blackbourne said that Greg had died of a drug overdose. But when Jerome explained how Greg detested drugs and would never even take an aspirin, Dr. Blackbourne mentioned the rumors of Kristin having an "improper relationship" with her boss, Dr. Robertson. He said he had personally questioned his chief toxicologist, who had denied anything improper. Dr. Blackbourne promised to re-examine the body.

Their next stop was Orbigen, where they spoke to Stefan Gruenwald and Terry Huang, who both shared their suspicions.

"We were all voicing our concerns," remembered Jerome. "They didn't understand what was going on."

Dr. Gruenwald mentioned that Greg had taken the previous Thursday afternoon off for family reasons, saying it was something he had never done before. And since Greg's death, Dr. Gruenwald had checked his computer, discovering some alarming e-mails from Kristin, which he now showed to Jerome.

One of them was the e-mail sent October 9 after the SOFT conference when Greg had searched her purse for drugs.

"You've hurt me beyond repair," she'd written Greg. "I wish that I had been able to talk to you about more, but ... [you] make me feel so uncomfortable, so alone. It's a very unhappy place to be."

"That was really disturbing," said Jerome, who suddenly began to realize the terrible ramifications of just who "Mike" was.

On Wednesday afternoon, Kristin's toxicologist colleague Donald Lowe called the UCSD Police Department, informing Det Sergeant Robert Jones that he had some important information regarding Greg de Villers' death.

"I told him that I felt Kristin Rossum and Michael Robertson were having an affair," said Lowe. "And I felt they needed to have [this] information regarding the circumstances."

Detective Jones listened carefully, realizing that this could provide a motive for murder. He also remembered how Robertson had spent nearly two hours lurking outside Kristin's apartment the night of Greg's death.

After putting down the phone, he walked down the hall to Chief of Police Maudie Bobbit, who agreed they should now hand over the investigation to San Diego Homicide.

"We're a small police department here," explained Det Sergeant Jones. "We don't have the experience or the logistic support to conduct homicide investigations."

He then called Det Laurie Agnew, telling her about Kristin's suspected affair with her boss in the ME's office. Then, armed with this new information and Jerome's suspicions, she asked her supervisor, Sergeant Howard Willams, to call the medical examiner's office and place a hold on Greg's body to stop the cremation. It would be another two days until the cremation would be stopped.

After meeting with Jerome, Det Agnew spent several hours confirming his account. She spoke to Cal Vine at the ME's office, learning that Greg's body had been autopsied at UCSD and his specimens were currently at the sheriff's crime laboratory, awaiting analysis.

The following morning, Det Agnew officially opened a Homicide investigation in the death of Greg de Villers. But it would be many months before she would have enough evidence to make an arrest.

On Wednesday afternoon, Kristin went to the medical examiner's office to clear out her desk. She had been granted bereavement leave, and spent time in the laboratory area, accepting sympathy from her colleagues.

"It seemed like she wanted to take work home to have something to do," remembered toxicologist Cathy Hamm. "Saying 'Hi' to people and possibly gathering some folders or files."

Earlier that day, Nicole Robertson had left for England for a vacation. Dr. Robertson would finally be able to stay the night at Kristin's apartment.

Soon after arriving at work that day, Dr. Robertson went to the ME's autopsy room, where he asked Bob Sutton if he could view Greg's toxicology samples, which were being temporarily kept there before being transported to Frank Barnhart in the sheriff's crime lab. Sutton allowed him to look at the organs, although he didn't touch them.

When Dr. Blackbourne discovered that Dr. Robertson had disobeyed his order to stay away from Greg's toxicology, he was furious, summoning Robertson into his office to explain himself.

"I was pretty irritated and let him know that," Dr. Blackbourne would later testify. "I made it clear that I expected him to cease any inquiries about the toxicology in this case."

A few hours later, Robertson told toxicologist Cathy Hamm that he had seen the contents of Greg's stomach and that they were red, speculating that he had maybe overdosed on cough syrup.

At 6:30 a.m. on Thursday morning, the ME's autopsy room supervisor, Robert Sutton, personally delivered a cardboard box to Frank Barnhart, at the sheriff's crime lab, containing vial samples of Greg's blood, stomach contents, urine and liver. The box was marked "Gregory de Villers, 2000–2088." Along with the toxicology, there was also a list of tests that Dr. Blackbourne wanted, including blood alcohol, drugs of abuse, a urine drug screen, aspirin, clonazepam and cyanide.

Barnhart decided to send the samples to Pacific Laboratories in Woodland Hills for analysis. He telephoned Pacific's director of toxicology services, Mr. Michael Dean Henson, to ask for the testing.

"He was not comfortable in doing the work himself," said Henson. "He knew the people involved in the case."

Henson promised to run a comprehensive drug screen on the samples, but it would be another five days before the results were ready.

Late Wednesday night, Dr. Yves de Villers had landed at Los Angeles International Airport. Bertrand went to collect him, and the following morning they drove to Huntington, where Jerome picked them up and took them to San Diego.

Earlier, Jerome had left a message with Det Sergeant Robert Jones saying that he needed to talk to Jones urgently.

"I called him back," said Det Jones. "He wanted to express his opinion that he didn't feel that this was suicide. He felt Kristin was involved in his death and he wanted me to know that."

Jerome also demanded an independent autopsy, and Det Jones assured him that he would make that happen now that he was in close touch with San Diego Homicide.

A couple of hours later, Jones drove to police headquarters on Broadway, where he officially handed the investigation over to Det Laurie Agnew.

As a trained medical doctor, Yves de Villers also wanted to meet Dr. Blackbourne, to ask him about the autopsy he had performed on Greg. Jerome decided to take his microcassette recorder with them and secretly tape the conversation, so he could have a record of everything said. In his job as a field appraiser for a nationally known insurance company, he was used to taping conversations with clients.

"I was real emotional," recalled Jerome. "The person who did the autopsy worked with Kristin. There was a conflict of interest, [so] I taped it."

During their meeting, Dr. Blackbourne again brought up the relationship between Kristin and Dr. Robertson, saying he was never certain that the rumors were true. He also told them that Kristin had recently attended the SOFT conference in Milwaukee with Dr. Robertson.

Then Dr. de Villers asked the medical examiner for a second independent autopsy on his son's body. Dr. Blackbourne tried to allay Dr. de Villers' fears, explaining that the bloodwork and organ specimens were going to be tested by laboratories outside his office.

After leaving the ME's office, Dr. de Villers and his two sons drove across San Diego to Orbigen, for another talk with Greg's co-workers. They told Dr. Stefan Gruenwald that the police were treating Greg's death as suicide, and many of his organs had been removed with Kristin's consent. Jerome said they had to move fast, as his brother's body was being cremated on Sunday.

Dr. Gruenwald, who had worked in forensic medicine in his native Germany, was amazed that Kristin had allowed her husband's eyes to be donated for cornea transplants, knowing they might hold the chemical key to his death.

"If you donate yourself," Dr. Gruenwald would later testify, "you donate the liver, heart, or something. Definitely not your eyes. That would never cross most people's minds."

Dr. Gruenwald agreed that they must stop Greg's cremation at all cost, until a proper outside autopsy and investigation could be conducted. So far, Dr. Gruenwald, who had collected a number of suspicious e-mails from Kristin off Greg's computer, had not even been interviewed by police.

They decided that all the Orbigen staff should send a letter to San Diego Homicide detectives, explaining why Greg de Villers may not have committed suicide.

"Dear Homicide Detectives," the letter began. "This statement is to express our strong belief that Gregory de Villers, who was our friend and co-worker for many years, has not shown any sign of suicidal tendency during all the time we have known him." The letter went on to portray Greg as a happy and ambitious person with exciting plans for the future, including reaping the rewards of Orbigen's financial growth and going to law school.

The Orbigen staff members concluded by declaring that "suicide is not an option for his death," and asking for an opportunity to discuss the matter with a San Diego homicide detective.

The letter was signed by Dr. Gruenwald, Terry Huang and five other Orbigen employees. Later, Dr. Gruenwald would estimate that Orbigen was worth $5 million at the time of Greg's death and his stock options added up to $150,000 on paper.

That afternoon, San Diego Homicide detectives officially placed a hold on Greg's body, to prevent it being cremated on Sunday. And at 6:00 that evening, the de Villers family pulled up outside Kristin's apartment at La Jolla del Sol. It had been decided that all three of them appearing might be too overwhelming for Kristin, as Jerome was unsure if he could control his emotions. So Dr. de Villers and Jerome went to get coffee, while Bertrand went in to see Kristin.

"I was concerned about how she was doing," remembered Bertrand. "I thought it was kind of odd that she would want to be in the apartment [where] my brother died. Her husband. And that she would sleep in the bed [where] his body was found."

When Bertrand knocked on the front door, Kristin answered—and she had male company. She introduced Michael Robertson to him, explaining that he also worked for the ME's office and had come to drop off her paycheck.

He was wary of Robertson, who looked extremely nervous, waiting in the living room while Bertrand asked Kristin how she was doing. But as soon as he began discussing his brother's death, Robertson disappeared into the kitchen.

"To be honest, I was a little scared of Michael Robertson," he said. "I had never met him before. I didn't know who he was."

A few minutes later, Bertrand left feeling uncomfortable that his recently bereaved sister-in-law was already entertaining men.

When Bertrand got back into the car with his father and brother, he told them Michael Robertson had been with Kristin in the apartment.

"I was really concerned," said Jerome. "I was being told about this possible affair, and then three days after Greg dies, he's in Greg's apartment."

So the two brothers went back to see Kristin, while their father waited in the car. Without even telling Bertrand, Jerome flipped the tape over in his microcassette recorder and set it to RECORD.

By the time they entered the apartment, Robertson had

left. Kristin seemed talkative, inviting them to sit around the dining room table with her. Then they asked about the events leading up to Greg's death.

She began by telling Greg's concern about her working around drugs in the ME's office.

"He said it was unhealthy for her, given her past drug history," remembered Bertrand. "She said that since her problem in the past, she had become interested in methamphetamine and its psychosis."

Kristin freely admitted Greg had suspected that she was back on drugs, telling the brothers that "it hurt her so badly." She also told them of Greg's ultimatum, after searching her purse a week earlier and finding Robertson's "old letter," that she either quit her job or he'd expose her "drug history."

When Jerome asked her point-blank if she was back on methamphetamine, Kristin categorically denied it.

"She was acting like Greg was wrongly accusing her," said Jerome. "As if Greg was out of line."

Then they brought up the conference that Dr. Blackbourne had told them she'd recently attended with Robertson. She explained that Robertson was her "lab supervisor" and a "good guy," pointing out that Bertrand had seen him in the apartment earlier, dropping off her paycheck.

"He wanted to make sure I was okay," she told them. "That's allowed. Because he knew how devastated I was . . . He knew that I would feel responsible."

Suspicious, Jerome then asked her exactly what her relationship with Dr. Robertson.

"She said they were just friends," he recalled. "Just good friends."

Jerome remembered what Kristin had said two days earlier in Claremont, when she'd mentioned Greg's concern that she wouldn't stop seeing someone from her past. Now he pressed for more details why Greg would be so upset about her friendship with Robertson.

"I told him that I had an emotional relationship with Michael," she replied. "And that was over—that was it."

When asked to elaborate, she said, "I was unhappy, or thought we were—it was something we shared. You know, find yourself. There was some flirting. But that was it. And it was over."

Then Kristin started hinting that Greg was taking drugs because of her relationship with Robertson. When Jerome said it was totally out of character for his brother to take drugs, she agreed, adding that he didn't even take aspirin. She told them that she had tried to give Greg cough medicine on several occasions, but he had stopped taking it, saying it didn't work anymore. Greg had some vicodin, she said, left over from the removal of his wisdom teeth a year earlier, but it upset his stomach.

Bertrand then asked about Greg taking half a day off the Thursday before his death. Kristin told him how Greg had come home and found Robertson's letter, which she had shredded. She said that Greg had then telephoned Michael Robertson to confront him, telling him to "stay away from my wife!"

Astonished, Bertrand asked why she would bring a love letter home.

"You don't leave that kind of stuff at work," his sister-in-law explained.

She then related how Greg had come home for lunch that Thursday, becoming "aggressive and accusatory."

"You are doing drugs," she remembered him saying. "I know you are on drugs."

Kristin's demeanor was constantly changing throughout the often-emotional conversation around the dining room table. One minute she would be calm, and then she would become defensive and emotional. The brothers wondered if she was on drugs.

She seemed particularly unnerved when they asked her about the day of Greg's death. She had called in sick for him, she said, as she didn't want his boss to hear him sounding slurry, like a drunk. After going to work, she had returned at about 9:30 a.m. to check on him and found him "sleeping soundly."

"I came back at lunch," she said, her eyes welling up with tears. "I made him some soup, and he didn't eat much of it at all. He pushed it around and seemed upset. So I went back to work."

She then told them how she had begun to worry about Greg.

"I shared that with Michael," she said. "And I took off a little early . . . because I was really scared, and didn't know who else to talk to about this. We took off early, around three o'clock. We were talking and then we stopped at the grocery store, picked up some more soup and stuff."

She then said she returned home about 5:00 p.m. to find Greg sleeping soundly and snoring. She made him dinner. When it was ready, she told him and he acknowledged her with a grunt, but never left his bed.

At about 6:00 p.m., she told them, she had suddenly remembered leaving her "instrument" on in the ME's office, and had gone there, stopping for gas on the way.

When she had returned to the apartment at 6:45, she had kissed Greg on the forehead, noting that he was warm.

"I regret that I decided to take a long bath," she told them, adding that she had been studying the policies of the various political candidates, so she could vote in the local elections the following morning.

After her bath, she said, she came into the bedroom to find Greg cold and not breathing, immediately calling 911.

Jerome told her he found it hard to believe that his brother had committed suicide, as he'd never seen any signs of depression.

"I don't think he did," replied Kristin enigmatically. "I don't think he did. I think it was accidental. I don't know if he had a reaction to something. Maybe he's allergic to a drug."

Jerome then asked about the clonazepam she claimed Greg had told her he'd taken. Kristin explained that they were from a five-year-old prescription of hers.

"Greg threw away the prescription bottles five years ago," she declared. "I saw him, and as you know, you always throw away the prescription bottle and drugs in separate places. He kept the pills, I guess, without the containers."

Bertrand said it would be "weird" for Greg to keep drugs, as he never took any.

"It seems weird," Kristin agreed. "It seems very weird."

Jerome pressed her further, saying that he had a problem with her explanation, as his brother loathed drugs.

"It's not a problem I have an answer to," she replied, adding that Greg may also have taken some cough syrup, although she had spilled most of it.

"It's very unfortunate," she said. "It's unlike him, yes. But so is his behavior. So is his depression."

Kristin theorized that Greg might have been depressed about the credit debt she had accrued since she had started college. But this didn't ring true to Bertrand, who recalled Greg recently boasting that he had worked off everything they owed and they were in the black.

"It was accidental," an exasperated Kristin finally told them. "Don't you understand? I'm grieving too. I am just as confused as you. I don't know all the answers."

Jerome and Bertrand left with even more questions about their brother's death. Bertrand would later admit he believed her that night. He even felt some guilt about probing so deeply, feeling that he should be there to support her and help her to grieve Greg. But Jerome was not so sure.

Later that night, the brothers transcribed every word on the tape, rewinding it over and over again, as some of it was hard to hear.

"It was kind of a long process," Bertrand remembered. "We would listen to it, write it down by hand. Try to make certain words out."

When Jerome gave Det Agnew a CD he'd made of the tape and his written transcript, it would prove a crucial part of her investigation.

• • •

At 8:00 on Friday evening, Greg de Villers' friend Bill Leger arrived at the La Jolla del Sol apartment to see Kristin. Now that police had put a hold on Greg's body, and there would be no cremation, Kristin had arranged a simple memorial service on Sunday, which would have been Greg's 27th birthday. Leger had planned to attend.

Kristin looked terrible, with fresh scabs on her once-beautiful face, her blonde hair unwashed and greasy.

"She was withdrawn," Leger remembered, "and a little distraught in her appearance."

Leger ordered in a large pizza, but when it arrived, Kristin did not have much of an appetite, managing to eat a few bites while Leger ate two slices. While he was there, the phone rang and Kristin talked for a few minutes.

She informed Leger that the call had come from her boss, Michael Robertson, asking if he could come over to see her that night. Then she surprised her husband's close friend by announcing that she had started to have "feelings" for Dr. Robertson, and that they had been to a toxicology conference together a few weeks earlier.

At about 10:00 p.m., Kristin said she was getting tired and wanted to take a bath before going to bed. Leger took the hint and, after wrapping the remaining seven pizza slices and putting them in the fridge, he left.

Leger and his mother returned to the apartment early the next morning, bringing food for the guests after the memorial service. When he opened the fridge, he was surprised to see that only one slice of the pizza remained. He was shocked to think Dr. Robertson had spent the night alone with the new widow in Greg's bed.

On Sunday, November 12, Kristin looked every inch the grieving widow at the small family memorial service for Greg. After the service, Jerome went back to Greg's apartment and noticed that Kristin had now removed every trace of him. The framed wedding pictures that had adorned every wall had been taken down, and he couldn't see any of Greg's possessions anywhere.

But when he left, he saw his brother's favorite Nike sandals lying in a trash can outside the apartment complex.

Chapter 19

Under Suspicion

On Monday, November 13, one week after Greg's death, Dr. Michael Robertson invited his laboratory staff to drinks at the 94th Aero Squadron Restaurant to show their support for Kristin. Only a handful turned up for the two-hour get-together, the majority preferring to stay away.

Kristin arrived late, looking sad and shaken-up, and appearing highly nervous and fidgety.

"She had scratches on her hands and face," recalled Christine Robertson, a student worker at the ME's office, and no relation to Dr. Robertson.

They all sat around a table at the restaurant, Kristin sipping a drink as she sadly told her colleagues about the arrangements she was making for Greg's funeral. Then she brought them up to date with what she'd done since her husband's death.

The gathering broke up after about an hour, and Kristin left to go home, followed shortly by Dr. Robertson.

A couple of days later, Pacific Laboratory's Director of Toxicology Michael Henson got the results of the tests he had carried out on Greg de Villers' samples, and was astonished. The comprehensive drug screen had tested positive for the obscure but lethal drug fentanyl, although the tests hadn't revealed exactly how much was present.

He immediately called Frank Barnhart in the sheriff's crime lab to inform him.

"Oh shit!" said Barnhart, who said he would get back to him.

Barnhart immediately called Dr. Brian Blackbourne with the news, who in turn alerted Lloyd Amborn. Dr. Robertson was immediately summoned into Amborn's office and ordered to break off all contact with Kristin, without being told why.

Although Barnhart liked Kristin, he was also determined to find out how Greg had died. So on his own initiative, he ordered the samples to be re-tested by Pacific Laboratories, and also by specialist labs in Las Vegas and Canada. He instructed them to spare no expense and do whatever testing was needed to confirm fentanyl and measure the quantities in which it occurred. It was something he had never done in his long career.

That week, Kristin Rossum made several trips to Tijuana, scoring methamphetamine from her taxi driver contact. Now on bereavement leave, she spent her days getting high at home and most nights with Dr. Robertson. At this time, they had no idea they were being investigated by the Homicide task force, believing they were now free to "pursue their destiny" together.

Since Greg's death, hospital social worker Diane Warren had become increasingly concerned about Kristin coping alone with her husband's death. She began calling Kristin leaving messages, but she never got a reply. In mid-November she called Michael Robertson's home number, which he had provided at the hospital, and his by-now estranged wife Nicole answered. When Warren asked for Kristin Rossum, Nicole went ballistic.

"You tell that whore not to call here!" yelled the angry Australian.

The social worker was so astonished by the outburst that, after trying to explain the circumstances, she put down the phone.

"She used words like 'whore' and 'bitch,' " Warren later testified. "Very strong language indicating that there was an inappropriate relationship between [Kristin] and this man."

Angela Wagner, who had conducted the official ME's office investigation the night of Greg's death, was also worried about how Kristin and her family were coping. So she went to Dr. Robertson's office to find out. He suggested they meet outside the office on a social basis. Consequently, she had dinner with Kristin and another colleague named Dan Maddox in the middle of November. Although he had arranged the evening, Dr. Robertson never showed.

A few days later, toxicologist Cathy Hamm happened to be using Dr. Robertson's telephone when she looked in his desk for a blank sheet of paper. In a drawer, she found a two-page handwritten love letter that Robertson had written to Kristin but never given her. After reading the "Hi Gorgeous," letter—which bemoaned the fact that he wouldn't be able to spend Thanksgiving and Christmas with her because of Greg—Hamm showed it to her colleague Donald Lowe. Then, believing it to be important evidence, he faxed it to Det Laurie Agnew, who seemed extremely interested.

Since opening the special investigation into Greg's death, Agnew and her team of three detectives had begun questioning potential witnesses. She was in daily touch with the ME's office and the UCSD Police Department, but so far had not approached Kristin Rossum or Michael Robertson.

On November 22, Sergeant Howard Williams told Agnew about the massive doses of fentanyl in Greg's body that Pacific and the two other laboratories—who had confirmed Pacific's results—had reported to Frank Barnhart the day before. The three labs had all run a series of tests that conclusively proved that Greg had had enough fentanyl in his body to have killed him many times over. In fact, his blood contained an astronomical count of fifty-seven nanograms per milliliter—nineteen times the amount that would have stopped his breathing.

In her twenty-three years in the police department, Det

Agnew had never come across fentanyl, and immediately ordered her team to find out everything they could about the lethal drug.

That morning, Agnew called Medical Examiner Dr. Brian Blackbourne to discuss the results and their ramifications, asking him to keep them secret. Around noon, she telephoned Kristin Rossum, asking her to come to the police department that afternoon, to be interviewed about her husband's death.

Kristin readily agreed to meet Det Agnew in the lobby at police headquarters an hour later, but when she put down the phone, she was shaken. She had been about to leave for Tijuana to score crystal meth, to help her cope with a visit she had received the night before from Jerome de Villers.

On Tuesday night, without warning, Jerome had shown up on her doorstep. He'd wanted to go through her story once again, convinced that Kristin knew far more than she was saying about his brother's death. He began interrogating her, trying to get at the truth.

"I worry about him, because he can't deal with this," Kristin would tell police the following day. "He just seems like he's going to explode."

Jerome carefully led her through everything that she had told him in the days after Greg's death, repeating that his brother had hated drugs. Kristin stood by her story, saying Jerome had no idea just how upset Greg had become. Eventually a frustrated Jerome asked her how she could possibly accept the idea that Greg had committed suicide. Grasping at straws, he even theorized that maybe a stranger had come into the apartment and murdered Greg while she was taking her bath.

"He just lets his mind go crazy," Kristin later complained to police. "He would rather believe some ludicrous conspiracy theory rather than his brother maybe has [problems]."

First thing the next morning, Kristin had gone out and bought a Rottweiler puppy she named Bear, for company and future protection.

At 1:30 p.m., Det Agnew met Kristin on the second-floor lobby of the Homicide Department at police head-quarters. She escorted Kristin to an interview room where they were joined by Det Jimmy Valle, who was also working the case. Earlier, they had decided not to mention that they now knew Greg had died from a massive fentanyl overdose, as they didn't want to scare her. A video-recorder was turned on, and Det Agnew began the interview, saying that Kristin was free to leave at any time if she felt uncomfortable.

The middle-aged detective began by trying to put Kristin at ease and relating to her, saying that she had a son Kristin's age. She said there were a number of discrepancies in the reports so far that she needed to straighten out, and began summing up the basic facts.

"[I was] a total basket case at the time," Kristin told her, before asking if it was standard procedure for the campus police to "pass off" cases to Homicide. Agnew explained that the campus police were not equipped to deal with real investigations.

Then she asked Kristin why she rarely used her married name.

"It's a lot of paperwork," replied Kristin. "And plus, he has this beautifully long, gorgeous French name that no American gets right."

Agnew then asked how she had first met Greg. Kristin admitted running away because of a drug problem, saying that he had saved her and cleaned her up.

"He was my angel, and I clung to him," she sobbed. "He helped me through the most difficult time in my life."

Saying she realized how hard it must be for Kristin, Agnew asked about the day of Greg's death. Kristin then went into a long monologue, telling the detectives how she had "freaked out" before the wedding. Things had only gotten worse, she said, after they'd married with his "constant clinging." Then the Saturday before he died, she had told him she was leaving him.

"He got really upset," Kristin explained to the detectives. "And, like he's done in the past a couple of times . . . he blows up, gets irate and won't talk to me . . . goes and hides himself in our bed."

After a sleepless Sunday night, he had "sounded like he was drunk or something" and was slurring. She had then gone to work, after calling in sick for him. She had tried calling him, and when there was no answer she returned to the apartment at about 9:30 a.m. and found him asleep. She drove back to the ME's office, but came home for lunch at 11:30 a.m. and made him some soup, which he pushed around.

"I said, 'What's going on? What did you take?' And he said that he took some old prescriptions that he hadn't thrown away. They were mine, like over five years ago. I said, 'Please don't take any more.' He said, 'There aren't any more.' I was so mad at him about that."

According to Kristin, Greg seemed to improve, so she then went back to work.

"I needed to talk to Michael . . . Dr. Robertson about some personal things," she said. "So I left work early and he also left early. I spoke to him for about an hour and a half in the afternoon before going home at about 5:15 p.m."

While she prepared dinner, Greg was "stirring a bit and snoring," so she told him it was too difficult for her to be there and went out to run some errands and buy a wedding gift for her cousin.

"I came back," she said. "He's quiet and started sleeping peacefully. I told him I was going to take a bath. I went in and gave him a little kiss on the forehead. Half-angry and just half-sad for him."

But after taking her bath and puttering around, she came into the bedroom to go to bed, discovering Greg cold and not breathing.

"I'm haunted by the image," she sobbed to the detectives. "I didn't know he was in distress. I didn't. I called

911 and I gave him CPR. And it was so hard 'cause—I'm sorry . . ."

Kristin then broke down completely and Det Agnew told her to take a minute to compose herself.

"And he was gone," Kristin continued after she had calmed down somewhat. "I can't believe he's gone. I really can't. He was my best friend. I did plan a separation, but I never expected this."

Det Agnew then asked Kristin to tell her about Greg. Calling the de Villers family "dysfunctional at best," she said Greg "hated" his father for every "bad thing" that had ever happened to him. Three years ago, Greg had cut him off and hadn't spoken to him since.

"His father is apparently a loose cannon," she told them. "The mom has a very short fuse too."

Kristin then rounded on Jerome, calling him "the angry middle child," and saying she was scared of him because he looks like "a pressure cooker that's about to blow."

But she was far more charitable to Bertrand, who she described as "well-adapted" and "well-adjusted." She also stressed that she came from a "different type of family."

Asked about Greg's reaction when she told him she was looking for apartments and wanted a separation, Kristin complained that he'd never let her have her own life or develop as a person. Becoming visibly angry, she said that Greg had tried to stop her going to the May 2000 CAT conference with Michael Robertson.

Kristin then told them how she had desperately tried to get Greg into marriage counseling, but that every time they'd argued, he became depressed, saying he couldn't live without her.

Det Agnew then asked her about the oxycodone and clonazepam that Kristin claimed Greg had told her he had taken. She explained she had gotten them in Mexico five years earlier to help her get off methamphetamine, which she had once had a problem with.

"Greg was not amused at my logic in that," she wryly observed. "He said, 'We're getting rid of them.' I saw him throw away the containers that they came in."

But Kristin reasoned that he must have secretly kept the pills.

"Hell, I'm a toxicologist," she suddenly announced. "I went to schools and graduated with highest honors in chemistry. It was something I really loved, because it was something I was really close to. Probably too close."

Det Agnew then asked for more details on how Greg's body had been found. Kristin said that, although she had often seen dead people in her job, she had panicked when she turned on the light, seeing him "pale white." The rose petals surrounding his body were Greg "trying to be melodramatic, I guess."

The detective pressed the point, and Kristin said that she had first seen the rose petals while she was on the phone to the emergency dispatcher.

"It seems so selfish now, but I was always wanting him to be more romantic," she explained. "I saw the red and the petals and I had to pull him down. His body just thumped and hit hard. It was just a mess. I struggled with that."

Then, telling the detectives to treat it in confidence, she began discussing her relationship with Michael Robertson, having no idea how they had his "Hi Gorgeous" love letter. She explained how she had met him at work in March, and felt that he possessed all the qualities Greg lacked. They were in similar situations with "questionable home lives" and soon they had developed a very close relationship. She had told Greg in early July, and it was weighing heavily on her.

"I said, 'Look, I'm sorry, we really do have issues. I'm questioning whether or not it was right to get married.' "

Telling the detectives that her relationship with Robertson was "real emotional" but "not physical at all," Kristin explained that they had agreed to just have a "working relationship," until they could figure out what was happening in their respective marriages.

She said Dr. Robertson had written her a "very sweet

letter," which she had kept at work, before bringing it home the Thursday before Greg's death, intending to store it in her "keepsake" box.

"You know women are stupid and sentimental sometimes," she told Det Agnew. "I was reading it when he came home, and I couldn't refold it up in my pocket. He basically wrestled me to the ground and read it."

She then claimed that Greg had become "mad and furious," phoning Robertson at home and telling him to stay away from her.

Calling Greg "vindictive" and "revengeful," she told Agnew that he had then given her an ultimatum: either she quit her job or he would tell the ME's office about her "drug history."

Kristin said she refused to give in to Greg's threats, insisting on a separation. On the afternoon of Greg's death, she had told her boss, Dr. Robertson, about her drug history, maintaining that it was all in the past.

"It's something that I'm not proud of," she claimed to have told him. "I just wanted to let you know, because someone might be informing you of this."

Det Agnew then asked Kristin if anyone else in the ME's office knew about their relationship. She admitted there had been a lot of gossip, and that three months earlier, Lloyd Amborn had called them both into his office to explain themselves. Although they had both denied any unprofessional behavior at the time, Kristin confided that, since her husband's death, Robertson had told Amborn they were close.

At this point, Det Valle began asking questions for the first time, trying to get a better idea of Kristin's relationship with Dr. Robertson.

"I'm curious about rumors at the office, especially since this incident of Greg's death," he probed. "Can you tell me any rumors you've heard?"

Kristin said it was just that they were "an item," but Valle pressed her to be more specific. Then Kristin began attacking Jerome, saying he refused to accept that his brother had "just made this stupid mistake."

"It's really hard for me," she sobbed. "It makes me feel horrible."

Det Valle than asked her why Greg would have over-dosed after scattering rose petals around his body and prop-ping up their wedding picture by his head. Kristin said it was a cry for help to show her how hurt he was.

Then Det Valle came right out and asked if she believed Greg had committed suicide.

"I don't think he did," she replied. "I can't believe he would. He had too much going for him. He really did."

Det Agnew then brought up her private journal, which had been found open near Greg's body. Kristin acknowl-edged that Greg knew about it, saying that it had bothered him. She explained that she had written it to try to figure herself out.

"I guess women are more complicated than guys," she rationalized. "I'm asking you to respect my privacy in this matter."

Det Valle, aware that Greg had died of a massive dose of fentanyl, said that suicide would have been very un-characteristic.

"What I see here is behavior that he's never exhibited before," he told her. "The petals, the picture, the slurring, the grogginess."

Kristin agreed, saying that it had been driving her crazy, wondering what had happened. And the hostility from her in-laws had only added to her grief.

"We're just looking for answers," she said. "I'm just saying 'Wait until the freaking toxicology report comes back before you start.' "

Det Agnew then took over, asking exactly where Dr. Robertson fitted into her wanting a separation.

"Michael—I cared for him a great deal," Kristin said. "He's a wonderful person and he possesses almost all the qualities that I would like to see in a relationship."

Describing Greg as "a great friend," she admitted that,

had he lived and they'd separated, she would have dated Robertson. Now that Greg was dead, she claimed not to be pushing Robertson into their being a couple until he had resolved his issues with Nicole.

"I just want to support him in whatever he decides to do," she told the detectives. "I just want to be there for him."

Now, after previously maintaining that there was nothing physical about her relationship with Dr. Robertson, Kristin told the detectives that Jerome had learned about the affair.

"His idea is that foul play must be involved," she said. "Either by me or Michael."

Then Det Valle asked if she had killed Greg. Breaking into tears, Kristin said it had been so painful, as she felt guilty by wanting a separation and hurting him.

"I was the cause," she sobbed. "I didn't control his actions . . . but I did provide the stimulus."

She said she was now seeing a psychologist who was helping her get through it.

Toward the end of the three-hour interview, Det Agnew suddenly produced the "Hi Gorgeous" letter that had been found in Dr. Robertson's desk, asking Kristin to explain. As she read it for the first time, Kristin seemed lost for words. But she agreed that it appeared to be his writing, and was very "sappy."

Det Agnew then moved to the offensive.

"All right, I'll be very blunt with you," she began. "I don't know you and I didn't know Greg. I don't know Mike. But we have somebody that's dead and we have two people that wanted out of a marriage. And we have somebody that wants somebody by the holidays. Just look at it as a mystery on TV, okay? Maybe you loved [Mike] enough that you guys had to get rid of Greg?"

Kristin started floundering, repeating how much she had loved Greg and that he was her best friend.

"That's disgusting," she sobbed. "That's horrible. That's ludicrous. I don't even know how to support that. Just because I may have wanted out of my marriage does not mean I'm capable of harming my husband."

"When I have somebody that's dead," Det Agnew continued, "my job is to determine why this person is dead and if there's somebody responsible for it. And I have questions that I don't have answers to do. I don't know why this young man is dead. He's a healthy individual. According to you, he took some drugs that he shouldn't have taken."

Then Det Valle moved in, as "good cop." Telling Kristin he was sure that her "mind [was] going a million miles an hour," he went on to say that some people thought she had murdered her husband.

"I don't even know how to deal with that," Kristin replied, after Valle refused to say who was pointing the finger.

"Some people say you could have put something in his food or drink," he continued, "because you have access to drugs at the office."

"That's ridiculous," she snapped.

Valle assured her that he and Agnew were not going to "blab" what they'd learned of her relationship with Dr. Robertson to other people.

Then steering the questioning around to skin patches, one of the ways fentanyl can be administered, he asked if she had any nicotine neck patches in the apartment, like the ones used to beat smoking. When Kristin replied that she didn't, he changed tactics, asking if she still had a drug habit.

"Look at me," he said forcefully. "Please don't lie to me."

Kristin broke down in tears, confessing that she had relapsed and was now working with a drug counselor.

"I need to heal," she sobbed, saying she was taking meth she got off the street. "I have slipped up a couple of times, but I haven't since Saturday."

She explained that she had started taking methamphetamine to build up the courage to leave Greg, admitting she had hidden drugs in her kitchen drawer that hadn't been found by the investigators.

She also told the detectives that Greg had suspected she'd been using drugs, but she had denied it to him.

"He was very upset about that," she said.

Finally, Det Agnew asked Kristin if she would be willing to take a polygraph test, and she agreed to, if necessary.

"If nothing else, that would probably put a lot of people's mind at ease," said the detective. "Take a lot of the rumors down the drain and get rid of a lot of pressure."

The interview finished at around 4:15 p.m., and Kristin agreed to let the detectives come to her apartment and collect her journal. They were so concerned about her state of mind that they offered to drive her to La Jolla, but Kristin insisted she was all right.

After getting the detectives' cards, Kristin drove Det Agnew back to 8150 Regents Road, with Valle following in his police car. During the twenty-minute drive, Det Agnew made small talk, deliberately trying not to prolong the emotional interview.

"She was upset," the detective remembered. "I was trying to keep her calm so we wouldn't have a crash."

Back at her apartment, Kristin handed over her journals and proudly introduced the detectives to her new Rottweiler puppy, Bear. When the detectives left her apartment, Kristin must have breathed a sigh of relief. For the moment, at least, the police appeared to have accepted her story.

Later, writing in her journal about her interrogation, Kristin said she was "shocked" that Greg's death was now being treated as a potential murder case. And she rounded on her in-laws for being responsible.

"Their wild imaginations started this whole thing," she wrote, calling Jerome "the primary instigator" and claiming that she was afraid of him.

Then she complained how that "stone-cold lady detective" had suddenly shown her Robertson's "lovey-dovey" letter that she had never seen before. She also considered it "an abomination" that a colleague of hers would go through Mike's trash bin—where she believed the letter had turned up—find the letter and then fax it to Homicide.

"Apparently the detectives are considering it as a possible motive. I can't even begin to comprehend how anyone could think that."

Chapter 20

The Investigation

Soon after the detectives left, Kristin Rossum telephoned Dr. Robertson, telling him about her interview with San Diego Homicide. She carefully went over what she had told detectives, and the timing of events leading up to Greg's death.

She said she had not admitted they were lovers, only saying that they had a close emotional relationship.

Later that night, she drove to Claremont to spend Thanksgiving with her family in the comparative safety of their home. The following afternoon she called Robertson, who was at a friend's Thanksgiving party. That evening, he called her back at her parents' home.

She drove back to San Diego on Friday morning, calling Armando, her Tijuana drug connection, twice from her apartment. The following day, Armando called to set up a meeting across the Mexican border, and Kristin withdrew $361.00 from an ATM at the Vons near her home, and went to Tijuana.

On Friday morning, Detectives Laurie Agnew and Jimmy Valle drove to Nicole Robertson's apartment at 8550 Costa Verde Boulevard, where Dr. Robertson was staying while his estranged wife was out of the country. After their first interview with Kristin two days earlier, they were suspicious of her relationship with Dr. Robertson and wanted to see if the couple's stories matched up.

The audiotaped interview began at 10:20 p.m. and Dr. Robertson readily acknowledged that Kristin had told him about her Homicide interview. Det Valle began by asking him what he knew of Greg's death. Backing up Kristin's account, Robertson said he'd sent her home on the morning Greg had died to check on him. Later that day, he had spent a short period of time with her outside the office.

He told detectives that he had been at a marriage counseling session with Nicole when Kristin called in tears, saying that Greg was in the ER and asking Robertson to come to the hospital.

"She was an emotional wreck," he told detectives. "She just said, 'He's gone, he's gone.' I tried to comfort her."

Robertson said he picked up Kristin at the hospital and took her back to her apartment, as she was cold and had a headache. The police investigation was under way by the time they arrived, so he waited outside the apartment before speaking with the officers. Then Professor Rossum had arrived, telling him to leave, as he was taking her back to Claremont.

Robertson told the detectives that he suspected it was a drug-related death. When Det Valle asked him how he could be so certain, Robertson said Kristin had told him that Greg had taken a large amount of "unknown medications."

"He may have taken some of these things to help him sleep," theorized the chief toxicologist. "However, the effects on him suggest to me that he took more than just to get some sleep."

Robertson said that Kristin had said she was worried about Greg's reaction when she told him she wanted a separation, as he was a "volatile type of individual," who was unpredictable.

Asked about their relationship, Dr. Robertson said that they had become "fond" of each other soon after he joined the ME's office, and had begun a "personal relationship." He said Kristin had no idea why the police were investigating her husband's death, except that Greg's family didn't believe her account of what happened.

He said his wife, Nicole, who was due back from her English vacation that afternoon, knew about Kristin and that he was aware of the rumors in the ME's office about him and Kristin.

"I had a discussion with my immediate boss [Lloyd Amborn] with regards to some concerns that he had about the rumors," said Robertson. "I make the point of trying not to get involved in rumors."

Det Valle told him that Kristin had been "very candid" about their relationship, asking him to do the same. Refusing to be drawn, Robertson downplayed it, denying that they had ever been to bed together. But he admitted spending the night in her apartment three or four times since Greg's death to comfort her, saying that she had never stayed over at his place.

"I told Kristin that if my wife and I separate, then I would certainly look to pursue a relationship with her, if she was also separating."

He said that after Greg had confronted him on the phone, warning him to stay away from his wife, he and Kristin had both decided to "re-focus" on getting their own relationships back on track. He was also aware of Kristin's past addiction to drugs and her relapse before Greg's death, saying he was "upset and disappointed" with her. But he had made "a personal decision" not to tell the ME's office that she was back on drugs, although as her boss, he had a responsibility to do so. He agreed with Valle that a "drug abuser" would be a problem in the lab, but strenuously denied knowing if she had stolen drugs from work.

Det Valle then asked him if he thought Kristin had had anything to do with Greg's death.

"I don't believe she has the ability to do it," said Dr. Robertson. "She's a sweet, caring, loving individual. Could she be fooling me? I guess."

Then, without mentioning the massive amounts of fentanyl found in Greg's organs, Valle told Dr. Robertson that he was giving him just one chance to tell police what he knew about Greg's death.

"This is the opportunity," said Valle. "Not tomorrow, not next week, not next month. Because the end of our investigation is gonna be concluded one way or the other. What did Greg die from? What drugs, and who had the ability to obtain these drugs?"

Robertson merely replied "Mm-hm," to all Valle's questions, refusing to be drawn any further.

"I'm not clear in my mind," he said, "whether or not [Greg's death] was a scare tactic that went wrong or it was an intentional overdose."

The detective then tried to trap Dr. Robertson, claiming that Kristin had told Homicide she was involved in Greg's death and he knew about it. But Robertson insisted he knew nothing.

For the next half-hour they played a cat-and-mouse game, with the doctor refusing to give an inch. Finally the tape ran out and Det Valle began taking notes for the remaining eighty-minute interview. Robertson stuck to his story and finally the detectives gave without the breakthrough they had hoped for.

After she'd heard that her lover had been interrogated by San Diego Homicide, Kristin voiced her growing insecurities and fears in her journal.

"I'm terrified of losing him," she wrote. "I know that we have nothing to hide (besides the full extent of our relationship). I put my faith in the legal system and pray."

On Monday, November 27, Lloyd Amborn returned from a vacation in Mexico to learn that fentanyl had caused Greg de Villers' death. He immediately checked his computer database for all cases the ME's office had handled involved the drug, and the ones where it had been impounded at death scenes.

The following day, he instructed toxicologist Donald Lowe to work with San Diego Police Department Detective Felix Zavala, searching all the cases in 2000 where fentanyl had been collected.

Two days later, Amborn summoned Kristin Rossum into his office and put her on administrative leave. He took her keys, so she could no longer have access to the ME's office.

"She had initially been put on compassionate leave," Amborn would later testify. "Based on the events we had learned about, I wanted to put her on administrative leave and restrict her access."

A few days later, Zavala and Lowe would discover that fifteen fentanyl patches were missing out of twenty-four that should have been locked away in the toxicology lab's drug storage room. A total of 127.5 milligrams of the drug could not be accounted for. And they also discovered that a further ten milligrams of fentanyl citrate, which Kristin had officially logged in on October 3, 1997, had disappeared from a two-inch vial.

In every one of these cases, Kristin Rossum had been responsible for logging in the fentanyl and benzodiazepine, and had screened them on the High-Pressure Liquid Chromatography (HPLC) machine she operated. When Detective Agnew was told just how much of the lethal drug was missing, she moved her investigation into high gear, convinced that Greg de Villers had been murdered.

On Friday, December 1, Lloyd Amborn telephoned Kristin, asking her to come to his office the following Monday to review her status at the ME's office. Suspecting that she was about to be fired, she wrote a letter to her parents, telling them about her relationship with Dr. Robertson, but not admitting they were lovers. She apologized for not telling them the entire story of Greg's passing, saying she needed their "love and support," fearing they would abandon her if they knew the real story.

"What I didn't tell you," she wrote, "was that I had met someone who I quickly developed a close, emotional relationship with."

The letter repeated Kristin's version of the Robertson relationship, emphasizing that she and Michael were both in unhappy marriages and that both tried to work out their marital problems. She blamed Greg for refusing to talk to her, especially after she first told him about the "emotional" involvement with Robertson. And she complained that Robertson was being investigated by the police, as well as in danger of losing his job.

Just as she had throughout her life, she played the sympathy card to her parents, saying that her entire life was crumbling.

"I'm scared," she said. "I feel so alone and feel helpless. The police see our relationship perhaps being a motive. That is ridiculous though."

Once again, she railed on the de Villers family for creating suspicion and pushing the idea that somehow foul play was involved. Why, she asked, would they do something "so stupid," to turn her into an "emotional wreck"?

Since Greg's death, Kristin had been seeing a counselor twice a week. She also acknowledged that she had become addicted to methamphetamine again.

"I was falling apart," she would later testify. "I was lapsing into much greater drug use. I needed a professional to talk it through with and help me overcome it."

Throughout December, Kristin made drug runs to Tijuana two or three times a week, each time withdrawing $360.00 from an ATM. She was now numbing herself with methamphetamine most of the time, and her behavior was increasingly erratic.

On Monday, December 4, Greg de Villers' body was at last released to his family by the police, and they could finally give him a proper funeral.

• • •

San Diego Homicide Detective Laurie Agnew was closing in on Kristin Rossum, calling in Robert Petrachek, a computer forensic examiner at the Regional Computer Forensic Laboratory (RCFL), to bring his expertise to the investigation. With more than twenty five years as a peace officer, Petrachek, who was attached to the California Highway Patrol, had worked on some of the most high-profile murder cases in the state. Later, he would work on the World Trade Center investigation and the murder of *Wall Street Journal* reporter Daniel Pearl in Pakistan.

Over the next few months, Petrachek would spend almost a thousand hours analyzing computer hard drives used by Kristin, Greg and Robertson, as well as floppy disks and CDs. And he would discover a series of incriminating e-mails between the lovers that would turn the case.

That afternoon, Dr. Robertson was summoned into Lloyd Amborn's office, where he found Dr. Blackbourne and Det Paul Torres from the San Diego Sheriff's Department waiting for him.

He was then fired from his $70,000-a-year county job for failing to report that he'd known Kristin Rossum was abusing drugs. In his official termination letter, his offense was described as "a key personnel issue with serious operational implications."

At 4:15 p.m. the same day, Rossum was also fired from her $35,000-a-year toxicologist job for breaking her probationary status by using illegal drugs. During the emotional meeting, Kristin looked like she was under the influence of drugs, with no make-up and unwashed hair.

"She didn't look her normal self," remembered Amborn. "It was clear that she probably was distressed and crying from time to time."

After leaving the ME's office for the last time, Kristin went home and called her Mexican drug dealer and then, after withdrawing $360.00 from the ATM of Vons, went off to Tijuana.

• • •

On Wednesday, December 6, San Diego TV reporter Kevin Cox, on an assignment for News 8, turned up unannounced at Kristin's Regents Road apartment for an interview.

Kristin answered the door, wearing a pullover and jeans, her once-long blonde hair now cut short and brushed behind her ears.

"She is really cute, and she is really trembling," Cox would later write in an in-depth feature for *San Diego Magazine*. "She looks like she's been crying all day and could start again."

Cox commiserated about Greg's death, asking what he was like. Instead of slamming the door in his face, as he had expected, she invited him in. The apartment was a mess and smelly, as Bear had still not been house-trained. Cox noticed that there were no pictures of Greg on the walls, although there was a framed one of Kristin and her dog.

Everything went well until Cox brought up the investigation, saying that the police considered her a suspect. Then Kristin told him to leave.

"The detectives, they lie," she sobbed, walking him to the door. "I really can't talk to you, but the truth will come out."

That night, News 8 broke the sensational story of a love triangle at the ME's office, and that Homicide detectives were investigating. Over the next few months, Cox would update San Diego viewers as the story built momentum.

Soon after Dr. Robertson was terminated, toxicologist Donald Lowe took over his job, moving into his office. While cleaning out Robertson's desk, Lowe found a number of articles on fentanyl, including a case study of twenty-five fentanyl overdoses by Robertson's friend Dr. Daniel Anderson, of the Los Angeles County Medical Examiner's Office. He immediately sent them to Homicide.

An investigator then called Dr. Anderson, as an expert, asking him specific questions on fentanyl. Although the detective was vague, never mentioning the specific case he was investigating, Dr. Anderson later warned Dr. Robertson that he suspected fentanyl had been found in Greg's body.

"Everything was being kept hush-hush," said Dr. Anderson. "I kind of put that together and talked to Michael."

A few days later, Lloyd Amborn asked toxicologist Cathy Hamm to clear Kristin Rossum's desk and box up her personal belongings. In a hanging folder, she found Mexican prescriptions for the drugs Aslenix, which metabolizes amphetamine in the body, and Somacid, a muscle relaxant. Nearby, she discovered the drugs, still in their Spanish prescription bottles. She also found the business card of Kristin's drug connection, Armando, as well as a hotel room key.

When she pulled out Kristin's pencil tray, she found reddish-orange rose petals in the desk, alongside a Post-it note reading, "Happy Birthday to my Sweetheart," in Dr. Robertson's writing. Hamm immediately told Donald Lowe, who alerted Homicide.

On Thursday, December 14, Robert Petrachek of the RCFL visited Orbigen, where he took for forensic analysis two Apple iMac computers that had been used by Greg de Villers. Taking the computers back to his laboratory, he began examining their contents for e-mails and Web sites that had been visited. But it would be another three weeks before detectives would seize Kristin's and Dr. Robertson's computers for forensic analysis.

The following Tuesday, Lloyd Amborn gave Donald Lowe a list of thirty-eight death cases involving methamphetamine, that had passed through the ME's office that year. He then ordered Lowe to audit eight of them in which the drug had been impounded in evidence envelopes. Out of those eight, Lowe discovered that the evidence was completely missing for seven of them. These had all been stored in a room where Kristin Rossum had easy access during her time working for the ME's office.

• • •

In late December, Kristin Rossum and Deputy Chief Medical Examiner Dr. Harry Bonnell, went to a ladies' Aztec baseball game at San Diego State University's Cox Arena. Frank Barnhart happened to be sitting one row in front of them, and heard them discussing the investigation into Greg's death.

"I recall Dr. Bonnell saying something to the effect that an investigation like this takes time, and it's hard to know where it's going to go," remembered Barnhart. "I honestly wasn't real comfortable."

Barnhart then turned around and told Dr. Bonnell that he shouldn't be discussing details of Greg's death with Kristin.

Dr. Robertson spent much of the week after Christmas at Kristin's apartment, where he accessed his e-mail on several occasions. When Robertson was not around, Kristin would make trips to Tijuana to score methamphetamine.

On December 30, she began accessing several drug addiction sites on her home computer, presumably now wanting to clean up.

"I'm really looking forward to the end of this year," she wrote in her journal, "and the beginning of a new one . . . A new year, a fresh start, a new life."

Writing that it seemed the perfect opportunity to rebuild her life, Kristin had decided to move on.

"[I don't want] to feel that I need to wait until the investigation wraps up. *God* I hope it's soon."

Chapter 21

The Net Closes

At 7:00 a.m. Thursday, January 4, 2001, the San Diego Homicide task force made their move. To prevent anyone from tipping off anyone else, they obtained simultaneous search warrants for Kristin and Dr. Robertson's apartments, as well as the medical examiner's office.

And as a team of detectives led by Laurie Agnew arrived at Kristin's Regents Road apartment, a five-officer surveillance team positioned itself outside Dr. Robertson's new Eighth Avenue apartment, awaiting instructions.

When Kristin answered the door, Agnew handed her a search warrant. Kristin went to read it in the living room. She looked terrible, and Officer Dan Dierdoff, whom Agnew had brought along because of his drug expertise, immediately suspected that she was high.

After reading the warrant, Kristin nervously told Det Agnew that she needed to talk to her in private, and they went into the bedroom.

"I have something to tell you," said Kristin, whose hollow-looking face was covered in acne and her breath was foul.

Det Agnew nodded and told her to go ahead. Kristin fidgeted as she nervously told the detective that they were going to find something in the apartment. The detective asked her what it was, and Kristin mumbled, "meth and paraphernalia." Then Agnew asked if she would voluntarily show them or if she wanted them to search.

Kristin walked over to a chest of drawers by the bed on which Greg had died, opened the top drawer and pointed at a box inside. Agnew opened the box to find a disposable Bic lighter, a glass pipe and some white powdered meth-amphetamine.

"She sat down on the bed," Det Agnew would later testify, "and started to cry."

"Please don't do this to me," she begged. "Please don't do this to me."

Scratching her face in desperation, Kristin asked the detective if she could flush her drugs down the toilet, begging the detective to get rid of them. Agnew refused, saying that that would be destroying evidence.

"She was crying," remembered the detective, "and probably three more times said, 'Please don't do this to me.' "

As the rest of the team searched the apartment, Dierdoff, at Agnew's request, examined Kristin as they sat on the living room couch. Her eyes were extremely dilated and he smelt a "bad odor" on her breath. She was dehydrated, her lips were chapped and she seemed very thirsty.

He checked her heart rate twice over the next couple of hours. Her resting heartbeat was 103 per minute. An hour later, after she had been arrested and taken to the police station, it had leapt to 133, compared to the normal rate of 60 to 90 beats per minute.

Throughout the examination, Kristin kept getting up from the couch to pet her Bear, and her mood kept changing for no apparent reason.

"It was shocking at first," Officer Dierdoff remembered. "There would be different times when nobody would be saying anything, and she would be sobbing. Almost an out-of-control sob. And then back to normal like nothing had happened."

He also noted her "caved-in jowls" and that she was almost skeletal.

He took a photograph of Kristin. Although normal pupils

constrict when the flash goes off, Kristin's remained dilated.

While Dierdoff was examining Kristin, a detective photographed the bathroom, careful to show the shower ledge on which the bath stopper was still resting. In the bedroom, Agnew found Greg de Villers' wallet, containing his California driver's license, credit cards and a yellow sticky Post-it with Michael Robertson's old apartment address and phone number on it. She also found his organ donor card signed by Greg and Kristin, with instructions to "donate my whole body."

Also in the bedroom, detectives found files containing a 1999 article by Frank Barnhart entitled "Drugs of Abuse." The sixty-four-page article, which mentioned Kristin by name as a researcher featured a discussion of methamphetamine and, of special interest to the investigators, fentanyl analogs. It listed the psychiatric symptoms of methamphetamine abuse as: "Violent behavior, repetitive activity, memory loss, paranoia, delusions of reference, auditory hallucination, and confusion or fright."

Kristin's latest journals were also found by her Compaq computer, which Bob Petrachek would later remove for forensic analysis along with Greg's iMac.

After the search finished, Kristin was read her rights and arrested for being under the influence of drugs. She was then driven to police headquarters by Officer Dierdoff, where she was re-examined. Later, her blood was found to contain 363 nanograms per milliliter of methamphetamine and 70 nanograms of amphetamine. Her urine had 17,700 nanograms of methamphetamine and 2,740 nanograms of amphetamine. And the white powder found in her bedroom was .36 grams of methamphetamine.

Kristin was then booked and given the opportunity to make a telephone call. She immediately called Michael Robertson's cell phone, asking if he could raise bail.

"I said, 'Sorry, I just can't,' " recounted Robertson, whose apartment was being searched at the time he got her call.

After putting down the phone, Dr. Robertson called his lawyer, Charles Goldberg, as investigators seized his computer and passport. Later they would discover several PowerPoint presentations and thirty-seven articles on fentanyl. Among them was a case called "The Crooked Criminalist," involving missing fentanyl patches, which was solved after the drug was detected in hair samples.

Robertson then called his wife, Nicole, warning her what had happened and that she would probably also be questioned by police. Nicole was furious, and told him to come over immediately and explain.

At 9:52 a.m., after the police had left the apartment, the five-man surveillance team saw Dr. Robertson come out of his upstairs apartment, carrying a white trash bag which he dropped into a large Dumpster at the back of the building. He was also observed putting something into his sports car.

He then walked south along Eighth Avenue, calling his attorney on his cell phone for a ten-minute conversation. After the call, he returned to his apartment, constantly looking over his shoulder to ensure that he wasn't being followed.

Ten minutes later he came out of the apartment again, carefully looking behind him, before returning to the Dumpster.

"His behavior was suspicious in nature," remembered Detective Randy Alldredge, a San Diego undercover narcotics officer, who was leading the surveillance team. "He actually walked past the Dumpster one time before approaching it again."

Convinced he was not being watched, Dr. Robertson went back to the Dumpster and opened the lid.

"I saw something in his left hand," said the officer. "Looked like he was moving the trash."

Robertson lifted up the trash and placed a manila envelope under it, before patting it down and closing the lid. He then walked to his car and drove off.

As some of the surveillance team followed Robertson's car, Officer Alldredge donned his evidence gloves and removed the large white trash bag and the envelope, storing them in a brown paper evidence bag.

After leaving his apartment, Robertson drove to I-5 toward La Jolla, where Alldredge rejoined his surveillance team. They observed Robertson pick up his wife Nicole, and then drive to Torrey Pines State Beach.

Detectives watched as Nicole got into a heated argument with her estranged husband. Still arguing, they walked down the beach until they were out of the surveillance team's sight.

"We became concerned with what was going on," said Officer Alldredge, "because of the verbal confrontation."

Alldredge then commandeered a Jeep from a lifeguard, having him drive north along the beach, until he located Robertson and Nicole, who were sitting on some rocks in deep conversation. He had the Jeep drive past them again, parking at a safe vantage point where he could observe them in case the discussion turned violent.

"Once I was satisfied it was just a conversation," said Alldredge, "the lifeguard brought me back to my vehicle so we could continue on with the surveillance."

Eventually the Robertsons walked back to the sports car, shouting at each other. Then a furious Nicole reportedly slapped her husband three or four times, as he tried to shove her away.

Dr. Robertson got into his car and drove off, abandoning Nicole on the beach. The team left her stranded as they resumed following Robertson, who drove straight to Kristin Rossum's apartment.

The following day, Kristin was released from custody and went to Claremont to explain her relapse to her parents. In an emotional family meeting around the kitchen table, she told them about her drug arrest, finally admitting that she and Robertson had been lovers before Greg's death.

"She told my family about it," her brother Brent later testified. "We were all very displeased with her. The floodgates opened. She let us know everything at that point."

Kristin's religious family was shocked to discover that she had been committing adultery for months before Greg's death, and Brent was said to have "gone ballistic."

"We were very disappointed," Constance Rossum would later tell *Good Housekeeping*. "I think it's terrible. But Kristin had decided the marriage was over."

A few days later, Kristin's high school friend Melissa Prager met her in San Diego and was shocked at her appearance. It was the first time Melissa had seen her since Greg's death, and she looked painfully thin, far worse than she had when she was addicted to drugs at Claremont High.

"She was deteriorating," Prager later said. "I remember her having black circles around her eyes, and obviously very stressed. She confronted me with the truth that she had been using drugs."

At the police station, Randy Alldredge would examine the manila envelope that Dr. Robertson had thrown into the Dumpster, finding Kristin's love letters and greeting cards, some of which had been torn into pieces. There was also a SOFT bag he had been given at the Milwaukee conference, containing love notes and a book on sex.

On Tuesday, January 9, Michael Robertson's lawyer, Charles Goldberg, called San Diego Homicide, requesting a meeting. Initially, Goldberg had resisted, but Robertson insisted he wanted another meeting with investigators, who had already interviewed Nicole. He also wanted the computers that had been seized from his apartment returned.

At 9:10 a.m. the next morning, Robertson and Goldberg arrived at police headquarters and were shown into an interview room at the Homicide Department. There, Detectives Laurie Agnew and Jim Valle joined them, and informed them that the meeting would be recorded.

"You are not under arrest," Det Valle told Robertson.

"In fact, I'm not even going to advise you of your rights."

Goldberg told the detectives that he didn't want Dr. Robertson to discuss his relationship or contacts with Kristin after Greg de Villers' death.

"This is a very sore point," said the attorney, "that has caused a problem with him personally in terms of his wife [and] his marriage."

After asking Dr. Robertson about routine procedures at the ME's office and the storage of impounded drugs and standards, Det Valle asked him if he knew that fentanyl had been found in Greg's body. Robertson admitted he had heard that from his friend Dr. Anderson, although he had still not been told officially.

Then Valle asked if an employee of the ME's office would know that the office did not routinely screen for fentanyl. Knowing that, might someone think he or she could get away with murder?

At this point, Goldberg stepped in, telling the detective to back off. But Dr. Robertson answered anyway, saying the fentanyl would eventually be found in a second round of testing.

Det Valle also told Robertson that they now believed Greg had been injected with fentanyl, but Robertson refused to be drawn into a discussion of how that could have happened and how much of the drug would be lethal. Frustrated, Valle changed course and tried to reason with him.

"You are a very intelligent young man," said the detective, adding that it wouldn't take a scientist to figure out they weren't buying the suicide story. "Someone had to have taken an active role in this. Possibly Kristin . . . or in this case, it just happens [that] you're having a relationship with her at the time."

Suddenly, for the first time in the interview, Det Agnew stopped her colleague's line of questioning, changing the topic to Kristin's relapse into drugs. Robertson maintained that he had become suspicious the weekend before Greg's death, and had searched her drawer and found some methamphetamine, which he disposed of.

On the Monday morning Greg died, Robinson said he had "dragged" Kristin to his office, telling her not even to try to deny she was doing drugs.

Detective Valle then said, "Take a gander," and produced the love letters and cards pulled out of Robertson's trash, asking why he had tried to dispose of them.

"In all honesty, I didn't want them in the house," admitted Dr. Robertson. "I'm not denying it. I did get rid of a couple of things."

Then Dr. Robertson told the detectives that he had ended his relationship with Kristin, telling her he didn't want any further contact.

Det Valle then asked whether he would tell police if he knew that Kristin had killed her husband.

"Absolutely," replied Robertson.

"Why?" asked Valle.

"Because I lost my job," replied Robertson. "I've lost my profession. I'm losing my wife. I want to get back with my wife. I don't want to be a part of this. I had a relationship with Kristin, [but] this isn't where I envision my life beginning in 2001—in the middle of a homicide investigation. I want it over and done with."

Then Goldberg asked if his client could have his Dell Latitude laptop computer back, as he had two conferences coming up. Agnew refused, saying it had not been examined yet and they would need a court order to return it.

"We'll look into it and see what we can do," replied Valle.

The interview finished at 11:00 a.m., with Goldberg refusing to allow his client to take a polygraph test unless his demands for limiting the questions would be met.

"Polygraphs are used as a tool of interrogation," said the lawyer. "They are not used to determine the truth."

On January 26, Lloyd Amborn asked Donald Lowe to audit all drugs for analysis in the ME's office for fentanyl and drugs of abuse. Amborn was shocked when Lowe discovered that there were eleven drug standards where whole vials of methamphetamine, amphetamine and cocaine were missing. Other drug samples that could not be accounted for were fentanyl and oxycodone, both of which had been discovered in Greg's toxicology.

Further audits of the ME's office during the next few months would reveal even more drugs to be missing.

"There were hundreds and hundreds of drugs stored in that office," Det Agnew would later tell a reporter. "Of all of them, only meth and the three drugs found in Greg's body were missing."

Chapter 22

In Limbo

In late January 2001, Kristin Rossum found work as an assistant chemist with a small Sorrento Valley biotech company called TriLink BioTechnologies, which produced synthetic DNA for gene therapy research. Since her arrest, she had stayed off methamphetamine, putting on weight, getting a smart new hairstyle and regaining her former beauty. Interviewed by a panel of executives, including TriLink Production Manager Kelly Christianson, she made a good impression.

Kristin never mentioned her arrest, or admitted being fired from the ME's office for drugs a month earlier. And TriLink never asked her to fill in an employment application, relying on her interview and the résumé she supplied.

Kristin was hired for a full-time position on the spot. She would use the same equipment she had operated in the ME's office.

"She was great," said Christianson, who became her boss. "She was a quick learner. She was always on time [and] did her job very well. In my experience as a supervisor, she's one of the best employees I've ever had."

On Friday, February 9, San Diego Deputy DA Daniel Goldstein, who was now overseeing the homicide investigation, asked Frank Barnhart to personally examine Greg de Villers' gastric contents. By coincidence, Barnhart ran into Kristin Rossum as they were standing in line for San Diego Padres tickets later that day. Kristin proudly told him about her new job at TriLink, inviting him to join her and her parents for dinner that night. Although he was actively working on the forensic toxicology side of the investigation for the sheriff's office, Barnhart presumably didn't see a conflict and agreed, enjoying a dinner with the Rossum family at a San Diego restaurant.

Now, trying to put her past behind her, Kristin developed a strict work routine. That was relatively easy at TriLink, where there were no illegal drugs to tempt her.

Feeling lonely, Kristin soon befriended Claire Becker, an English girl a year younger than she. Becker, who had started at TriLink three months earlier, was put in charge of training her, and they soon started lunching together and going out after work.

"As soon as we met, we basically became friends," remembered Becker, who now lives in Great Yarmouth, England. "We became close very quickly. She said she didn't feel very close to anyone, and we got along so well."

Initially, Kristin never mentioned that she had been married, but soon after they started taking lunch together, Becker went to her apartment for the first time and saw her wedding picture on the mantelpiece.

"I asked her about it," said Becker. "And she just went through the whole story."

In floods of tears, Kristin explained how she had always seen Greg as more of a brother than a husband. Whenever she had tried to tell him this, he would say they could work it out and he couldn't live without her.

"And then, when she got involved with Michael, she told [Greg] about that," said Becker. "She told me that she was always very open and honest with him and let him know what was going on. And when she did say she was finally leaving, he committed suicide."

Kristin also told her that she was the "prime suspect" for Greg's murder, and under investigation by San Diego Homicide.

Although Becker never got to meet Dr. Robertson, Kristin would constantly talk about how much she loved him, and their plans for the future.

"Her lawyer told her to cool the relationship, but she didn't," Becker said. "She used to tell me how Michael would park a few blocks away from her house and then try and sneak in without being seen, in case they were being watched, which they were. But they couldn't stop seeing each other."

Dr. Robertson was using his contacts in forensic toxicology to look for a new job, and went for several job interviews in San Francisco. He spent a lot of his spare time playing Australian football with the San Diego Lions. He now took precautions with his love letters and presents to Kristin's mailing them to TriLink instead of her apartment.

But if Dr. Robertson was trying to be discreet, Kristin made no secret of their affair at TriLink, placing a stuffed kangaroo toy he had given her on her desk.

Kristin often talked of marrying Robertson and having his kids and settling down, either in San Francisco or his home town of Melbourne, Australia.

"She seemed very proud of him," said Becker. "She never tried to keep it a secret, and would tell other people at work too. Some of them even went out to dinner with her and Michael on occasion."

Kristin also told Claire about her problems with methamphetamine.

"She never seemed like a druggie," said Claire. "Or ever under the influence when I saw her."

Kristin regularly socialized with her boss Kelly Christianson and a small group of other female colleagues. They would often take in happy hour at a local Mexican restaurant called El Torito after work, and Kristin was always sociable and in good spirits.

That April, Kristin moved into a new apartment at 831 26th Street, in downtown San Diego. She moved Greg's remaining clothes to her parents' house in Claremont, and later donated them to a church bazaar.

She also joined TriLink's softball team, playing every Friday through the summer and becoming close friends with Jessica Vanella, who was leader of the company's HPLC group. At one of the first Friday softball games, Jessica's mother Kathy met Kristin and liked her a lot.

"It was after the game, and everybody was excited," remembered Kathy. "And this little voice in the crowd asked everybody to please not swear. And it was Kristin."

It became a Friday night ritual for everyone to go out after the game to dinner, and Kristin always came along, sometimes bringing Michael Robertson.

"We went bowling," said Jessica. "We went to the movies [and] several times as friends to a downtown club."

By May, Dr. Robertson returned to Australia, abandoning Kristin to her fate. He had been unable to find a new job because of his notoriety in his field, and his work visa was contingent upon him working at the ME's office.

Detectives returned his passport, as his mother was dying of breast cancer. "[They] had seized my passport in a search warrant," he later explained. "When I said I was going back to Australia, they basically handed it back to me."

Kristin was heartbroken when Robertson left, crying on Claire Becker's shoulder.

"I knew she was vexed," she said. "Kristin had only told me that Michael was engaged, but not that they were actually married."

After Robertson returned to Melbourne, Kristin began socializing even more. She also found a new boyfriend, who began appearing at various functions with her.

But if Kristin was trying to put the homicide investigation behind her, Det Laurie Agnew was working harder than ever. She and her team were now relentlessly interviewing everyone from Kristin's past, examining her and Robertson's computer hard disks and obtaining deleted e-mails from their Internet servers, methodically building up murder case against her.

At the beginning of April, Kristin's replacement at the ME's office, Tina Martinez, was searching for a filter in the HPLC room, when she came across a small glass pipe, hidden in a box. Not knowing what it was, she left it there. But two days later, when Martinez found a manila evidence envelope out of place on a cabinet, she told her supervisor Cathy Hamm.

"The envelope was kind of rolled up and put in the box," remembered Hamm. "One end had been completely cut off."

Looking inside, Hamm discovered a collection of glass pipes, some of which were broken, and a small piece of foil.

Police forensics would later determine that the pipes contained traces of Kristin's DNA on one end and methamphetamine on the other.

Homicide detectives were so determined to bring Kristin to justice that money was no object in the murder investigation. San Diego police forensic expert Randy Gibson worked six weeks with a special computer program to digitally reconstruct Robertson's love letter, which Kristin had shredded after Greg had found it. And Robert Petrachek spent almost three-and-a-half months gleaning evidence from a battery of computers used by Kristin, Greg and Dr. Robertson.

That spring, Kristin was asked to come to Homicide for a second interview and to take a polygraph test. She told her grief counselor, who urged her to get a lawyer, so she hired San Diego attorney Michael Pancer.

"It was a horrible reality check to actually seek a lawyer," she wrote in her journal. "It really hit home the gravity of the entire situation."

At the last minute, on the advice of her new attorney,

Kristin cancelled the interview with Det Agnew and stopped communicating with her.

"I wanted to just go down to the interview without an attorney," she wrote. "I was afraid of how getting a lawyer would look. Is it really to my benefit or does it imply that I have something to hide?"

For the next few months, detectives kept Rossum on a long lead, and they did not pressure her further. But they continued watching her.

Every once in a while Kristin would drop her gregarious façade, breaking down in helpless frustration.

"She would cry a lot about it and it always seemed to be on her mind," said Claire Becker. "I would always ask her about the latest news and what was going on with the case. Underneath she was worried just because it took so long, as they were questioning her evidence. She didn't know what was going on, and she just had to wait it out."

Finally, all the pressure of the investigation, and the possibility that she would be arrested for Greg's murder, proved too much for Kristin. Soon after Robertson left, she relapsed into methamphetamine again in order to cope.

On Sunday, June 24, as Det Laurie Agnew and her team prepared the search warrant for Kristin's imminent arrest, she made her final trip to Tijuana to buy methamphetamine.

Chapter 23

Arrest

On Monday, June 25, after having Claire Becker hide some of Robertson's love letters and her koala bear, Kristin Rossum returned to her Golden Hill apartment, where police were waiting. After reading Kristin her rights, they arrested her on suspicion of murdering her husband. Suspecting she was high on drugs, detectives took her downtown to police headquarters, where samples were taken of her urine and blood, which were later found to contain methamphetamine.

Investigators also served a search warrant on her apartment, where they found a mega pocket torch, used for smoking meth; her address book, containing four phone numbers for her drug dealer Armando; and the latest installments of her writings in a blue notebook entitled "Meditation Journal."

The following morning, as Kristin woke up in a holding cell at Las Colinas Women's Detention Facility in Santee, her arrest made the front page of the Metro section of *The San Diego Union-Tribune*, under the headline "Ex-County Toxicologist Faces Charges in Death of Husband." In the article, San Diego Police Homicide Lieutenant Ray Sigwalt said that Rossum and Dr. Robertson had been having an affair, and, although he was back in Australia, Robertson too was considered a possible suspect in the death of Greg de Villers and could be brought back to America for further questioning.

"The sheer nature of the death was suspicious," Lieutenant Sigwalt said. "There was no [suicide] note. Rose petals were sprinkled on his body in bed. Most men don't do those sorts of things."

Lieutenant Sigwalt also noted that Kristin had told investigators that *American Beauty* was her favorite movie.

Although police sealed Greg's autopsy report after Kristin's arrest, refusing to name what poison had killed Greg, sources close to the investigation told a reporter it was fentanyl, and that investigators believed Kristin had stolen it from work.

On Wednesday morning, twenty-four-year-old Kristin Rossum appeared in court for the first time since her arrest. The previous day, her lawyer, Michael Pancer, was notified that the district attorney was considering adding a special circumstance allegation in his charges, which would allow the prosecution to request the death penalty.

A tearful Rossum was led into San Diego Superior Court in bright orange prison garb and handcuffs. Her shocked parents were in the public gallery, which was packed with reporters.

At the hearing, the prosecution officially filed a felony complaint, charging Kristin Rossum with one count of first-degree murder of Gregory de Villers by the administration of poison.

The only time she spoke at the hearing was when Judge David Szumowski asked if she agreed with her attorney's request to delay her arraignment.

"I do, Your Honor," she sobbed inaudibly.

The judge then postponed the arraignment until the following Monday, when Rossum would have to enter a plea. He ordered her held without bail.

Outside the courthouse at 200 West Broadway, an emotional Professor Rossum gave his first interview to reporters, calling the charges against Kristin "devastating."

"[The authorities] are making a victim of our daughter,

who lost a husband," he said defiantly. "She does not have it in her to commit these charges."

Jerome de Villers also spoke to reporters that day, saying his late brother knew that Kristin had a problem with drugs before they married, and believed he was rescuing her.

"Then something happened," he said. "I don't have all the pieces to the puzzle . . . I hope the truth will come out."

By now the story was gathering momentum in the press, and going national. It had all the ingredients to get the headline writers excited: murder, a love triangle and, best of all, what one magazine photo editor would call. "The most beautiful potential murderess in living memory."

On Thursday Kristin's bosses at TriLink stood by her, saying they were holding her job open. Describing Kristin as "a rising star" in the biotech company, TriLink president Rick Hogrefe said he had never seen any indication that she was on drugs.

"It is a shockingly sad story," he told *The San Diego Union-Tribune*. "From our side, it doesn't fit."

But Orbigen's general manager Terry Huang told the newspaper how he had been suspicious when Greg hadn't called on the day he died.

On Thursday, seventy-two hours after Kristin's arrest, her father gave an exclusive interview to *Los Angeles Times* reporter Tipton Blush, proclaiming his daughter's innocence. He accused prosecutors of trying his daughter in the media, vowing to set things straight, as her husband had committed suicide.

"We were astonished at how many factual matters were wrong," he said. "I know that she is innocent."

Professor Rossum said he had known that homicide detectives had been investigating Greg's death for months, but he never believed anything would come of it.

"It struck me always as absurd," he scoffed, "that a bright toxicologist would do something that would incriminate her."

Lawyer Michael Pancer's partner, Gretchen von Helms, also joined the fray, adding that prosecutors were trying to make it seem like "this creepy Hollywood thing." There was no motive, she said.

But Deputy DA Dan Goldstein had the last word in the article, saying that investigators had left no stone unturned by using outside agencies to test Greg's toxicology.

"The evidence in this case is immaculate," he announced resolutely.

Back in Claremont, the town was stunned by the arrest of the daughter of one of its most prominent citizens. Professor Rossum's colleagues at Claremont McKenna College rallied to his defense, offering their support. But some of Kristin's old friends were not so certain she was innocent.

"Well, I was shocked," said former boyfriend Ted Maya, who was now studying to be a lawyer. "My initial reaction was certainly 'Yeah . . . she did it.' And most of the people that knew her then had the same reaction. It was just such a fantastic story. In fact, I don't know any [of her friends] who actually didn't think that she had done it. I mean, she lied so well it was like she really believed her own lies."

By the weekend, the story had gone international, and was covered extensively in Australia's Melbourne *Herald Sun*, Michael Robertson's hometown newspaper. Under the banner headline, "American Beauty and the Beast Within," the paper concentrated on Robertson's affair with Rossum, interviewing his old Monash University mentor, Professor Olaf Drummer.

"I was not aware of any of this," said the professor. "But I know he is back in Melbourne. To my knowledge, he is not working."

At her arraignment on Monday, July 2, Kristin Rossum pleaded not guilty to the first-degree murder of her husband. Looking haggard and skeletal, her greasy hair falling into reddened eyes, she was escorted in chains into court by a bailiff.

After making her plea, Kristin burst into tears, as her father stood up in court to request Judge Szumowski grant bail. Professor Rossum said there was no chance of her running away, noting that she had not fled to Mexico during the eight-month police investigation.

"She would jeopardize our love and financial future," he added.

Deputy DA Dan Goldstein opposed bail, saying that the charges against her carried the death penalty.

The judge ordered her to be held without bail, setting a preliminary hearing for July 16. He also appointed a public defender to represent her, after Professor Rossum claimed that hiring a private lawyer was beyond his means.

Outside the court, the well-to-do professor told reporters that he could not afford the legal fees, which could run into the hundreds of thousands of dollars. He said he would rather spend the money for Kristin's bail.

One week later, the preliminary hearing was postponed until October 9, to give Kristin's new defense team time to prepare their case. The San Diego Superior Court assigned the high profile case to Judge John M. Thompson.

The following day, faculty members of Claremont McKenna College set up a legal defense fund for Kristin.

"We have known Kristin and the family for years," read a press statement from the fund, "and know that she could not have committed this crime."

The Rossum family also cooperated on a special ABC *Good Morning America* segment, featuring the case.

Professor Rossum described his daughter's drug taking and adulterous affair with her boss as "examples of moral weakness," admitting that she'd displayed bad judgment.

"But that is very, very different from . . . committing murder," he said.

The tabloid TV show *Inside Edition* also sent a team to San Diego, to prepare an in-depth story which was broadcast the following week.

On the other side of the world, Dr. Michael Robertson gave his first interview, denying reports that he'd "fled" to escape prosecution. Speaking from his parents' home in Melbourne, he proclaimed his innocence, saying he'd returned to Australia because his mother was ill.

"I stayed [in San Diego] for many months after this happened in order to facilitate the investigation as much as I could," he told a local reporter. "To say I fled is not the case."

But while the Rossums were busy exerting spin control on behalf of their daughter, the de Villers family hired top San Diego civil lawyer Craig McClellan, filing a wrongful death suit against San Diego County. This would be the first step in a $2.1 million family civil action against the ME's office, Kristin Rossum and Michael Robertson.

The de Villerses accused the ME's office of negligence, by hiring Rossum without running background checks, and placing her in charge of logging dangerous street drugs into the lab evidence locker. It also claimed that the ME's office should have prevented her from donating Greg de Villers' organs, so a proper autopsy could have been conducted.

On August 7, County Medical Examiner Dr. Brian Blackbourne fired his long-time deputy, Dr. Harry Bonnell, just a day after the Board of Supervisors had given him a commendation. Dr. Blackbourne refused to discuss the matter with reporters, who questioned if it was related to Rossum and Robertson.

"Dr. Bonnell is no longer working for the county," Dr. Blackbourne told a TV reporter. "This is a confidential personnel matter, and I really can't go into it."

On July 16, three weeks after Kristin Rossum's arrest, Det Agnew's superior officer, Sergeant Howard Williams, left a message on her parents' answering machine, requesting an interview. The next day, when he checked his voice mail, there was a message from Professor Rossum, declining to be interviewed on the advice of an attorney.

"I chose not to respond at that point, because it was subsequent to Kristin's arrest," Rossum would later testify. "I saw nothing that could be of value at that point by speaking to that officer."

However, a week later, Professor Rossum went on San Diego's Channel 10 News, vigorously defending his daughter.

Asked about the red rose petals scattered around his late son-in-law's dead body, Rossum had his own interpretation of what had happened.

"My reading on that," he said, "is, this was Greg telling Kristin, not in a letter but symbolically, that the romance that could be embodied in a single rose was now over." Insisting that Greg had committed suicide, Rossum claimed that Kristin's affair with Dr. Robertson did not provide a motive for murder. As for fentanyl, Rossum said that no one knew how long it had been missing from the ME's office.

In an earlier interview, Constance Rossum had compared Greg's behavior the Friday before he died to a scene straight out of the Stephen King movie *The Shining*.

"We saw a man spiraling down," she would tell *The San Diego Union-Tribune*.

In her cell at the Las Colinas women's jail, Kristin spent her time consulting with her defense team to prepare for her preliminary hearing. She was also working on a scientific paper for TriLink, and receiving regular monthly visits from the supportive company president, Rick Hogrefe.

Since their daughter's arrest, her parents had spent at least four hours daily speaking to attorneys and giving interviews to media outlets, in a dogged attempt to put forward her case before it could go to trial.

To counter this, the de Villers family, talking through their attorney, Craig McClellan, claimed that Kristin had been lacing Greg's food and drink with drugs in the days before his death.

As the preliminary hearing drew nearer, it was fast becoming San Diego's highest-profile case in years, making front-page headlines almost daily with the latest twists and turns.

Public defenders Alex Loebig and Victor Eriksen had now been assigned Kristin's case, but they had found themselves spending more time fielding media inquiries than working on her defense.

"In the first couple of months I put all my time and energy in dealing with the press," remembered Loebig. "All the shows—*48 hours, Dateline* and everyone else—wanted to interview her. I tried to coordinate Kristin's screening of prospective interviewers so that she had the final choice of who to cooperate with."

Ultimately the Rossums would decide to allow CBS's *48 Hours* exclusive coverage, hoping for a sympathetic story.

Additionally, Professor Rossum allowed *MSNBC*'s Mike Brunker to send him a list of questions about the case. In one of the questions, Brunker asked: "How does the defense explain the presence of the controlled substance fentanyl in de Villers' body? Is there a theory of how the drug was administered?"

Professor Rossum responded that "Greg had knowledge of, past use of, and his own independent access to fentanyl."

Later, when asked where that information had been obtained, Professor Rossum said it had come from his daughter.

In mid-September, Deputy DA Dan Goldstein took an unprecedented step for a San Diego prosecutor, asking Judge Thompson to allow television cameras into his courtroom. He argued that the Rossum family had now given so many "erroneous" interviews to national media outlets that they had prejudiced his case. Usually it is the media organizations that request television coverage of criminal trials, and the prosecution that opposes it.

Judge Thompson, one of the few San Diego Superior Court judges never to have allowed cameras into his courtroom, denied Goldstein's motion, only allowing reporters to take notes.

Two weeks before the preliminary hearing, the DA's

office offered to fly Michael Robertson back from Australia to testify as a witness, all expenses paid. But unless he was charged, there was nothing they could do to compel him. A spokeswoman for the DA's office said they were giving him the opportunity to clear his name, as he had repeatedly said he wanted to do.

"By Australian law, he doesn't have to come back," said the spokeswoman. "We can't force him back."

Asked whether Dr. Robertson might also be charged with Greg de Villers' murder, the spokeswoman said the investigation was ongoing, and by no means over.

Ultimately, Dr. Robertson would refuse to return to the U.S. to testify, instead closely following coverage from his parents' home.

Chapter 24

"She Will Be Held to Answer"

On Tuesday, October 9, Judge John Thompson's Courtroom 38, on the third floor of San Diego County Superior Court, was packed for the first day of Kristin Rossum's preliminary hearing. Under California law, the district attorney would have to prove there was a case to answer before it could go to trial. The defense would not even have to call witnesses. Outside in the corridor reporters milled around, discussing the case.

Inside, Greg de Villers' mother, Marie, and two brothers, Jerome and Bertrand, took their seats, averting their gaze as Kristin's parents entered, taking their places on the opposite side of the public gallery. A handful of reporters who had managed to secure seats filed in. The atmosphere was electric.

Then Kristin was escorted into the court, wearing a stylish maroon dress, and looking nothing like she had in her police arrest photo. She had put on weight and regained her looks, after three months at Las Colinas women's lock-up without methamphetamine.

Prosecutor Dan Goldstein was all business, going through his notes at the prosecution table. The youthful 42-year-old deputy district attorney, who had won convictions in some of the city's most high-profile murder cases, had been a paramedic before he graduated from law school. He was careful and methodical, having deliberately not rushed into arresting Rossum until he was certain he had an iron-clad case against her. He also planned a run for a Superior Court judgeship in 2002, and knew that this might be his last case on this side of the bench if he won.

On the other side of the courtroom were the two public defenders, Alex Loebig and Victor Eriksen, whom the county had appointed to represent Kristin. Loebig had spent more than thirty years as a defender, starting his career in the 1970s working gang-related murders in Los Angeles. He then spent four years in Guam, as the Pacific island's head public defender, before moving to San Diego in 1981. The Rossum case was the biggest in his career, and he knew he had a tough battle ahead.

"She was difficult to defend," Loebig would admit eighteen months later, "in that [the prosecution] had a lot of evidence against her that was difficult or impossible to explain."

His partner in the case, Victor Eriksen, was also a highly experienced public defender, having successfully defended murder suspects for many years.

Dan Goldstein began by calling a procession of witnesses who had been at Kristin's apartment on the night of Greg's death, to demonstrate inconsistencies and contradictions in her story.

His first witness was UCSD Campus Detective Sergeant Robert Jones, who had first investigated the possible suicide. Jones said he had arrived soon after Greg had been taken to the hospital, and seen the red rose petals littering the bedroom. Then, on a cursory search, he discovered the Ziploc bag containing Dr. Robertson's shredded love letter, the "Hi Sleepy" note in the dining room, and Kristin's journal on the coffee table.

Kristin looked stoic, taking notes at the defense table, as Jones expressed surprise at seeing the bathtub stopper suspiciously out of place, resting on a shower shelf and not in the bathtub, as would have been expected after the leisurely bath she had claimed to have taken.

Det Sergeant Jones said the investigation had changed

from suicide to homicide after toxicologist Donald Lowe tipped him off that Rossum and her boss were possibly having an affair. Then Jones had turned it over to San Diego Homicide.

In Victor Eriksen's cross-examination, the detective admitted never removing any evidence from the death scene for further analysis, or cataloguing the contents of two trash cans on the apartment balcony. He had also not impounded the rose-streaked sheet or two cups of clear liquid, which had been in the apartment but later disappeared.

Asked by the public defender whether he had initially considered passing the case on to Homicide, Det Sergeant Jones said he had, but that there had not been enough information until Lowe's call supplied a motive.

Then Campus Police Officer Edward Garcia took the stand, describing how he and his partner, Bill MacIntyre, had arrived at the apartment as paramedics were battling to revive Greg de Villers. Garcia told Judge Thompson that Kristin said her husband had taken oxycodone and clonazepam to help him sleep. He had then searched the apartment for any remaining drugs and a suicide note, but all he found was a half-empty bottle of cough syrup.

"I asked her, 'What happened to him today?' " said Officer Garcia. "She answered like she didn't know."

The prosecutor then asked when he had first seen the rose petals. Garcia said Kristin told him that she'd thought they were on the bed and that when she'd pulled the blanket back, they had fallen to the floor.

Then Officer Garcia described driving her to Scripps Hospital in the back seat of his police car.

"She acted like she was crying," he told the court. "Her face would wince and she would look upset."

Then, while in the hospital waiting for news of Greg, she called Michael Robertson on her cell phone, and he arrived about twenty minutes later.

"They were whispering," said the officer. "I couldn't hear what was said at all."

Garcia had then returned to the Regents Road apartment

to secure the death scene for ME Investigator Angela Wagner, who was on her way. A few minutes after he got there, Kristin had walked in with Michael Robertson.

Paramedic Sean Jordan then took the stand, telling the judge how he and his partner April Butler were first at the scene after the 911 call. Finding Kristin talking on a cordless phone, they went straight into the bedroom to see Greg lying on the floor, surrounded by rose petals. By his head, resting up against the dresser, was his wedding photo.

"[It] was like he propped it up and was looking at it," Jordan remembered.

Goldstein asked about Greg's skin temperature when Jordan first tried resuscitation.

"When I walked in, it was warm, fresh. Like he was newly deceased," he said. "He didn't have any rigor mortis."

The paramedic then explained how he had fought to revive Greg with cardiac drugs and narcan, in case he had overdosed. By this time, another team of paramedics had arrived, and Jordan told of making two puncture wounds in Greg's left arm, attempting an IV. Another paramedic, Joseph Preciado, made another one in the right arm.

The prosecutor then asked if he was certain that he hadn't made three puncture wounds in Greg's left arm. Jordan said he was.

Public defender Alex Loebig, knowing the prosecution's contention that Greg's left arm had been injected with fentanyl, asked if the paramedic had looked for any prior injection marks. Jordan said they'd done exactly that, but had not seen any.

"We looked for needle track marks," he said. "That was one of the first things I looked for."

The next witness was EMT April Butler, who'd thought Rossum's behavior "weird," as she spent most of the time on the cordless telephone in the kitchen and living room. Prompted by Goldstein's questions, Butler testified that Kristin had told her that, on the orders of the 911 dis-

patcher, she had placed Greg's body on the ground before
starting CPR.

"Did you see any rose petals in the bed or on the bed?"
asked the prosecutor.

"No, there were none," Butler replied emphatically.

In his cross, Victor Eriksen asked why Butler had said
that Kristin was a "little distraught," when she was in fact
hysterical. The EMT admitted Rossum had been hysterical,
saying that was only to be expected with her husband lying
dead in the bedroom.

There was much anticipation in the courtroom as Jerome
de Villers took the stand. He was the prosecution's most
powerful witness, and Kristin Rossum began nervously
playing with her blonde hair as he began to testify. He told
the court how he and his brothers Bertrand and Greg had
first met Kristin on a "fun" night out in Tijuana in 1995.
Greg had hit it off with her right away, and she spent that
night in his bed.

"She came home with him," he said. "She moved in with
us that night."

Jerome told of the last time he had ever seen Greg alive,
at a wedding two weeks before his death. He had seemed
highly positive about the future and was organizing his
birthday trip, planning to go snowboarding in Mammoth
with his brothers and Kristin.

"He seemed happy," Jerome said. "Appeared healthy."

Judge Thompson then recessed for lunch and Professor
Rossum gave an impromptu interview to reporters outside
the courtroom. He described the case against his daughter
as "a house of cards," that would come crashing down.

After lunch, Jerome retook the stand and Deputy DA
Goldstein took him through the emotional night of his
brother's death. Jerome said he had been in his Thousand
Oaks apartment when his mother called, saying Constance
Rossum had phoned with the news that Greg was in the
hospital, after having a bad reaction to medication. Later

that night, at his mother's home, he heard that his older brother had died.

Jerome said that the following day, they had gone to Claremont to see Kristin, and a couple of things she'd said had made him suspicious.

"She told me Greg was upset because she wouldn't stop seeing a past relationship," he told the court. "She told me that she didn't mean to hurt him. I remember when I tried to get more detailed information ... she was crying. I couldn't get specifics."

Jerome then explained how he had never believed that Greg had committed suicide, and had come to San Diego with his father and brother to investigate. He spoke of his horror at learning that Kristin was planning to have Greg's remains cremated as soon as possible.

The atmosphere in court was electric as Jerome described how Bertrand had gone to Kristin's apartment three days after Greg's death to find Michael Robertson there. He had then decided to record the conversation on microcassette, as he had done earlier when he met County Medical Examiner Dr. Brian Blackbourne.

Jerome's tape of his and Bertrand's emotional meeting with Kristin was then played in court in its entirety. As the tape ran, Kristin broke down at the defense table in tears.

After the tape was finished, Alex Loebig cross-examined Jerome. Loebig asked him about Greg's demeanor at the wedding, and what he had spoken about.

"Having kids," said Jerome. "He really wanted to get a house. Kristin said she wasn't ready to have kids."

Loebig then noted that Jerome had "no fondness whatsoever for Kristin" after his brother's death.

"I thought she had something to do with my brother's death," he replied resolutely. "So obviously, it wasn't a fondness issue."

Then the public defender asked if Greg had wanted to be with Kristin as much as possible.

"It appeared to me that he was in love with her," said Jerome. "If she was having affairs and other things that he found out about, maybe it was more that he didn't want her to be alone."

Then, after hearing testimony from several La Jolla del Sol apartment complex employees on how Kristin was rushing around on the day of Greg's death, his boss and friend Dr. Stefan Gruenwald took the stand to give critical evidence. He testified that he had met Greg at Pharmagen and hired him when he'd set up Orbigen. Describing him as "rational" and "a problem solver," Dr. Gruenwald said that Greg had had no enemies and was very popular.

Dr. Gruenwald said that when Greg didn't turn up for work on November 6 without calling in, he and General Manager Terry Huang had both become worried, telephoning his home many times that day. Kristin finally answered one of his calls at 9:30 p.m., while the paramedics were trying to save Greg.

"She was totally in tears and a little bit hard to understand," he said. "Something severe must have happened."

He then described receiving a call from a stranger named Michael Robertson the following morning, telling him to call Kristin's parents. Constance Rossum had then told him the "sad news" that Greg had passed away from an allergic reaction to pills. He then called his employees together to tell them.

Later they had checked Greg's computers, including the office iMac he'd used at home, discovering e-mails between Greg and Kristin, including the one where she wrote, "You have hurt me beyond repair. You make me feel so uncomfortable, so alone."

Then Judge Thompson recessed, saying they would resume the next day at lunchtime. That night, Kristin returned to her detention center cell, confident that the judge would decide there wasn't enough evidence to bring the case to trial. But she still had to endure another three days of testimony before it would be resolved one way or another.

On Wednesday afternoon, Kristin Rossum seemed composed as she took her place at the defense table dressed conservatively in a white blouse and blue blazer. Prosecutor Dan Goldstein resumed questioning Dr. Gruenwald, asking about the Web sites someone had visited on Greg's home iMac the weekend before his death. Dr. Gruenwald said that someone had hit a couple of sites that dealt with drug abuse and how to synthesize methamphetamine.

"There was at least thirty or forty clicks around that site, regarding methamphetamine," he said, adding that most of the searches had been done on the Saturday before Greg's death, with just a few on Sunday.

In his cross-examination, Alex Loebig asked Dr. Gruenwald if Greg had been nervous during the last week of his life. Greg had been "more hyper," Dr. Gruenwald said, as he was upset because a friend of his had ended up costing Orbigen $30,000.

"That was something I found kind of unusual," he said. "He was so mad the last day . . . because he said, 'He used to be my friend, and he had kind of screwed me over many times.' "

Dr. Gruenwald said that he and Greg had never discussed his marriage to Kristin, except that when Greg was working late, he would say he had to go home because Kristin would be mad if she had cooked a meal.

In his redirect examination, Goldstein asked Gruenwald about the letter Orbigen employees had written to San Diego Homicide.

"We believed that it was definitely not a suicide case," said the doctor. "Because Greg did not appear to be a suicide candidate."

Later that afternoon, Greg's Palm Springs High School friend Christian Colantoni took the stand. Describing Greg as one of his closest friends, he said he had often stayed at Greg's family summer home in Canada in the early 1990s. Greg and Kristin had also stayed at his house when they'd attended Aaron Waldo's wedding in Palm Springs.

"He seemed in a good state," Colantoni said. "Just seemed normal Greg: happy, positive, outgoing."

Then Goldstein asked him about Kristin's strange comments about the best way of using drugs to kill someone, while they were watching the *Office Space* video.

"She mentioned a specific combination of drugs," he said, "that would, if taken, end your life in a non-painful and undetectable way."

Eriksen tried to counter Colantoni's damaging testimony, asking whether he had discussed the fact that Greg had died of fentanyl poisoning with the friends who had been at his home the night of the video. He said that he had, but could no longer remember the exact drugs Kristin had mentioned.

The prosecution then called Bertrand de Villers to testify, asking him about his brother's mental state prior to his death.

"Greg seemed to be normal," replied Bertrand. "I think he was actually excited about his life at the time."

Bertrand said his final conversation with Greg was on the Sunday afternoon before his death, when he'd called about setting up an America Online account for his mother. Greg had sounded fine, but tired, and Bertrand had asked why.

"He had told me that he and Kristin had been drinking the night before," said Bertrand, "and that he felt tired in the morning."

Bertrand said he had never known Greg to use drugs, and that he hated to be around chemicals.

For the defense, Alex Loebig got Bertrand to admit that Greg had once tried marijuana in his presence, but had disliked it.

The next witness was toxicologist Donald Lowe, who said he had been acting laboratory manager at the ME's office prior to Michael Robertson's appointment. Then Lowe had started reporting to Robertson. Lowe had worked with Kristin Rossum from the time she had first joined the ME's office as a student worker in 1997, until her firing.

Lowe said that she was responsible for the High-

Pressure Liquid Chromatograph machine (HPLC), where she often worked alone in its special room. The prosecutor then asked him about his recent drug audit. Lowe said a large quantity of fentanyl was missing, including fifteen Duragesic patches, designed to slowly dispense the lethal substance and a small vial of the drug.

The senior toxicologist also testified that quantities of methamphetamine and amphetamine were missing from the lab's office. All of them had been logged in and signed for by Kristin Rossum. An evidence envelope containing two syringes, a plastic bag with a black tar substance and white granular powder were also missing.

A few months after she had been fired, Lowe said he had been given a glass pipe that had been found in the HPLC room by Rossum's replacement. It was later tested and found to have Kristin's DNA on it. In December 2000, Lowe testified, he was cleaning out Dr. Robertson's desk after he had been terminated, and discovered articles on fentanyl.

In his defense cross, Eriksen got Lowe to admit that other employees used the HPLC room at various times, and his client did not have exclusive access. Lowe also agreed that office procedure was lax during that time at the ME's office and that drugs recovered from death scenes often overfilled the lock box where they were stored. They were then brought into the laboratory and left on workbenches or desks.

"It was possible that someone could reach in and remove evidence from that lock box," said Lowe. "Even when [it] was locked."

Lowe also said that his 2001 audit was the very first he was aware of in the thirty-two years he had worked at the ME's office.

The final witness on the second day of the hearing was Lloyd Amborn, who ran the day-to-day operations at the medical examiner's office. On Goldstein's direct examination, Amborn confirmed approving county funds for Rossum and Robertson's travel and hotel for the Milwaukee

SOFT conference the previous October. He also testified that after Greg's death, he had ordered Dr. Robertson not to have anything to do with the toxicology, which was being sent out to avoid any possible conflict, as Kristin was an office employee.

But the following day, Dr. Robertson had ignored Amborn's instructions, viewing Greg's stomach contents.

"When I questioned him why he violated my instruction not to be involved," said Amborn, "he said he was feeling an obligation to keep the Rossum family out of the case."

On the third day of the preliminary hearing, the county chief medical examiner, Dr. Brian Blackbourne, who had performed Greg's autopsy, was the first witness. He testified he could not determine a cause of death until later, when it was discovered that Greg had died of acute fentanyl intoxication. His lungs were very congested and there were signs of early pneumonia, suggesting that Greg had been in a coma for up to twelve hours before he died.

Dr. Blackbourne said that the bladder was also very distended, filled with 550 milliters of urine.

"The first thing we think of," said Dr. Blackbourne, "is someone who has been unconscious for a period of time."

He also confirmed finding three needle puncture marks on Greg's left arm, although paramedic Sean Jordan had earlier testified that he had only made two, as he tried to set up an IV line.

Responding to Goldstein's questioning about fentanyl, Dr. Blackbourne said there would have been two methods of administering it: by Duragesic patch or intravenously.

"Like the NicoDerm patch, there's a fentanyl patch called Duragesic," he said. "Usually it's placed on the upper chest of cancer patients, someone with chronic intractable pain."

Dr. Blackbourne said that the fentanyl levels found in Greg's blood and urine were "excessively high," and could have killed him many times over. Additionally, clonazepam and oxycodone were also found in his body.

In his cross-examination, defender Eriksen tackled Dr.

Blackbourne about the congestion and early signs of pneumonia in Greg's lungs. The medical examiner agreed that Greg may not have been in an actual coma six to twelve hours before death, but his breathing and heart functions had certainly slowed down. And then, attempting to neutralize the prosecution's theory that the third puncture wound on Greg's left arm was where fentanyl had been injected, Eriksen asked if there was any way of knowing when the marks were made.

"No," said Dr. Blackbourne.

The next witness was San Diego Homicide Detective James Valle, who had questioned Rossum and Robertson with his partner, Det Laurie Agnew.

A tape of the first interview with Dr. Robertson was then played in court and Goldstein asked Valle what Robertson had told them about his relationship with Nicole.

"One of the areas we were trying to ask him was if he in fact [had] separated from his wife," said Valle. "He would deny that. He had difficulty admitting he's separated."

The detective testified that in Dr. Robertson's second interview in January, he had admitted staying over at Kristin's apartment three or four times after her husband's death. But Robertson had emphatically denied having a physical affair with Kristin, either before or after Greg's death, although he admitted they were very close and had discussed starting a relationship once they had left their respective marriages.

After the afternoon recess, Det Laurie Agnew took the stand, testifying how she'd first gotten involved with the case when Jerome de Villers telephoned a couple of days after his brother's death. Jerome had told her he was suspicious about how Greg had died and wanted an independent autopsy.

Then, after hearing that Kristin and her boss were having an affair, Agnew put a hold on the body to stop cremation and took over the investigation from the campus police.

She described her November interview with Rossum at

the Homicide Department, and going to the apartment the following January to serve a search warrant.

"She told me we were going to find meth or drug paraphernalia," said the detective. "She asked me to get rid of it."

Det Agnew said she'd refused, taking Rossum to the police department, where she tested positive for methamphetamine and was arrested. She also described searching the Regents Road apartment after Rossum's arrest on June 25, finding more love letters from Robertson and a thirty-six-page journal.

Friday, October 12 was the final day of the preliminary hearing. As she was escorted into the courtroom, wearing a smart navy blazer, Kristin Rossum seemed confident, as if certain she would be going home that night.

Goldstein resumed questioning Det Agnew, asking her about her interview with a friend of the Robertsons named Mary Wright. Agnew said that Wright had initially claimed just to be good friends with Michael Robertson, but after seeing e-mails between them, she had re-interviewed her and her story had changed.

"They had a sexual relationship," said the detective. "Several years back when they all knew each other in Pennsylvania."

Wright also said she and her husband had had dinner with Dr. Robertson in summer 2000, where he had admitted having sex with Rossum.

In his cross, Eriksen asked the detective whether she had told Kristin at the November interview that it was a possible homicide investigation.

"No, I didn't say that," she admitted.

The detective had not asked if she had wanted to consult an attorney or told her that the interview would be video-taped.

The prosecution then called a procession of employees from the ME's office, who provided detailed background about the office's procedures and its lax security.

Toxicologist Cathy Hamm testified that Kristin had told her that her favorite movie was *American Beauty*, and that she had seen it three or four times. She also described cleaning out Rossum's desk after she was fired and finding two bottles of Mexican prescription drugs, as well as a card from Dr. Robertson. The defense did not have any questions for Hamm.

Another toxicologist, Ray Gary, told the court that one Sunday he had gone to the lab and Dr. Robertson had been there. He'd happened to notice that there were fresh flowers in Robertson's gym bag, and the next morning they were on Kristin's desk.

He had then become concerned about their relationship, and some time later had seen what appeared to be a small brown gift box on Rossum's desk.

"I lifted the cover and looked," he said. "There were typed notes that said "I.O.U. A night of lovemaking.""

Gary said the box had disappeared from her desk two days after Greg's death. Later, after she was terminated, the toxicologist said he was present when Kristin's desk was cleared out and saw red rose petals in it.

Eriksen asked if he had ever seen signs that Rossum was on drugs at work. Gary said he hadn't.

The next witness was Rossum's friend and mentor Frank Barnhart, who had spared no expense to retest Greg's toxicology at three outside laboratories, where the fentanyl had been discovered. Barnhart, who'd nicknamed Kristin "Li'l Bandit," said he had once worked at the ME's office, but was now a supervising criminologist at the San Diego County Sheriff's Regional Crime Lab.

He testified that he had hired Kristin as a student intern in June 1997 and that she had been an excellent worker.

"She's incredibly talented in the field," he said. "And really grasps toxicology."

Barnhart told how he had been called by Dr. Blackbourne, who asked him to take over custody of Greg's toxicology. On the medical examiner's instructions, he had sent the tox to Pacific Labs for general testing, but not at that time for fentanyl. Later, when the results came back showing unspecified amounts of the drugs, he had had it re-tested by three independent laboratories.

Then Dan Goldstein called his final witness, Professor Ralph Rossum, to the stand. There was a hush in the courtroom and all eyes were on Kristin's father, as he walked past the gallery to testify. Professor Rossum would be the only witness fully sympathetic to his daughter. And he was well-prepared, having carefully read all 4,400 pages of the case discovery.

The deputy DA began by asking about the Friday before Greg's death, when they'd celebrated Kristin's birthday. Professor Rossum said his son-in-law had acted atypically throughout the evening.

"It began when we arrived in the apartment," he said. "We saw on their dining room [table] a single rose in a vase. Suddenly Greg starts waxing eloquent about [it]. Well, we looked at each other, thinking we hadn't heard this kind of comment from Greg in the past. It put us a bit on edge."

Goldstein asked why he hadn't told Det Sergeant Robert Jones that story when he'd interviewed him by telephone the day after Greg's death.

"I did not consider that an interview," snapped the professor.

Rossum conceded that he had discussed that point with Jones, but not gone into "great detail." The prosecutor then read the professor back the statement he had given Jones, where he said they'd all had "a pleasant evening" and gone for a "nice meal," never mentioning Greg's outburst about the single rose.

"I don't recall using those words," he said. "I had been up virtually all night driving down and spending a very distressful evening with my daughter. I talked to this officer. I assumed that he was a campus guard."

The prosecutor also wondered why he had refused to

talk to Sergeant Howard Williams of Homicide in July, and the professor said he could see "nothing of value" in being interviewed. But he admitted giving interviews to a plethora of local and national journalists.

Then the nationally recognized expert in juvenile justice said he had hesitated to be interviewed by the DA's investigator, Frank Eaton, as the request had only come eight days before the preliminary hearing. He also noted that he had been approached just an hour before Dan Goldstein was scheduled to be interviewed by CBS News, claiming that that was the real reason Eaton had called him.

"I said we would save it for the appropriate time," declared Rossum, who in the end had granted the investigator a brief interview.

After recessing for lunch, the professor retook the stand, and his exchanges with the prosecution became more and more confrontational.

Tempers became heated when, under questioning, Professor Rossum put forward an entirely new theory about the origin of the fentanyl that killed Greg. In what he presumably considered a case-turning *Perry Mason* moment, he announced that he had photographic evidence to prove Greg had obtained the fentanyl that had killed him.

A few weeks earlier he had written a response to a question from an MSNBC reporter, claiming that his son-in-law had had "independent access" to fentanyl. Now, questioned by Goldstein about that statement, Rossum said it had come from his daughter. Countering the prosecution's case that Kristin had stolen fentanyl from the ME's office, her father stated that he had photographic proof supporting his daughter's claim that Greg had taken the drug from his father's medical supplies, kept in storage in Thousand Oaks.

A week before his death, Greg and Kristin had gone to the storage locker to photograph Dr. de Villers' medical equipment, hoping to sell it on eBay. The reason, claimed

Professor Rossum, was that his mother was about to be evicted from her condo and he wanted to help her.

"We have photos," he said defiantly. "It logs the time and date on the pictures."

Asked to elaborate, Rossum said Kristin had told him that she and Greg had found three boxes of medical supplies in Dr. de Villers' locker, one of which contained fentanyl.

"[Greg said] he would take care of disposing of these contents," he said. "And that was the last she saw of it."

But when the prosecutor asked whether the photos showed fentanyl, Rossum had to admit it was only "equipment and boxes." He had no idea how Greg had self-administered the lethal drug.

Questioned why he had never told DA Investigator Eaton about Greg's alleged access to fentanyl, the professor said he had told him that it would come out at the appropriate time.

"Do you think this is a game?" asked the visibly angry prosecutor.

Suddenly Professor Rossum said he wanted to clear up a misconception about his son-in-law and drugs. Despite Goldstein's objections, Judge Thompson allowed him to go ahead.

"During the course of this preliminary hearing," he began, "I have repeatedly heard the word 'drugs' used to refer to even prescription and over-the-counter products. And to that extent, it is the case that Kristin had reported Greg to be a kind of medicator, using things to deal with pain and with emotional problems."

As the de Villers family bristled with anger in the public gallery, Rossum emphasized that he was not referring to illegal drugs.

"Greg would often be in bed when we would call Kristin and him," he continued. "On several occasions when we would go down, intending to go out to dinner, having reservations made, Greg would not join us. Because we'd learn Greg isn't feeling well and is in bed all day. We learned that he was often ill on weekends. And in fact we said, 'Kristin, for this guy who claims to be this vigorous outdoor guy, hiker, camper, he seems sickly a lot.' "

When Goldstein questioned Rossum about his daughter's drug use, he claimed she had never been arrested or charged, despite her Claremont arrest for possession in January 1994.

Rossum said his daughter had taken drugs up to 1995, when Greg had helped her give them up. She had only relapsed two weeks before her husband's death to help her deal with "emotional problems." He had discovered that Kristin was back on drugs only after Det Agnew had arrested her for possession in January.

The deputy DA had no further questions, and the defense waived its right to cross-examine or call any witnesses.

Judge Thompson did not take long to make his decision.

"The court finds there are sufficient facts to indicate that the crime alleged in the complaint was committed," said the judge, as Kristin sat impassively at the defense table. "That the defendant was the perpetrator thereof. She will be held to answer." Kristin Rossum, young, beautiful, highly intelligent—the wild child daughter of a conservative academic who had made his career demanding that society hold kids responsible for their trespasses—was going to be put on trial for murder.

On October 25, Kristin spent her 25th birthday behind bars in solitary confinement at Las Colinas Women's Detention Facility. She was granted special permission from the jail to receive Holy Communion from an Episcopal priest in a visiting room. Later that day, her parents spent half an hour with her, communicating by telephone through bullet-proof glass.

Back in Melbourne, Michael Robertson read that he was

still under investigation for his role in Greg's death.

"There is compelling circumstantial evidence against Mr. Robertson," Dan Goldstein told an Australian reporter. "We are actively investigating his involvement in the death of de Villers."

Chapter 25

A Last Gasp of Freedom

On November 9, 2001—three days after the first anniversary of Greg de Villers' death—San Diego DA Paul Pfingst decided not to go for the death penalty at Kristin Rossum's murder trial, now scheduled for next June. But she still faced life in prison if convicted.

"It's good news," Ralph Rossum declared. "It means that the jurors who may be riding the fence can't split the difference by saying, 'I'll vote to convict, but not on the other [death penalty].' This means you can't be a fence-rider."

Five days later, Greg de Villers' parents filed a $2.1 million wrongful death suit against Kristin, Michael Robertson and the county for negligence. Their attorney, Craig McClellan, contended that the ME's office bore some responsibility for Greg's death, for failing to run a background check on Kristin's drug history and then not supervising her access to dangerous drugs.

The suit read: "As a former drug user, in charge of the log book for the evidence locker containing dangerous drugs, she was not subjected to any random or even scheduled drug tests. She began having illicit sexual intercourse with her boss, Michael D. Robertson, who was the Chief Toxicologist of the Office of the Medical Examiner, and the person in charge of the toxicology evidence locker, containing the street and dangerous drugs."

The suit maintained that Rossum had been allowed to

take drugs she stole at work, even storing them in her desk.

"Robertson, her lover, knew that the woman he was sleeping with was on drugs, having declared himself an expert on the classic side-effects and signs of . . . drug . . . intoxication."

It alleged that the ME's office was aware of the improper affair, even paying for the couple to travel to Milwaukee for the SOFT conference.

On November 5 or 6, 2000, said the suit, a methamphetamine-addicted Kristin, had administered drugs to Greg and put him in a catatonic state, with Dr. Robertson's knowledge and help.

Then, on the day Greg died, "she administered fatal doses to her unconscious, unknowing and unsuspecting husband. Either shortly before or shortly after the administration of the fatal dose of fentanyl, Rossum and her lover, Robertson, anticipating de Villers' death, spent several intimate hours together."

It alleged that Kristin dialed 911 only after she was certain that Greg was irretrievably dead.

After Greg's death, it contended, the ME's office had given its permission for Rossum to donate her husband's "skin, eyes, veins" and other crucial organs before an autopsy could be carried out.

"The Office of the Medical Examiner intended to quickly release the body to its Chief Toxicologist's lover, Rossum, for immediate cremation," it continued. "But the protestations of family and friends of Gregory de Villers, the intervention of the police department at the family's request, and a court order prohibiting the destruction of Mr. de Villers' remains, put an end to what would have been a near perfect crime."

Six months later, Kristin filed Chapter Thirteen bankruptcy, halting the civil proceedings in their tracks. She claimed she had credit card debts of $30,862, offering to pay off a chunk of it over a three-year period at $330 a month.

Attorney McClellan argued that her filing was intended

to "delay or interfere" with the civil case, and made in bad faith. Eventually a U.S. Bankruptcy Court judge granted a motion from Marie de Villers that the civil case resume.

Just days after Kristin Rossum was ordered to stand trial for the murder of her husband, her mother gave an exclusive interview to *Good Housekeeping*. The seven-page feature, which would run the following March, was entitled, "My Daughter Is Innocent."

Illustrated with pictures of Kristin as a beautiful young child and at her graduation, the savvy marketing executive portrayed her daughter as an innocent victim of circumstantial evidence and damning lies, spread by the de Villers family.

"The details of this case have unfolded like a Hollywood thriller," wrote journalist Joanna Powell. "The Rossums, now battling to save their daughter, claim that their side of the story has not been heard and that they have evidence that could exonerate Kristin."

Constance said she and her husband were "angry, frustrated and scared," describing it as "a living death" for Kristin, who could spend the rest of her life behind bars. She accused the media of "making things up" and spreading misinformation, claiming that everyone wanted to cash in on Kristin's misfortune. She explained how Kristin had gotten into drugs after a serious injury derailed her dreams of becoming a professional ballerina. She'd then left home to move to San Diego to get away from drugs, and met Greg de Villers, who helped her get clean.

Saying she considered Greg "our angel," Constance described him as "bright, charming and attractive." But when Kristin had told him she wanted out of the marriage, he could not accept it.

"Greg loved Kristin to the point of obsession," she said. "She was like his pretty prize."

She claimed that her son-in-law was "spiraling down" during the last year of his life, becoming "nervous and irritable."

Then, she said, he had killed himself, and the scattered rose petals and framed picture of their wedding were his suicide note.

After accusing Greg's family of being unable to accept that he had either committed suicide or accidentally died in a "theatrical bid for sympathy," she repeated the claim her husband had made at the preliminary hearing.

"We know that Greg had taken fentanyl before and had liked the effect," she stated. "And we also know that he had independent access to the drug."

Since her daughter's arrest, said Constance, both she and her husband have sought medical attention for stress-related illness. She said it had been very hard on them mentally, but that they were carrying on the best they could for their daughter.

"It's frightening because it's so wrong," she said. "Kristin has been accused of murder and she's innocent. But the truth will come out when we finally get to court."

Finally, Kristin Rossum had some good news at the end of November, when Judge Thompson agreed to release her from jail on 1.25 million dollars bail.

"[It's] a nut we can crack," Ralph Rossum confidently told reporters. He said they would put up their house for bail bond collateral, and dip into their retirement savings. The Kristin Rossum Defense Fund, he added, now stood at $30,000.

At 3:00 p.m., Friday, January 4, 2002, Kristin was released on bail, returning to her parents' home in Claremont. With a crew from CBS-TV's *48 Hours* filming, the prodigal daughter alternated between laughing and crying as the Rossums celebrated her release with a champagne toast to their "innocent" daughter. This was an image that would later come back to haunt her as it was repeatedly shown on television.

"I did not harm my husband in any way," Kristin defiantly told reporters as she left jail, wearing a black sweater and gray pants, a simple string of pearls around her neck. "I look forward to proving my innocence in court this summer."

Professor Rossum was visibly emotional when he was reunited with his daughter after her six months of incarceration.

"I'm going to be able to hug my baby," he said. "She is delighted, happy, and looking forward to having a kind of semblance of normalcy in her life."

And he thanked Judge Thompson, along with friends and family who had helped swell his daughter's defense fund to $40,000. To make bail, the Rossums had put up $125,000, which was non-refundable, as well as their home and her two brothers' investment accounts as security. Her TriLink boss Rick Hogrefe, who had kept her job open, also generously contributed, as did a retired judge who was a friend of the family.

But Deputy DA Dan Goldstein was less pleased, telling an Associated Press reporter, "This is a woman who, every time the police have come in contact with her, was either under the influence of methamphetamine or in possession of methamphetamine. I have serious concerns that she is going to be in the public."

Two weeks after she was released, Judge Thompson called am emergency hearing, placing a gag order on Kristin and all the attorneys and investigators involved in her case. Accusing the Rossums of attempting to try the case in the media, the judge voiced frustration that he was unable to find a law to muzzle Kristin's parents.

He told Professor Rossum that he firmly believed the extensive press interviews he had been giving were an attempt to "poison the jury pool."

"If I could, I would issue a gag order on him as well," thundered the judge, who threatened to move the trial to Imperial County. He also took a hit at Professor Rossum, advising the renowned constitutional scholar to review the landmark Supreme Court ruling in the famous 1954 Dr.

Sam Sheppard case, which inspired the movie and long-running TV series *The Fugitive*.

"I'm going to do what I should have done when this case came to me," he snapped, warning lawyers for both the defense and prosecution, and all police and support staff not to talk to reporters.

Kristin spent the rest of January with her parents, before leaving to return to her apartment in San Diego. She resumed her job at TriLink in February, starting part time but going full-time within a few weeks.

The TriLink staff were highly supportive and utterly convinced of her innocence. They believed she had been railroaded by the DA's office. How could such a beautiful, quietly spoken, friendly girl murder her husband?

Kristin was now something of a celebrity in San Diego, and when she went out on the town with her friends Claire Becker and Jessica Vanella, heads would turn. During her six months in jail, Jessica had been a regular visitor and they'd become close friends. Soon after she returned to TriLink, Jessica and her mother Kathy invited Kristin to stay over at their home several nights a week, so she wouldn't have to make the long drive back from Orange County to her downtown apartment.

According to the Vanellas, Kristin was the perfect house guest. She got on well with Jessica's grandmother Dee Dee, and every Thursday night she would join the Vanellas and their friends to go remote control racing on a track they'd built on their forty-acre lot. Kristin even found a new boyfriend named Zack Hoover, who promised to stand by her through the upcoming trial.

In March, *San Diego Union-Tribune* writer Caitlin Rother wrote a feature on the Kristin Rossum case for *Cosmopolitan* magazine. It contained a wedding picture of Kristin and Greg that they had sent out to friends and family the previous Christmas. The magazine had first approached the

Rossums for the picture, but they had refused. Editors then secured one from the de Villerses.

Soon after the article came out, Constance Rossum wrote a letter to the de Villerses' attorney Craig McClellan, demanding $2,000 from their in-laws, citing the "illegal" usage, and demanding a penalty. The letter also said, "We will hold you/them responsible for any misuse of any photos."

"It's the standard fee as I understand it," Constance would later explain. "It was *my* picture for use in *Cosmopolitan*, and I had told them so."

On April 10, *48 Hours* broadcast a half-hour segment on the Kristin Rossum case, featuring interviews with all the principals, including the Rossums and Michael Robertson. The program had been recorded before Judge Thompson's gag order in January, and had the full cooperation of the Rossum family.

In a dramatic jailhouse interview from Las Colinas jail, a teary-eyed Kristin denied stealing fentanyl from the ME's office, saying that all the other employees had access too.

"It is above and beyond any nightmare I could ever imagine," she sobbed to reporter Bill Lagattuta. "I am not a murderer. I did not harm my husband."

Kristin also offered up her bizarre theory that Greg had deliberately killed himself in order to frame her and Dr. Robertson for his murder.

From Melbourne, Dr. Robertson also proclaimed his innocence, denying that he was hiding out in Australia. But he agreed that if the prosecution theory that Greg was injected with a massive dose of fentanyl was correct, he would never have lived long enough to get rid of the needle, which was never found.

"It can look suspicious," he said nervously. "Absolutely."

Admitting that he understood why he was under investigation, Dr. Robertson said he was certain that Greg's death was not homicide and Kristin was not the type of person who would even consider killing her husband.

Dan Goldstein also weighed in on the program, describing the prosecution's case against Rossum as "immaculate."

One day after the broadcast, Judge Thompson angrily reacted, sealing all pre-trial documents to prevent further contamination of an "already polluted jury pool."

"There has been a concerted effort to indoctrinate or otherwise influence the potential jury pool in this case through the media," wrote Judge Thompson in his ruling. "The public banter back and forth between both sides in this case, fueled by what we see as an insatiable appetite of the media for the latest chapter in this macabre saga, left the court at the outset with little choice but to issue a gag order, precluding either side from commenting further on the case."

Judge Thompson rejected a motion from *The San Diego Union-Tribune* to gain access to court documents for the case.

The *Union-Tribune* immediately appealed Judge Thompson's ruling, and on April 23, the 4th District Court of Appeal ordered him to unseal the documents and release them to the media.

But the media were not Judge Thompson's only problems with the case. In March, prosecutor Dan Goldstein won his election to become a Supreme Court judge, and would take his place on the bench the following January. The Rossum defense immediately filed a motion to have Goldstein removed from the case, saying it would be a conflict of interest and lead to an unfair trial as he was a potential judge when the trial was scheduled.

The Ethics Committee of the California Judges Association weighed in, asserting that his being a judge-elect would not be a conflict of interest. Thompson denied the motion.

That spring, while it was still uncertain whether Dan Goldstein would remain on the case, another deputy district attorney from the Family Protection Division named Dave Hendren was drafted in as a possible replacement. A graduate of UCLA Law School, Hendren was a boyish-looking

42 years old and had been a San Diego prosecutor for eleven years. Married with two children, he was a veteran of more than one hundred trials, including five murder cases.

When he was appointed to the Rossum case, he had just one month to acquaint himself with it. The sheer volume of material was staggering. By the time it came to trial, the case had generated more than 25,000 pages of documents, the equivalent of eighty novels. There was also a massive amount of electronic data, including hundreds of e-mails, and Web sites visited by Kristin and other people involved in the months before Greg's death. It was estimated that if all the electronic data was ever printed up, it would tower higher than the Washington Monument.

And when Hendren was assigned to the case, there was a good chance he might have to prosecute it alone, if the defense successfully appealed Judge Thompson's ruling on Goldstein.

"I had to become a fast learner," said Hendren. "I had a lot to read, there was no doubt about that."

Over the next few months, Hendren became consumed with the voluminous case, spending almost every waking hour reading it. He said he began with an open mind, but before long he became convinced of Kristin's guilt.

"There were a large number of coincidences, if she was to be innocent," he said later. "I started seeing more and more things piece-by-piece, and the puzzle started to fit perfectly."

He even enlisted his 110-pound wife Marissa in an experiment in their bedroom to see if it was possible to give CPR while talking on the telephone. Hendren, who weighs 165 pounds, almost the same as Greg de Villers, lay on the bed as his wife tried to pull him off, as Kristin had claimed she had. They found it was impossible while talking on the phone.

"It didn't seem like she could have done everything she said," he said. "So one of the things was: could she even pull her husband off the bed by herself? If she did, how would she do it?"

Soon after he came on board, Hendren got a break when Judge Thompson delayed the trial date until October 4, to give him, and the other attorneys, more time to prepare for the case. It also gave Kristin Rossum a few more months of freedom.

In June, as Kristin Rossum tried to live as normal a life as possible, another sensational San Diego murder case competed for the public's attention. David Westerfield went on trial for the murder and kidnapping of 7-year-old Danielle van Dam. The case, which was covered gavel-to-gavel by Court TV, made front-page headlines daily, throwing the spotlight off Rossum. Ultimately, Westerfield was found guilty and sentenced to death. Court TV had also wanted to broadcast the Rossum case live, but Judge Thompson had ruled to prohibit cameras in his courtroom.

Behind the scenes, Kristin's defense team was busy. In August they filed a motion to move the trial to another county, claiming that it would be impossible for her to have a fair hearing after all the publicity. The defense even commissioned San Diego State University to conduct a telephone poll, asking 303 San Diego County residents what they knew of the Rossum case. Fifty-seven percent said they had heard of it, out of which twenty percent thought she was guilty and only four percent believed her innocent.

Judge Thompson postponed ruling on a change of venue, saying he would decide after he had determined if an impartial jury could be found.

On the same day, the defense also filed court papers claiming that fentanyl is not a recognized poison, and is not defined in state law. The prosecution countered that California criminal jury instructions defined *poison* as any substance introduced into the body that can cause death.

The prosecution told the judge that fentanyl, combined with the two other drugs found in Greg's body, would certainly cause substantial injury or illness, and fall under the definition of *poison*. After considering the motion, Superior Court Judge Judith Hayes sided with the prosecution, refusing to dismiss the allegation that Kristin had poisoned her husband.

Dan Goldstein and Dave Hendren were also working around the clock, subpoenaing Kristin's bank records and other paper trails she may have left in the days leading up to Greg's death. The DA's paralegal, Meredith Dent, worked the Rossum case full-time, and on September 30, as a lengthy jury questionnaire was finally agreed to by the defense and prosecution, she hit the jackpot.

While sifting through Kristin's ATM withdrawals, the 32-year-old paralegal noticed that Kristin had gotten money from Vons on the day of Greg's death. Meredith then contacted the store, requesting all records for that date. A security officer then sent her the records for Kristin's Vons Club Card for November 6, 2000, which listed every item she had purchased that day.

"I was going through the records," remembered Dent, "and at the bottom of the page it said 'single rose.' I said, 'My Gosh!' and literally jumped up and told Dave Hendren, 'Look what she purchased from Vons on November sixth.' "

Hendren was so excited, he rushed into Dan Goldstein's office, yelling at him to get off the phone. Proof that she had bought a single rose at Vons at midday on the day of Greg's death was damning evidence against Kristin, providing almost undeniable proof of where the rose petals scattered around his body had come from.

It was a major victory for the prosecution, and not well received by the defense the following day when Hendren informed them about it. Public Defender Alex Loebig would later describe this key piece of evidence as "devastating," saying that the prosecution had been lucky, only discovering it through "an intuitive lark" by a paralegal.

On Monday, October 7, Kristin had an appointment to meet with her defense team to discuss the implications of the new single rose evidence. That morning she called 911 from the hotel room where she was staying before the trial, complaining that she was having a panic attack. When paramedics arrived, they found her face-down in bed clutching a teddy bear.

Later, she would deny that the panic attack had been brought on by the explosive new evidence that she had bought a rose the day of Greg's death.

"That had nothing to do with it," she claimed. "The whole process was starting. I was scared to death."

Chapter 26

The Trial

On Friday, October 4, 2002, jury selection began for the Kristin Rossum trial. One hundred and fifty potential jurors turned up at the West Broadway court and were given a twenty-eight-page questionnaire to fill in. It included such questions as: "Do you believe that a person who maintains a sexual or romantic relationship outside his or her marriage is more likely to commit an act of domestic violence against his or her spouse? If yes, please explain"; and "What television and radio programs do you view or listen to on a regular basis? Do you watch *Court TV*, *Law and Order*, or *Crime and Punishment*? If yes, which show(s) do you watch and do you watch regularly?"

Judge Thompson immediately sealed the questionnaire and a list of 135 potential witnesses, but relented a few days later, after *The San Diego Union-Tribune* protested. The witnesses included Michael Robertson, although he had told his civil attorney he had no plans to leave Australia to testify.

The judge also reversed his earlier decision to reserve two rows of bench seating for the press during the trial, saying he didn't see why reporters should get preferential treatment over the public. And the tough-talking judge warned that if any reporter attempted to interview a juror, he would "throw his ass in jail."

It took one week to whittle down the vast jury pool to

just twelve jurors and four alternates, who saw Kristin
break into tears as they were selected. The five men and
seven women who would decide her fate included a soft-
ware engineer, a public relations executive and a cryptol-
ogist.

"You will, in essence, be the judges of the facts," the
judge told them. "You must keep an open mind in this
case."

On Tuesday, October 15, the trial of Kristin Rossum began
at 9:00 a.m. sharp. Kristin and her parents, who were staying at nearby hotels, were swarmed by TV crews and reporters as they arrived at the courthouse. They went
through security before taking the elevator to the third floor
at Judge Thompson's Department 38 courtroom, where a
line of reporters and members of the public had gathered.

Looking more like a fashion model than a defendant in
a murder trial, Kristin was dressed in a stylish black suit
with a white top. Taking her place at the defense table she
appeared composed, even smiling when the jury was seated.

Prosecutor Dan Goldstein then stood up to deliver his
opening statement, cutting straight to the chase.

"Good morning, ladies and gentlemen," he began. "Kristin Rossum was a toxicologist at the San Diego Medical
Examiner's. She murdered her husband by stealing a little-
known drug called fentanyl. She stole it from the medical
examiner's office, and she administered it to her husband.

"She did this to protect two relationships. One was her
love for a drug called methamphetamine. She also murdered him for another love, and that was for the chief toxicologist. His name is Michael Robertson."

Telling the jury that they would never see Dr. Robertson
in the courtroom, the deputy DA called him as "an unindicted co-conspirator," saying that he would be an integral
part of this homicide.

"She saw the medical examiner's office as a veritable
candy store of drugs," he continued. "There are so many

drugs missing . . . most of them she's either used or they were in Greg de Villers' body at the time of his death."

Likening the case to a "murder mystery," Goldstein told the jury it was packed with "sex, drugs, motives and innuendoes," but they would see that everything led to Kristin's guilt.

"Now, what this trial is is merely an intersection," said Goldstein. "It's an intersection of all the lies that the defendant has told in the cover-up of this homicide, prior to the homicide, and during her relationship with Greg de Villers."

Throughout Goldstein's opening statements, Kristin shook her head, mouthing comments under her breath and trying to make visual contact with jurors. She would continue doing this with all the prosecution witnesses and it did not go unnoticed by Judge Thompson.

Goldstein told the jury that Kristin came from a background of wealth and privilege, but had "terrible insecurities" that led to her drug addiction.

"To Kristin Rossum and the Rossum family, image is everything," said the prosecutor. "That's why it was so important for Kristin Rossum to hide her addictions and her affair from her parents."

Greg de Villers, he said, came into her life as a savior, rescuing her from drugs. Over the next few years with Greg, her life changed and she went through university, finding a good job as a toxicologist. But she also had easy access to methamphetamine in the ME's office and became infatuated with her boss, Michael Robertson.

"What's interesting, though," said Goldstein, "is the extent to which the defendant was able to burn the candle at both ends. In one hour of the day, she would be e-mailing Greg de Villers, saying, 'I love you more than anything in the world. How come you don't e-mail me more often?' Twenty minutes later, she's e-mailing Robertson, saying, 'I love you and want to spend the rest of my life with you.' "
Goldstein told the jury they would receive a color-coded

comprehensive notebook of all e-mails between Kristin, Robertson and Greg.

He told the jury that Kristin had lied and deceived Greg about Dr. Robertson, but he finally found out and confronted her lover. And when Greg threatened to reveal her drug use and her affair to the chief medical examiner, said Goldstein, she decided to kill him.

"She was out of control, using dangerous drugs," he said, dramatically holding up a single red rose in front of the jury. "She had an affair that had reached an apocalypse. [Greg] was going to turn her in for an affair and using meth. She knew that she would lose her job, and she knew that Michael Robertson would lose his work visa and he would be out of the country. The defendant is guilty of murdering Greg de Villers. We are going to prove that."

Then, after four hours on his feet, Dan Goldstein sat down and, following a short recess, public defender Alex Loebig began his opening statement to the jury. He would speak for just forty-five minutes while Kristin wept at the defense table.

Loebig began by telling the jury that Kristin would later testify, telling in her own words what had happened. He then started to paint a picture of Kristin far different from the prosecutor's version.

"I don't think that Ms. Rossum was brought up with the silver spoon that was alluded to," he began. "This is not a blue-blood family with a black sheep in it."

It had been "love at first sight," said Loebig, when Kristin and Greg had met in Tijuana. But after he helped her kick her drug problem, Kristin began to have doubts about their relationship.

"It wasn't too long after the wedding that Kristin determined that maybe Greg wasn't the soul mate for her," said the public defender. "When Michael Robertson walked in, he had an accent, he had a Ph.D., he played rugby. He was one smooth guy."

He accused the prosecution of greatly exaggerating Kristin's drug use. He also said that Greg couldn't face the thought of living without her when she told him she was leaving.

"He wasn't in a happy place," Loebig told the jury. "It's very possible that that lethal drug was in the glass by the bed and that Greg drank it shortly thereafter. Greg told Kristin Rossum any number of times, from very close to the beginning of their relationship, that he didn't want to live without her. On November 6, unfortunately, before he could tell anybody else, he showed Kristin that he couldn't live without her."

Once opening statements were over, the prosecution began its elaborately prepared case against Kristin, which would take almost two weeks to present. Dan Goldstein and David Hendren called a procession of paramedics, homicide investigators, ME's office employees and experts, who all presented damning evidence, just as they had in the preliminary hearing.

One witness, drug expert Dr. Theodore Stanley, told the jury he had never seen such high levels of fentanyl present in a body in his thirty years of studying the drug as an anesthesiologist. Greg de Villers had 57.3 nanograms per milligram of fentanyl in his blood—fourteen times the fatal dose that would stop breathing.

He testified that it was possible that Greg had been given the tasteless, odorless drug orally, maybe in water. Within twenty to thirty minutes, he would have exhibited slurred speech and other signs of sedation.

"If he had one huge amount, he could have [had] enough to kill him in a couple of hours," testified Dr. Stanley. "I have never seen this high of a blood level."

The expert told Goldstein that the fentanyl could also have been administered by Band-Aid–like patches, but it would have taken fifteen to twenty of them to achieve such high levels.

Goldstein then asked about the effects of injecting fentanyl into a victim.

"If the injection is intravenous, the peak effect will occur in about five minutes," he testified. "If the injection is intramuscular, the peak effect will probably take fifteen to twenty minutes."

In his cross-examination, defender Victor Eriksen asked Dr. Stanley if, given the fentanyl levels in Greg's blood, urine and stomach contents, he could determine the amount of the drug "that was actually taken by Mr. de Villers?"

Dr. Stanley replied that there was no way of knowing, as it is not routinely measured in the stomach contents.

"In all my career, I haven't ever seen such high gastric levels," said the doctor. "So, it's a large amount."

Another crucial prosecution expert witness was the emergency room physician, Dr. Jack Stump, who had studied the behavioral and physiological effects of methamphetamine and trained police officers in how to deal with addicts. Asked by Goldstein to describe the drug, Dr. Stump said that frequent use could actually change the chemistry of the brain.

"What methamphetamine does for you is give you what's called supernatural pleasure," he explained. "A pleasure you could not obtain anywhere else in nature. There aren't enough vacations, aren't enough births of babies, not enough pleasant events in life to get remotely close to what methamphetamine can do for you."

But he said that after a few weeks on the drug, an addict would lose the ability to get the "supernatural high," and become acutely depressed. Soon they would be taking it just to feel normal. Long-term use, he said, leads to "extreme paranoia" and even hallucinations.

"When a person has used long enough," he told Goldstein, "we see several things. We see, oftentimes, weight loss. We see skin lesions. Part of the methamphetamine is an obsessive disorder in which they will start to scratch their skin. Face and arms are most common. They will scratch until they wear an ulcer in their skin. It's, on the street, called 'crank bugs' or 'meth bugs.'"

The prosecutor then showed Dr. Stump a picture of Kristin Rossum soon after her arrest, asking if he saw meth bugs on her face.

"Yes," he replied, saying that he saw several on Kristin's forehead and face, one with a scab on it and others in the healing process.

In his cross-examination, Victor Eriksen asked if a habitual meth user could function at work. Dr. Stump said that at low levels of the drug, a person could without too much difficulty, but the more they took, the more difficult it would become.

"Would it strike you as unusual," asked Eriksen, "that a heavy meth user would be able to graduate with a B.S. degree in chemistry at the summa cum laude level?"

"That would be unusual for a heavy meth user," conceded the doctor.

On Friday, October 25, Kristin Rossum passed her 26th birthday. She had little to celebrate—on the stand, the DAs paralegal Meredith Dent described how she had accidentally discovered that Kristin had bought a single rose from Vons the day Greg died. She also testified how Kristin had called her drug dealer four times that day and numerous times later, and how she usually withdrew $360 from her ATM before going to see him.

Later that day, the prosecution screened the three-hour video of Kristin's interview with Detectives Laurie Agnew and Jimmy Valle for the jury. Throughout it, Kristin remained composed at the defense table, taking notes and whispering to the two public defenders.

The following Monday, two weeks after the start of the trial, the prosecution's last witness, Jerome de Villers, took the stand, emotionally testifying that he had refused to believe his brother had committed suicide. He told of growing up with Greg in Palm Springs after their father had left, and how they had literally bumped into Kristin on the Mexican border.

"She was alone," he said. "She asked to hang out with us."

She moved into Greg's room that night, but never paid her share of the rent. Soon, valuables began disappearing from the apartment, like Greg's gold ring with the Tremolet–de Villers family crest, and a gold necklace, as well as some checks. But Greg had initially refused to believe that Kristin was the culprit.

Jerome said he was shocked when Greg announced they were engaged, but after they married, his brother seemed happy in the relationship, and had no idea that Kristin was being unfaithful.

After Greg's sudden death, Jerome said he had been suspicious of Kristin's behavior and gone to the police, prompting the investigation.

Throughout his testimony, Kristin seemed agitated and upset, continually shaking her head at the jury and saying "No!"

When Judge Thompson recessed that night and dismissed the jury, prosecutor Dan Goldstein took the defendant to task.

"Your Honor," he told the judge, "I have been fairly patient during this trial about the defendant's conduct in this courtroom. During my opening statement, in twelve or thirteen years' experience of doing cases, I've had very few defendants chipping at me during opening statement. I think the defense counsel noted it. I don't know if Your Honor did?

Judge Thompson said he had noticed it too.

"I'd ask the court to tell her to stop, knock it off," said the visibly angry deputy DA. "This is the victim's brother who is on the stand, who doesn't deserve this type of conduct." Goldstein accused Kristin of "interfering with the court process," demanding it stop immediately.

Alex Loebig said that, although he was sitting next to

her, he didn't see her do anything more than reacting "to some degree."

"All right," Judge Thompson told her. "Don't do it again."

"Yes, Your Honor," replied Kristin smugly.

Angered by her tone, the judge then launched into her in an uncharacteristic burst of profanity.

"You are smiling at jurors," he thundered. "Absolute bullshit. I think it's really hurting you. I don't think they are buying it for a second. It's up to you. You are to have no contact with any witnesses one way or the other. Don't sit there and tell me you are not doing it. I'm not a fucking idiot."

Before seating the jury the next day, Judge Thompson apologized to the court for losing his temper and using profanities.

"To the extent anyone was offended by the language that was used I apologize," he said. "But, as I said, I will not apologize for the message."

Chapter 27

In Her Own Defense

Since the beginning of her trial, Kristin had dominated the television news in San Diego. Every night the city's viewing public was treated to footage of Kristin and her parents entering the court in the morning, and then leaving at night to return to their hotel. Now that the trial was under way, her parents had stopped giving interviews to the scores of reporters and TV news crews camped out on West Broadway outside the modern courthouse.

Some reporters noted that Kristin had adopted the air of a runway fashion model, sashaying into court wearing a smart new outfit each morning. She dressed conservatively in somber suits and white shirts, but appeared to be enjoying all the attention, even smiling for cameras on occasion.

On Tuesday, October 29, Kristin seemed upbeat for the start of her defense. Her legal team would have an uphill battle trying to prove that Greg had died a tragic suicide. One of the first defense witnesses was Melissa Prager, Kristin's best friend since Claremont Junior High School.

Calling Kristin "my dear friend," Prager told the jury that she had found Greg "overly protective," saying he'd discouraged his wife from seeing her old friends without his permission. Finally, she said, Kristin had told her that she had fallen in love with her boss, Dr. Michael Robertson.

"She finally found someone who truly respected her for

her mind and appreciated her beauty," Prager testified. "Someone who she was in love with."

Defender Victor Eriksen then asked if Kristin had expressed reservations about telling Greg she wanted a separation.

"She seemed terrified," said Prager. "She informed me that she had told Greg about her affair and that [he] was very upset about it."

During his cross-examination, Dan Goldstein tried to demonstrate to the jury how Melissa Prager was part of the Rossum family PR machine, asking about interviews she had given to *The San Diego Union-Tribune* and *Good Housekeeping*.

"I was interviewed by so many people," she said. "I don't remember *Union-Tribune*, but it could have happened."

The defense's next witness was Constance Rossum, who recounted Kristin's childhood and adolescence. She told the jury of Kristin's early career as a child model and how she had dreamed of being a prima ballerina. But everything changed, said her mother, when Kristin was seriously injured in a ballet accident and had to give up dancing.

"Without her ballet, she felt very unhappy," said Constance. "She said, 'Mom, after being the Sugar Plum Fairy . . .' "

Then Kristin's grades started to fall and her behavior changed as she started keeping bad company at Claremont High. Constance started sobbing as Loebig asked her about the time police had been called to the house after her brother had discovered drug paraphernalia.

"I felt very stupid that I probably did not see or connect the signs," she said. "I wouldn't know a drug if I fell over it."

Describing her first meeting with her future son-in-law, Constance thought he had "very kind eyes." Soon afterward she had personally found the couple an apartment on the UCSD campus and helped pay rent and expenses. She had even prepared a three-page summary of all the money they had lavished on the couple over the period of their relationship and marriage, saying it totaled $74,425.

"It was our initiative," she stated. "They would remind us if the rent check was late."

Constance said that, soon after they'd met, Kristin had come home, saying she and Greg planned to be married.

"I asked them to please wait," she said. "I wanted Kristin to go back to school."

Kristin dutifully agreed and was accepted into SDSU, where she became a straight-A student.

"They seemed very hard-working," she said. "We were quite proud of them."

Constance told how, a few weeks before the wedding, Kristin had burst into tears, telling her she wanted to cancel it. Thinking she had "wedding jitters," Constance asked her daughter if it was wise after all the arrangements had been made.

"I gave her the wrong counsel, I'm afraid," she said. "I thought it was best at the time."

Throughout her testimony, Constance painted Greg as an angry, immature man, emotionally dependent on Kristin. By the beginning of 2000, she said, her daughter had told her that the marriage had no future, and her doubts about Greg had resurfaced. By September, testified Constance, Kristin had told her over lunch that she planned to leave him, but didn't want to hurt him, as his mother Marie was facing eviction.

"I said, 'Kristin, you can't stay with a man simply because you don't want to hurt his mother's feeling.'"

Constance had encouraged her daughter to walk out on Greg, even offering to help her move out that day.

Then she described how she and her husband had gone to San Diego to take Greg and Kristin out for a birthday dinner. When they arrived at the apartment, she commented on a single red rose in the dining room.

"It was strange and scary," she testified. "He was facing me. He said, 'Of all the roses, that single rose survived.'

Ralph and I looked at each other. We thought, 'Wow, you are waxing poetic there.' "

Later, over dinner, she described Greg as "agitated" that his mother had still not received her copy of the wedding album. Then, according to Constance, her son-in-law began shouting and making a scene in the restaurant about a friend who had let him down in a deal to raise funds for Orbigen.

"He was very upset," she said, "and wanted him to burn in hell. I kicked [Kristin] under the table. And that's a signal that Mom wants to talk to you."

According to Constance, Kristin then told her it was "really bad" with Greg and that she was leaving next week. The following morning, she and her husband went out to search for available apartments for their daughter. In his often-combative cross-examination, Dave Hendren challenged Constance about her defense testimony. He questioned her closely about when Claremont High School had called in the police, concerned that Kristin was being physically abused at home.

Saying that her daughter was engaging in "self-harm," she described how she and her husband had searched Kristin's backpack, finding a meth pipe. Constance admitted that she then "got physical" with Kristin, and Professor Rossum had "grabbed her arm" as she was attempting to run away.

"I slapped her in the face," she said, adding that her husband had given her a "spanking" on her buttocks. "I was very worried. I was very angry. She did things we could not handle."

Hendren then asked about Kristin's second encounter with Claremont police, after the Rossums had found methamphetamine in her bra.

"We confronted Kristin about drugs again," Constance answered. "And she said, 'Oh, I'm sorry. I'm so embarrassed.' "

She said her daughter had then picked up a kitchen knife and held it up, before running upstairs and going into the

bathroom. She denied that Kristin had tried to cut herself
with the knife, but confirmed that she had taken a razor
blade and drawn blood.

" 'Perhaps I'll slit my wrists,' " Constance remembered
her daughter saying. "But she didn't."

She said her daughter's continued drug use had devastated the family and put her at her wits' end.

"Image is not important if your daughter's life is in danger," she said, referring back to Dan Goldstein's opening
statements. "How can you teach ethics if you don't keep it
at home?"

The deputy DA also asked her whether she had hired an
agent to handle book and film rights on Kristin's story.
Constance admitted that she had been approached on the
subject, and had talked to a couple of agents, but "We told
them our focus is on our daughter's trial," she said. "Please
don't bother us until after the trial." So far she had only
hired a professor at the UCLA School of Communications
for illegal use of copyright.

Pointing out her extensive marketing and public relations background, Hendren asked if she realized the importance of accuracy. Then he brought up an interview she
had given *Good Housekeeping*, intimating that Greg had
Hepatitis B, and linking it to drug use and multiple sex
partners.

Constance claimed she had been misinformed that he
had the disease after Greg's eyes were rejected for donation
after his death.

"You were suggesting to a national news media," said
Hendren, "that Mr. de Villers either used needles or had a
sexual partner outside of his marriage, weren't you?"

"That's what we'd been told," she said. "That was our
understanding."

The next defense witness was Kristin's twenty-three-
year-old brother Brent. In line with defense strategy to
show Kristin's unhappy marriage, he told of a series of e-
mails in 2000, in which his sister spoke about her relation-

ship with Greg. He confirmed that in a May 23 e-mail, Kristin had told him she should have listened to her instincts and called off the wedding. But she had never mentioned her affair with Michael Robertson, or that she had relapsed into methamphetamine prior to Greg's death.

On his cross-examination, Dan Goldstein asked Brent what Kristin did when she was taking drugs in the early 1990s.

"She was picking at her knuckles," he replied. "Fidgety. That's the behavior I associated with the meth use."

Describing his late brother-in-law as "a good guy," Brent said they often played golf together. But in the months before his death, Greg's behavior changed and he became "distant."

Kristin's aunt, Marguerite Zandstra, then took the stand, describing how Greg had gotten angry the night before his wedding at the thought of his estranged father turning up.

"He said to me, 'If he shows up, I'll kill him,' " said her aunt.

Then, under questioning by Goldstein, Zandstra said that in the three times she had met Greg, she had found him "wimpy" and "immature," and that "he didn't act like a man."

The following day, the defense called its own medical expert, Dr. Mark Wallace, to try to show that Greg could have taken fentanyl himself. He testified that it would be hard to deliver the drug orally, as it gets destroyed by stomach juices and only twenty-five percent of the hit is absorbed. Unlike the prosecution's drug expert, he described fentanyl as "very bad-tasting," saying it would be impossible to deliver raw fentanyl without masking the taste.

Asked by Victor Eriksen if someone would taste ten milliliters of fentanyl dissolved into an eight-ounce glass, Dr. Wallace said it would taste bitter.

On cross-examination, Dan Goldstein challenged the doctor's claims about the drug's taste.

"Obviously 'bitter' is kind of a subjective word," said the deputy DA. "Let me ask you, how bitter is fentanyl?"

"I don't know," replied the doctor, who admitted that he had never seen a dose as high as the one in Greg's body.

Kristin's youngest brother Pierce then took the stand, describing how Greg had changed after the wedding.

"He stopped playing video games," said the 16-year-old. "Stopped talking with the family. Just became over-protective of Kristin and very clingy."

Asked by Eriksen how his sister had reacted to Greg's "clinginess," Pierce said she got annoyed at times and wanted her own space. He mentioned one time when Greg had come to Claremont for the Rossums' wedding anniversary, and insisted on watching a video of Kristin dancing the Sugar Plum Fairy again and again.

"I said, 'Come on, Greg. Let's play. You have seen that enough times. You have your own copy in San Diego.' "

When the Defense was finished, Dan Goldstein stood up, asking Pierce about some notes he had written, and whether he'd heard his mother and aunt testify. Pierce said he had written up the notes the night before, but had not discussed them with his parents.

The next witness was Professor Ralph Rossum, who described the family's repeated attempts to break his daughter's drug addiction. As he had in the preliminary hearing, he described Greg's dramatic outburst about the single rose on November 3, 2000, and his angry behavior later. And once again, under cross-examination, Professor Rossum acknowledged never mentioning either incident to the campus police investigating Greg's death.

When Dan Goldstein suggested that, like any father, he was protecting his daughter so she wouldn't get hurt, Professor Rossum became evasive.

"Depends on what it means to protect my daughter," he replied. "For example, I did participate in calling the police on her when we knew that there was this meth problem.

So protecting her, in one sense, could be just to hide it. Protecting her in another way would be to do the right thing."

At the end of that afternoon session, Alex Loebig called Kristin Rossum to the stand. There was a hush in the courtroom as Kristin, her blonde hair tied back, walked nervously over to the stand to be sworn in. Loebig began taking her through her life story and the circumstances that had led to her meeting Greg de Villers.

She seemed dreamy, as if reliving a movie, as she spoke about her early childhood in Germantown and Chicago. Some wondered if she had taken tranquilizers.

"I don't have too many specific memories from Tennessee," she said, staring straight at the jury. "More flashbulbs and fuzzy images."

Saying she had a "wonderful childhood," Kristin sounded like the all-American girl, as she described her successes at school and her aspirations to become a professional ballet dancer.

Prompted by Loebig, she spoke about her first drug experiences in sophomore year at Claremont High School and how a girlfriend had turned her on to methamphetamine at a football game.

"I knew it was illegal," she said. "I figured I was open to experimenting with it."

As she dabbed her eyes, she told how she had gotten deeper into drugs, losing friends as she retreated into using it alone at home. Her class grades slipped from A's to B's, and she started finding it hard to study.

Loebig asked when she realized she had developed a drug problem and how she felt.

"Just worn out, tired," she said tearfully. "It had gotten to the point where what started off as a good feeling was just something I really needed to feel normal."

She sadly told the jury of her two early brushes with the Claremont Police Department, and how she had gone to the

University of Redlands to break away from the Claremont drug crowd.

But in her second semester there, she had fallen back into methamphetamine with a vengeance.

"I thought I could study harder," she said in a breaking voice. "Work better, not realizing my limitations and how quickly that would snowball into more regular use."

Then she described how she had run away on Christmas, 1994, winding up in San Diego with $200 in her pocket. She had decided to go to Tijuana for the night for something to do.

"I began walking on the path to go over the border," she said. "I think I dropped my jacket. I bent down to pick it up and kind of bumped into Greg, literally. We kind of hit it off from there."

After bar-hopping in Tijuana, Kristin said, he'd invited her back to his apartment for the night.

"To be candid and blunt," asked Loebig, "did you guys have sex?"

"We did," she replied. "It felt safe and I didn't want to feel alone."

Within a week, she said, Greg had told her he loved her, inviting her to move into his room. When she told him about her problem with drugs, he was supportive, pledging to help her. But before she cleaned up, she confessed to stealing some checks belonging to Greg's roommate Christopher Wren, saying she had never been able to cash them.

At this point, after Kristin had been on the stand for one hour, Judge Thompson recessed for the day. Outside the court, Kristin, wearing wraparound dark glasses, walked back to her hotel chased by television news crews, refusing to even acknowledge them. It was her fifteen minutes of fame, and she appeared as jaded to the reporters' shouted questions as any movie star.

On Friday morning, *The San Diego Union-Tribune*'s city edition carried the front page headline, "Rossum Testifies at Trial: Drug use began in high school 10 years ago, defendant says." Above the story was a three-column-wide picture showing her leaving court, being chased by the media.

Re-taking the stand later that day, she told the jury she'd had misgivings six weeks before her wedding. But she had gone through with it, putting it down to normal wedding jitters.

Loebig then asked if she had loved Greg when they were at the altar exchanging vows.

"I loved him very much," she replied, her voice wavering with emotion.

Prompted by her attorney, she described how the relationship had soured after she graduated from SDSU and began working for the ME's office. She said Greg had felt threatened by her growing self-confidence, and became overly possessive.

"I was becoming more disheartened with our marriage," she said. "I just felt like I had married the wrong person."

Then Michael Robertson had started working at the ME's office, and they soon became close, finding much in common.

"Were you attracted to him?" asked Loebig.

"I sure was," replied Rossum. "I remember distinctly the moment I first saw him."

She said they had first slept together that June and that they were in love.

"It was very romantic," she declared. "Very exciting, very passionate."

Soon afterwards she told Greg that she had "developed very strong feelings" for her boss. Her angry husband had then called Dr. Robertson, telling him to stay away from his wife.

Kristin said that over the summer, as her love affair blossomed, her marriage had disintegrated. She told Loebig she had spoken to Greg about her fears for their marriage and he'd taken to his bed for a couple of days.

"I was devastated, too," she said. "It was pretty painful to see someone you love hurt so much."

After returning from the SOFT conference, she had told Greg, at her mother's suggestion, that she wanted a trial separation. He had not taken it well, and after finding a love letter from Dr. Robertson in her pocket, they had argued all through the last weekend of his life.

By this time she had begun taking methamphetamine again, and Greg was highly suspicious. Then, on the weekend before his death, Greg had threatened to expose her relapse into drugs and her affair with Michael Robertson.

"Were these threats so serious that you planned to take your husband's life?" asked Alex Loebig.

"Absolutely not," declared Kristin.

Then Loebig gently led her through the final hours of Greg's life. Sunday night, she said, Greg had snored a lot, at one point getting up complaining that he couldn't sleep. On Monday morning his speech was slurry and she had called in sick for him, before going to work.

When she arrived, she said, Dr. Robertson had called her into his office, accusing her of using drugs again.

"I broke down sobbing," she testified. "I was very upset. I was devastated and humiliated, disappointed in myself."

After the showdown with Dr. Robertson, she claimed, she had driven home to check up on Greg, staying for ten minutes before returning to work. Later, she went back again for lunch. Since the revelation that she had bought a single rose at Vons, Kristin now incorporated this into her story for the first time.

"I bought a rose bouquet with baby's breath that was wrapped up," she told the jury, adding that she'd also purchased two cans of soup, a bottle of NyQuil and an over-the-counter sleeping aid.

Two years earlier, she had told Homicide detectives that she had made Greg soup at 11:30 a.m., but now her story had changed to ninety minutes later. She then returned to work, but at about 2:30 p.m. she left to meet Michael Robertson, who wanted to discuss her drug relapse.

"He had a lot of questions for me about it," she said. "We agreed to meet at a spot in La Jolla where we had met on frequent afternoons, just to chat and walk along a little trail."

She said they spent an hour and a half at the spot they called "the Willows," and then returned home at about 5:00 p.m.

"Greg was still sleeping," she said. "I figured he was up at noon; he went back to bed. I didn't want to disturb him."

Then at about 6:30, she said, she left to run some errands at a local mall and bought some gas, before quickly returning to the ME's office to make sure she had shut down some equipment.

When she returned at 8:00 p.m., Greg was "sleeping peacefully," so she took a bubble bath, shaved her legs and had a shower.

"I changed into my PJ's," she continued. "And I towel-dried my hair. I went out. I had a booklet." The next day was going to be Election Day. "I was reading the voting polls for the next day, deciding how I would vote."

She claimed that, after brushing her teeth, she went into the bedroom, turned on the light and discovered Greg not breathing.

"I was petrified," she told Loebig, beginning to sob. "I called 911."

She said she had followed the emergency dispatcher's advice, pulling Greg off the bed and onto the floor to administer CPR.

"By the time Greg passed away," asked her attorney, "did you love Michael Robertson so much that you intended to take your husband's life so that you could have Robertson?"

"Absolutely not," declared Kristin. "That's what divorce is for."

When Alex Loebig finished questioning his client, it was near Friday lunchtime. Judge Thompson then recessed for the rest of the day, giving Kristin Rossum two-and-a-half days to prepare for her cross-examination by prosecutor Dan Goldstein. And she could be sure that it wouldn't be as easy a ride as her attorney had given her.

Chapter 28

"I Wasn't Telling the Whole Truth"

A little after 9:00 a.m. on Monday, November 4, prosecutor Dan Goldstein began his cross-examination of Kristin Rossum. He walked over to the witness box, looked straight into her eyes and asked: "Have you taken any drugs within the past ninety-six hours?"

Unfazed, Kristin said she had.

"Those medications are prescribed or non-prescribed?" Goldstein demanded to know.

"They are prescribed," she answered blandly.

"What are you taking?"

"I took last night a sleeping pill to help me sleep," said Kristin, her eyes darting around the courtroom. She had also taken a drug called Sonata, which had been prescribed by her primary care physician. Asked what other drugs she had taken in the last four days, she admitted taking half a Xanax, which the doctor had told her to take if she was particularly anxious or nervous.

"So you have taken medication, Xanax, which is some type of mood elevator, before you testified?" asked the deputy DA.

"It's not a mood elevator," snapped Kristin, adding that she had not taken any other drugs over the weekend except ibuprofen.

Over the next day and a half, the veteran prosecutor would rapid-fire salvos of questions from all directions to prove she was a liar, highlighting the many inconsistencies between her story and the evidence surrounding Greg's death. And although she had often sobbed during the testimony of defense witnesses, she now remained surprisingly restrained, a fact not lost on the jury.

Early on, he asked why she hadn't told detectives she had used her new cell phone to call Michael Robertson on the Sunday night before Greg's death. Kristin said she had forgotten making the call until she had seen the phone records.

"You graduated summa cum laude?" said the prosecutor sarcastically.

In another exchange, Goldstein questioned her about why she'd called her drug dealer four times in rapid succession on the morning Greg died.

"Two things had happened, correct?" he told her. "One, you weren't trying to stay clean anymore, were you?"

"That's not true," replied Rossum angrily.

"Were you calling [your drug dealer] to go golfing with him?" Goldstein asked mockingly.

Defense counsel objected and Judge Thompson sustained the objection. The question was argumentative.

Then Goldstein began asking her about keeping a stash of methamphetamine at the ME's office. Kristin admitted she had, as Greg had started searching her things, suspicious that she had relapsed. She admitted lying to her husband that she was back on drugs, saying that she hadn't told him the truth since she was about to walk out on the marriage.

Asked why she had left a bindle of meth at work, Kristin said she hadn't wanted to bring it home because of the tension. But she did admit having a supply at home the night of Greg's death.

Goldstein then asked her to show the jury how she smoked methamphetamine in foil.

"You can arrange it so that it can hold just a little bit of crystalline powder," she answered, starting to pantomime constructing a tin-foil pipe with her hands. "And just hold a flame of some sort, a heat source, under it. And it will eventually melt and produce a little bit of smoke, which you can inhale."

He then asked her why she had told Det Laurie Agnew that drugs were in her past, although she had smoked meth before the police interview.

"I wanted to keep my current drug use out of it," said Kristin. "So yes, it was a lie. I was in a police station, of all things."

The prosecutor asked her about hiding a meth pipe near the fume hood of the HPLC room at the ME's office, pointing out that the machine removes fumes from the building. He then moved his questioning to her e-mails, asking about the one she sent Greg after the SOFT conference, accusing her husband of hurting her beyond repair, and listing a number of drugs including diazepam, zolpidem and Seroquel.

Kristin said that Greg had searched her purse and found dietary supplements and an over-the-counter drug, and that she had deliberately misled him, claiming the drugs were anti-psychotics and a hypnotic given to her by a friend because of her marital stress.

"Those pills didn't actually exist," she admitted. "I was sending Greg on a wild goose chase to show him how wrong he was. I was making a point."

Goldstein asked whether she had told her husband that she'd had sex with Robertson in a hotel room at the conference. He then asked why she had lied to detectives about having a sexual relationship with her boss and why she hadn't told investigators about it right away.

"I'm very sorry I wasn't more forthcoming with that information," she replied. "I was too ashamed to talk about the sex stuff."

Questioned why she had told Det Agnew that she and Robertson had only met for coffee the summer before Greg's death, Rossum was forced to admit that she had lied again.

"I wasn't telling the whole truth, no," she conceded.

"Because it might make you look bad?"

"Yes, I was very embarrassed."

She also admitted lying to Jerome and Bertrand de Villers when they'd found Dr. Robertson at her apartment a couple of days after Greg's passing.

"And you told them that Robertson was merely dropping off a paycheck, correct?" demanded Goldstein.

"No, he didn't bring over a paycheck," she said, adding that she had direct deposit.

Then, under intense questioning, Goldstein forced her to admit making up the whole Natalie Merchant concert raffle story she had told Greg.

"Michael asked me to go to the concert," she explained. "I wanted to create an excuse to go."

Kristin became emotional when Dan Goldstein produced some photographs taken of her and Greg by her parents at the Prado Restaurant, three days before his death. She suddenly burst into tears when she looked at the affectionate pictures, showing her head resting on Greg's shoulder.

"We were celebrating our birthdays," she sobbed.

The deputy DA then asked why she had criticized her husband for not giving her flowers. After saying that she often exchanged roses with her lover, she said Greg thought that being romantic was too expensive.

"I liked the romance of a single rose," she declared. "I had mentioned [to Greg], actually, back on our anniversary, that it didn't cost that much for a single rose."

Kristin then offered the theory that Greg had seen rose petals in her desk when he'd visited the ME's office on October 26, and had spread them on his chest before he killed himself.

"So he had seen rose petals in your desk," asked Goldstein incredulously. "Ergo, when he decided to kill himself, he was going to put rose petals on his chest as a symbolic event. Is that what your testimony is?"

"Yes," she replied.

Judge Thompson then recessed for the day, and Kristin Rossum left the witness stand after five-and-half hours of intense questioning.

. . .

On Tuesday, November 5, Kristin Rossum entered the witness box for the second straight day of withering cross-examination. The consensus among the reporters in the court was that she was holding up remarkably well. Although she had already admitted lying on numerous occasions, she showed no signs of breaking down on the stand and confessing all.

Continuing his relentless questioning, the prosecutor asked why she had never mentioned Michael Robertson in the journal that she had given Det Agnew after her interview with Homicide on November 22, 2000.

"I talked about love and what love means to me," she replied. "But I didn't mention his name specifically."

Goldstein then asked if she had lied in her journal, intimating that it was part of an elaborate staging of her husband's murder. Kristin maintained that she had written it to express her feelings, conceding it was also to help Greg understand why the marriage wasn't working, so as not to hurt his feelings.

"You wrote this diary," asked the prosecutor, "this alleged diary, didn't you, for Greg to read?"

"That wasn't the sole purpose," she replied. "If he would read it, I wanted him to be able to get an understanding from it."

At the end of his cross-examination, Goldstein questioned Kristin about her husband's death, and the positions of her wedding picture and the rose petals. In his final salvo, Goldstein showed the jury that it was impossible for Kristin to have performed CPR while talking on the phone. And it would prove that she had reset the scene of Greg's death after the 911 dispatcher had instructed her to move Greg's body off the bed.

She admitted telling Det Agnew that she had seen the framed photograph just under the pillow on the bed.

"When you were doing CPR on Greg," he asked, "after

you pulled him off the bed, did you notice the wedding photo propped against the bottom of the dresser?"

"No," she replied. "When I pulled back the covers, I remember seeing him on the bed with the photo there and the petals. I pulled him off, and the photo came off with him. I'm assuming that I just picked it up and set it aside when I was on 911. I don't recall either way."

Asked why she had never mentioned touching the photograph before, Rossum said that she hadn't realized that it had been moved and propped up against the bed.

Goldstein wondered why she had told her father that Greg was clutching the photo in his hand. But Kristin denied ever saying that.

"When you pulled Greg's body onto the floor," Goldstein continued, "there were no rose petals in the bed, correct?"

"Not that I saw," she replied.

"And the rose stem ended up right along the base of this dresser?" said the prosecutor, holding up a photo of the death scene for the jury to see.

"That's where it was in the photo, yes."

"How did the stem get there?"

"I don't know," she faltered.

"The rose petals were farther down, correct?"

"Yes."

"As you look at [the photograph], the rose petals go along the side of the bed, correct?"

"That is true."

"And the stem is up by the top of the dresser, correct?"

"Right. I don't know how long it had been there."

"I didn't ask you how long it had been there."

"Sorry."

"When you called 911, were you using the cordless?"

"Yes, I was."

"Thank you, nothing further," said Dan Goldstein, walking back to the prosecution table after almost a day and a half of dramatic cross-examination.

· · ·

In his rebuttal, public defender Alex Loebig attempted to repair some of the damage done to his client by the prosecution. But it would be an almost impossible task.

In desperation, the defender showed Kristin three different photographs of herself and Greg. The first one was taken at Aaron Waldo's wedding, a couple of weeks before Greg's death. On seeing it, Kristin burst into tears, as Loebig asked her if she had already decided to kill Greg when it was taken.

"Absolutely not," she sobbed.

He then showed her a picture taken the weekend before Halloween 2000.

"By that date," asked her attorney, "had you reached an agreement with Michael Robertson that the two of you would kill your husband?"

"No, we did not," she replied tearfully.

The third photograph was of the Prado birthday dinner, three days before Greg died. Loebig asked if she'd loved her husband when it was taken.

"I loved him very much," she said, saying that she had also loved Michael Robertson.

"Did you, with or without Michael Robertson, kill your husband?" he asked.

"I wouldn't hurt Greg," she said as Loebig finished his rebuttal questions.

Dan Goldstein then stood up for re-cross, noting how emotional she had become at seeing the pictures again.

"It's very hard, yes," sobbed Rossum.

Goldstein now questioned her about the discrepancies of the times she said she had gone shopping at Vons, telling Jerome and Bertrand that she had gone between 3:00 and 5:00 p.m. with Robertson. Her Vons card later revealed that she had bought a single rose at 12:41 p.m.

"That was taken, like I said, out of context," said Rossum, her voice faltering. "I lost my train of thought. I combined two ideas. So I never went to the store with Robertson."

Suddenly Kristin announced that petals from the rose she

had bought could not have been the ones found on Greg's body, as she had purchased a yellow one.

"How do we know it was a yellow rose?" snapped the prosecutor.

"We don't," she was forced to admit.

Goldstein asked what had happened to the yellow rose. Kristin claimed she had given it to Robertson later that afternoon and it had never left her car.

"We had been arguing," she explained. "I wanted to make peace. Yellow stands for friendship in our little lingo."

Then Goldstein revealed to the jury how Kristin had dialed 911 from her San Diego hotel room a couple of days after she had learned that investigators had proof she had purchased the rose.

"You were having a panic attack because you found out that we discovered you purchased a rose on November 6 at 12:41 p.m., correct?" asked the prosecutor.

"That had nothing to do with it," she replied meekly.

At that point, Alex Loebig had exhausted his questions, and after four days of testimony, Kristin Rossum was excused from the witness stand. Then the defense rested their case and Judge Thompson called a recess for lunch.

In the brief afternoon session, Dan Goldstein called four additional witnesses for the People, including Kristin's old boyfriend Teddy Maya. When he arrived at court and was waiting on a bench outside Judge Thompson's courtroom, he saw Kristin for the first time since she had abandoned him at the Redlands hotel room seven years earlier.

"She kind of smiled at me," he remembered. "We didn't speak."

Officer Laurence Horowitz, the Claremont policeman who had arrested Kristin for possession in January 1994, after being called in by her parents, also testified. Constance Rossum had told the court that her daughter had never been arrested, so Goldstein had called Horowitz to prove that she had been.

"I'm the guy that put her in handcuffs," he said later. "Took her down to the station, had her fingerprinted, had her photographed. She was arrested and processed like any other minor."

The final witness of the trial was Greg's mother Marie de Villers. A defense investigator had unearthed the de Villerses' divorce papers to try to show that there was a history of domestic violence in the family. Now the prosecution had no alternative but to head it off.

Looking emotional and frail, she slowly walked across the court and entered the witness box. But Deputy DA Dave Hendren had just one question.

"I don't want to keep you up there and make this hard for you," he said sympathetically. "Did your ex-husband, Mr. Yves de Villers, ever, in any way, shape or form, hit you or injure you or make domestic violence upon you in any way?"

"Never," she replied resolutely, and was excused from the stand.

Then Judge Thompson addressed the jury, telling them that they had now heard all the testimony, and closing arguments would take place the next day. By Thursday they would start deliberations to decide Kristin Rossum's fate.

Later that afternoon in an empty courtroom, prosecutor Dave Hendren requested that Judge Thompson instruct the jury on conspiracy, despite the defense's objections. And he laid out the part that prosecutors believed Michael Robertson had played in the murder.

"It is the People's position," Hendren told the judge, "that Michael Robertson is an uncharged, unindicted co-conspirator in this case."

He said jurors could conclude that Robertson may have administered the lethal dose of fentanyl to Greg de Villers.

"If he did so," Hendren continued, "it's the People's

contention that he did so in conjunction with Ms. Rossum as part of a conspiracy to kill her husband. They both had the same motive."

According to the deputy DA, Dr. Robertson had a vast knowledge of the drug, with thirty-seven articles and a PowerPoint presentation on his computer. He also shared a motive with Rossum, as they were both involved in a "secret relationship" outside their marriages. But although Hendren believed there was "abundant evidence" to establish a conspiracy between the two, Dr. Robertson remained uncharged in the murder.

Judge Thompson agreed, overruling the defense objections and finding that there was sufficient evidence to suggest a conspiracy.

An hour later, the jury was unexpectedly called back into the courtroom to hear further testimony from Marie de Villers. A private investigator for the Rossum family had tracked down Dr. and Mrs. de Villers' divorce papers, which directly contradicted Greg's mother's testimony. The prosecution claimed never to have been told about its existence, and Loebig did not want to impeach "the poor woman" for perjury. But both sides agreed she should be recalled to wrap up the case properly.

So the jurors were reseated and Alex Loebig continued his cross-examination of Marie de Villers, by reading a part of the 1981 divorce, which she had signed.

"In the past [Dr. de Villers] has, on many occasions, beat me with a closed fist and police reports have been made. After he beat me, [he] sent me to a doctor for treatment, and I had black-and-blue marks all over. I'm afraid of him, and he's stated he will break my teeth and mouth and will make me an ugly person."

Although Marie de Villers agreed that she had signed it, she said she could not remember ever saying those words.

Chapter 29

Guilty

On Wednesday, November 6, 2002, the second anniversary of Greg de Villers' death, the People of California demanded his young wife serve the maximum sentence—life without parole—for his murder. As he had in his cross-examination of Rossum, prosecutor Dan Goldstein pulled no punches in his closing argument.

"On our road to truth is two families," he told the jury. "The de Villers family and the Rossum family. This is not the Hatfields and McCoys. This has nothing to do with any quarrel that exists between Rossum and de Villers. Both families have suffered at the hands of the defendant and her narcissism and her self-centered behavior."

Accusing Rossum of "playing God" by murdering her husband, Goldstein said it was irrelevant whether she had injected him with fentanyl, used patches, or had given it to him orally.

"Who knows?" said the prosecutor. "She's the expert. He didn't just die and fade away. He was murdered."

Reminding the jurors it was the anniversary of Greg's death, Goldstein said that his final hours had to have been harrowing.

"Greg's lungs filling up with liquid is unpleasant," he said. "Greg's bladder filling up with urine. Greg having shallow respirations. Greg not being able to get to a phone and call 911. Greg not being able to merely pick up that

Princess phone right next to his bed while his bosses are calling.

"He doesn't answer the phone because he's comatose. There are drugs in his system killing him . . . he's dying."

Then Goldstein dramatically pointed to an empty chair behind the defendant's table.

"Robertson is sitting in that chair right there," he thundered. "He is an integral part of this homicide. He and the defendant are involved in a conspiracy. They are working together. They want Greg dead."

Refuting any of the Rossum family's theories that Greg had committed suicide, Goldstein said it would be "bizarre" and "not reasonable" for him to be sitting at home all day, self-administering fentanyl.

"Remember what both Dr. Stanley and the defense expert, Dr. Wallace, said: 'We have never seen this much fentanyl in a human being.' "

Calling him an ambitious, goal-oriented young man who despised drugs, Goldstein said Greg had discovered that his wife of seventeen months had relapsed into drugs, five years after he'd helped her quit. He'd also suspected that Kristin was having an affair with Michael Robertson and had given her an ultimatum: either she quit her job or he would expose her history of drugs.

"There's an ultimatum, and she's stressed out of her mind," he said. "One of the critical factors of methamphetamine abuse is that people get paranoid. They get violent. They act rashly. Pour a little methamphetamine on a love affair that's going to be turned in, you have a disaster that's about ready to happen."

He also drew the jury's attention to the fact that a large amount of fentanyl was missing from the ME's office, and Kristin had been the last person to log it in. He accused her of viewing the ME's office as a "candy store," and using "these tools of her trade" to murder her husband.

"Look at the drugs that are involved in this case," he said. "Oxycodone, clonazepam and fentanyl. They are missing from the medical examiner's office. They happen to be inside her husband's body. Soma, methamphetamine. Who takes those two drugs? The defendant. Coincidence? No. Theft."

Goldstein then told the jury not to be taken in by Kristin Rossum's beauty, intelligence or the fact that she'd graduated summa cum laude. He said even he found it hard to believe that somebody who looks like her could be a murderess.

"It's pretty basic," he said. "Either she poisoned him or she didn't. It wasn't a cry for help."

At the end of his dramatic closing argument, Dan Goldstein described Rossum as "manipulative" and a "habitual liar," who had conspired with her lover to murder her husband.

"That crime scene was staged," said the prosecutor, staring straight at Rossum. "The numerous lies that the defendant made about her husband's death, her drug use, her affairs, and the staging of that homicide scene are tantamount to a confession. The defendant is guilty of murder. That's what this case is about."

The following morning, Alex Loebig delivered his closing address to the jury. His co-defender Victor Eriksen was unable to attend, as he was at home with the flu. The genial public defender began by telling the jury that in life, things weren't "black and white," as the prosecutor had presented them.

"We are not here to judge her sex life against ours or anyone else's," he declared. "And by and large, that's not the essence of this case."

Telling the jury that "passion does not translate into violence," Loebig said that Rossum had no motive to kill her husband, as she was trying to walk out of the marriage. He also noted that security at the ME's office was so bad that any one of the fifty-six other employees could have taken the drugs.

Then, risking alienating the jury, he brought up Marie de Villers' divorce petition, which the Rossums' investigator had unearthed, saying that it had played a part in

Greg's make-up. He suggested that if true and Dr. de Villers had been violent, the jury should judge both defense and prosecution witnesses by the same standards.

At the end of his final address to the jury, Loebig told them that it was a circumstantial case and there was reasonable doubt.

"I know that there's a lot of evidence in front of you," he said. "Look at it as carefully and at as much length as you need to."

In his rebuttal, prosecutor Dave Hendren applauded Jerome de Villers for his relentless fight to bring Kristin Rossum to justice, saying that she may well have gotten away with murder, using the "perfect poison," if Jerome had not been so diligent.

"[He] loved his brother and knew it didn't make sense," said Hendren. "Fortunately, you had a demand for the first time to send those tox samples out. Without those, Greg de Villers would not get justice."

The prosecutor then catalogued all the points the jury would have to believe in order to acquit Rossum: they would have to decide that her testimony was credible, even though she had repeatedly lied to police, family and friends, and had contradicted herself on numerous occasions. That Greg de Villers, who despised all drugs, was capable of taking them to kill himself, and had then hidden all the evidence of pill bottles, syringes or fentanyl patch wrappers. That there was another employee at the ME's office who had stolen all the drugs from the laboratory. And finally that someone else, who was infatuated with roses like Kristin Rossum, had sprinkled red rose petals over Greg's chest while he was comatose.

Hendren then appealed to the jury not to judge the case on sympathy or pity, or let Kristin Rossum's pretty looks enter into their decision.

"You say, 'Wow, that's a pretty girl,'" he said. "She doesn't look like a murderer. She looks nice. Probably loves her mom, dad. They probably love her. Greg de Villers loved his mom," and indicating Kristin, "he loved her."

Greg could not be in the courtroom to tell them what happened, Hendren said, but his body, containing fentanyl, was "crying out for justice."

"We are asking, on behalf of Greg de Villers, on behalf of his family, on behalf of his community, to hold this woman accountable for what she did to take his life away."

Judge Thompson then sent the twelve jurors out to start their deliberations, to decide whether Kristin Rossum was innocent or guilty. The grueling trial had lasted a month from jury selection to closing arguments, and the five-woman/seven-man panel had plenty to discuss.

After two hours' deliberation on Thursday afternoon, the jurors were sent home with the judge's instructions not to discuss the case, or look at the coverage on television or newspapers. They returned to the jury room on Friday, where they deliberated for another three hours before going off for a long Veteran's Day weekend. Judge Thompson ordered them to resume on Tuesday.

On Sunday, November 10, *The San Diego Union-Tribune* carried a front-page story asking why Michael Robertson had not also been charged with murder.

"A key player in the love triangle involving Kristin Rossum and her dead husband has been conspicuously absent from the courtroom," wrote Caitlin Rother, who had covered the story from the beginning. "The jury has deliberated over parts of two days without reaching a verdict, and testimony ended without any clarification about Robertson's absence."

Noting that Judge Thompson's gag order was still in effect, so none of the attorneys involved could answer the question, Rother had interviewed Kristin's first attorney, Gretchen von Helms, who said that prosecutors may have offered Kristin a plea bargain at the beginning in exchange for implicating her lover, but before von Helms could discuss it with her client, she had been replaced by public defenders Loebig and Eriksen.

"I couldn't be the only one they made the offer to," she reasoned.

While Kristin Rossum spent the long weekend with her family at a San Diego hotel, prosecutors were confident they'd get a conviction. Dave Hendren expected the jury to take up to two weeks to come to a decision, as there was so much evidence to absorb.

"Before it came to trial," said Hendren, "Dan and I talked about the fact that it could take a jury a significant period of time to make their determination. But there's always a certain level of anxiety from the time the jury goes out."

Soon after they returned to court on the morning of Tuesday, November 12, which would have been Greg de Villers' 29th birthday, the foreperson sent word that they had reached a verdict. Immediately, the Rossum and de Villers families took their places on opposite sides of the public gallery.

At the defense table, Kristin Rossum, dressed in a white V-neck shirt with her long blonde hair tied back, waited for the decision which could send her to jail for the rest of her life.

Then Judge Thompson entered his courtroom and called in the jury.

"Mr. Foreperson," he said, "has the jury reached a verdict?"

The foreperson said they had, handing it to the court bailiff to read out.

"In the matter of the State of California versus Kristin Rossum, we, the jury in the above-entitled case, find the defendant guilty of the crime of murder, in violation of penal code section 187 as charged in count one, fixing the degree thereof as murder in the first.

"We further find that in the commission of this offense, the Defendant did intentionally kill Greg de Villers by administration of poison, within the meaning of penal code section 190.2 (A) (19)."

As she heard the guilty verdict, Kristin Rossum began shaking her head in disbelief and gasping for air. She started weeping softly. Her father, sitting two rows behind her, hung his head and stared at the floor of the courtroom, wiping his brow with a shaky hand. Constance Rossum just looked exhausted, her face not registering any emotion. Sitting across the aisle, Marie de Villers and her two surviving sons held hands, bowing their heads as they heard the verdict.

Then Judge Thompson asked the jurors one-by-one if this was their verdict, and they all said, "Yes."

After thanking the jury, and warning them not to talk to the press for compensation for ninety days, he thanked them for their public service and dismissed them.

As the jury filed out, Kristin stood up, but her legs appeared to give way. She buckled, grabbing the defense table for support, as a bailiff helped her sit down.

Judge Thompson then revoked Kristin's bail, remanding her to be held at Las Colinas Women's Detention Facility until sentencing. She was then handcuffed and led out of the courtroom by bailiffs, as she turned around and stared imploringly at her parents.

Sentencing would come a month later, but she and her parents were well aware that her crime carried a mandatory sentence of life without parole.

Four days later, Michael Robertson gave an interview to Melbourne's *Sunday Herald Sun* reporter Shelley Hodgson, who believed in his innocence. He described the past two years as a "roller-coaster ride," saying that he lived in fear of spending the rest of his life in an American prison.

Robertson, who had now found a full-time job in the science field, complained that he had not been given the opportunity to defend himself, and was innocent.

"I had absolutely no knowledge or participation in the

very sad events that led to Greg's death and, in the end, with Kristin's conviction," he said. "It's like a sad end to two lives."

Admitting he was "scared" that San Diego prosecutors would extradite him to stand trial, in which he could face the death penalty, he admitted seeking legal advice in case that happened.

"That was a fairly scary concept," he said. "But I was always confident that I would ultimately be exonerated."

He even joked that he was now regarded by his friends as a "walking advertisement" for what could go wrong with cheating on your wife.

"My only regret is that I had an extra-marital affair," he declared. "But that was my only crime—if that was a crime."

He also said that, although he believed in Kristin's innocence, if she was guilty, she should pay the price.

"She's someone I still care for," he replied when Hodgson asked if he still loved Rossum. "But a lot of damage has taken place through all this."

On December 6, one week before she was due to be sentenced, Rossum's defense team asked for a new trial on a technicality. They claimed that the jury had not been instructed to consider that she did not attempt to flee while she was under investigation or during the nine months she was out on bail. They also asked the judge to remove the allegation that she had used poison to kill her husband.

Her defense also claimed that saturation media coverage had influenced the jury's decision.

"The local media in effect became a large and powerful witness for the prosecution," read the motion. "Jurors had to have been influenced."

Prosecutors quickly responded, filing a motion in San Diego Superior Court that defendants have no rights to an absence-of-flight instruction.

Six days later, before Judge Thompson passed sentence

on Kristin Rossum, he denied her motion for a new trial. Sitting nervously at the defense table in a black pin-striped shirt and handcuffs, Kristin looked drawn and stressed, as she waited to hear the judge hand down her sentence. She would sob continually during the thirty-minute hearing.

The judge began by stating that he had no alternative, except sentencing her to life without parole.

Then Alex Loebig read a statement from Ralph and Constance Rossum, who were in court for their daughter's sentencing.

"We are horrified by the verdict and sentence," it said. "Our innocent daughter has been wrongly convicted. We know Kristin did not murder Greg. We understand there are solid grounds for appeal and intend to pursue them vigorously. Keep us all in your prayers."

Then Bertrand de Villers stood up to read a statement that his father had written for his former daughter-in-law. Finally the de Villers family would have one public opportunity to tell her what they thought of her. There was a deathly silence in the courtroom, punctuated only by Kristin's continual sobbing.

"Kristin," read Dr. de Villers' message, "you have totally destroyed so many people: Greg, me and my family, your family and yourself. You show no remorse and ask for no repentance for any of your actions. You cried fake tears for Greg and real tears only for yourself.

"On the outside you are a smart, beautiful woman. On the inside, you are a lying, calculating, manipulating person that cares only about herself. You either, by yourself or with someone else, murdered my first-born child, a child I delivered myself.

"My family and I have been nothing but good and tolerant to you. Even though you knew you stole Greg's family crest and gold necklace, I had the rings remade for you as a wedding present because I knew Greg loved you.

"Greg did nothing but help you and love you. When he tried to help you get off drugs for a second time, you repaid him in the worst imaginable way. You killed him, and then you lied about it."

Bertrand then asked for the opportunity to address the defendant. During his moving statement, Kristin looked up and stared at him. It would be the only time she would make eye contact with any of her former in-laws.

"Kristin, this is my chance to talk to you," began Bertrand. "To tell you how you have changed my life forever and express how I feel about you. Whether you choose to listen to me or not, you will hear what I have to say."

Brimming with emotion, Bertrand described her betrayal as *the* most despicable act imaginable.

"Like Medea, you wielded your black magic to poison your husband. Your cunning and deceitfulness went undetected by Greg because, in his world, a person as evil as you did not exist.

"He saved you from the deepest valley of despair and lifted you to the highest peak of success that you will ever attain. When you reached the top, your reward to him was to push him off the cliff when he wasn't looking.

"You are an example of the most sinister darkness that exists in the world, and your darkness encroached into my life.

"Kristin, you are the only person in the world that I hate. I do so with all the strength and all the feeling that I possess within me."

Then Jerome stood up to personally tell Kristin the horror he had been through since his brother's murder.

"The circumstances of Greg's death were unbelievable, and had huge emotional and psychological effects on me," he said in a shaky voice. "The idea that Greg took his own life was unbelievable. I was determined to discover the truth about what happened.

"For months I spent all of my free time thinking and researching the possibilities. I was angry and obsessed with finding the truth, so much so that I stayed up at night thinking and questioning everything over and over again. At times I could not sleep or I would wake up in the middle of the night. I missed several weeks of work and lost productivity. I would be constantly distracted.

"I became reclusive and tended towards social avoidance. I did not go out with my friends. I shut people out. I became paranoid that the Rossums were plotting against my family. I worried that someone might harm me, Bert, my mom, or girlfriend. It became hard to trust anyone.

"Not long after Greg's death I suspected that Kristin killed [him] or in some way was involved. I want and have always wanted her to tell the truth. It has taken two years to prove this ultimate crime of betrayal in court. This does bring some closure; however, I'm still without my brother.

"Kristin took Greg from my life and from the world and to date has never shown remorse. My family is still struggling and hurt. I don't understand why this happened to us. I don't want this to happen to anyone else. I want justice for Greg and I want Kristin behind bars for the rest of her life. She's a danger to society."

Finally, Greg's mother slowly rose and put on her glasses to read what she had written about her son's murder.

"This has been a very long journey to seek the truth in the murder of Gregory," she began. "His death brought eternal turmoil in our lives. We were left with conflicting information. We had to find out what happened, and we had faith in the judicial system.

"Our world crumbled after his death, like after the destruction of the World Trade Center in New York. By an act of terrorism so brutal and unthinkable, she caused damage that cannot be rebuilt. Our beliefs were shattered, our hopes have been torn apart.

"Greg paid the ultimate price for his goodness, because Kristin Rossum's poor choices and irresponsible judgments led to his murder. He could not save someone drowning in turbulent waters mainly because this person was only thinking about surviving herself.

"The images we have of his murder will never leave our minds. We were left with the detailed horrific nightmare of his last hours. Kristin has destroyed our family by destroying the gentleness and goodness Gregory brought to our life. We will be forever shaken by her cold disrespect of life. She played a dangerous game with feelings and perpetually tried to cover up her secrets. Her actions escalated to a killing and the involvement of so many persons being hurt and betrayed.

"By sentencing Kristin Rossum to the fullest extent of the law, only then justice will be levied. It will not bring back Gregory. We have only memories saved in our mind, deep scars in our heart and severe sadness in the core of our soul."

Then, a visibly moved Judge Thompson pronounced sentence, as Rossum slowly stood up to face him.

"Ms. Rossum," he said, "it's the order of the court that you be committed to the Department of Corrections for the remainder of your natural life without the possibility of parole."

He also ordered her to pay $10,000 in restitution, refusing a defense motion to set her free on bail, pending appeal.

Epilogue

On December 5, 2002, a week before her sentencing, Kristin Rossum was interviewed by a probation officer at Las Colinas Women's Detention Facility, and was totally unrepentant. Once again she recounted her version of events as she had at her trial. But now she had added a new twist, claiming that she and Greg had had a custom of exchanging roses when one of them was ill. Besides, she stressed, the single rose she had purchased the day he died was a yellow one and not red, like the petals found on his body.

Asked by the probation officer about her conviction, Rossum vowed to exonerate herself, declaring: "I still can't believe the jury convicted me. We're going to keep fighting this."

Asked about her future plans, now facing the rest of her natural life behind bars, Rossum said she would take advantage of any available educational opportunities the prison she was sent to offered.

"It's hard to think about right now," she said sadly, adding that if she was freed on appeal, she planned to go to graduate school and get a Ph.D. in analytical chemistry and return to the bio-technical industry.

"I want to have a family," she said. "That's it."

Soon after her sentencing, Alex Loebig filed notice of appeal, which would be handled by the appellant branch of the public defender's office with new attorneys. Loebig said he had no regrets about allowing Rossum to take the stand and testify.

"She wanted to testify," he said in February 2003. "I had no reservation about it, because that was really the essence of the defense. We couldn't prove definitively, or much in any fashion, the potential source of the fentanyl. Nor could we particularly establish the way that he might have self-administered it."

The defender said his client was surprised when she had been found guilty, hoping for a hung jury and a new trial.

On December 20, 2002, Kristin's parents sold the exclusive rights to their daughter's story to a Hollywood production company called Brubaker-Recht Entertainment, for an undisclosed figure.

The de Villers family's civil attorney Craig McClellan vowed that any money the Rossums might make out of the deal would ultimately go to his clients in the pending $2.1 million wrongful death lawsuit.

McClellan said he wasn't surprised that the Rossums had made a deal for a movie and book about the case.

"It was always my impression that what they were after was ultimately to profit from it," he said.

A few months later, the de Villers family would also hire a Hollywood agent and entertainment lawyer to field the many offers coming their way for books and movies.

Six days after her sentencing, Kristin Rossum became Inmate No. W97094 at Chowchilla Maximum Security Prison. The convicted murderess was designated a high security inmate because of the nature of her crime and her life sentence, meaning she'd be counted six times a day.

Placed in a dormitory with seven other prisoners, Kristin had no access to a computer, although she can have a television if her parents buy her one. In early 2003 a prison spokesman said she had settled in well and was working as a janitor, cleaning assigned areas of the prison at eight cents an hour.

Her parents visit her as often as regulations allow, and she is planning to appeal.

During the summer of 2003, there were reports that Kristin had started corresponding with accused killer Scott Peterson in a bizarre jail romance. Peterson, who will go on trial in 2004 for the murder of his pregnant wife Laci, is said to find hope in Kristin's letters.

In late February, Deputy DA Dave Hendren and Homicide Detective Laurie Agnew flew to Melbourne to further investigate Michael Robertson, who was now analyzing chemical components for a food company. They spent a week with detectives from the Victoria Homicide Squad, interviewing friends, associates and members of Robertson's family.

Detective Inspector Chris Enright told the Melbourne *Herald Sun* that prosecutors were gathering enough evidence to charge and extradite Robertson. He said he had accompanied Hendren and Agnew on a dozen interviews, and that they'd also looked into his background training as a toxicologist.

Dr. Robertson himself refused to be interviewed, referring them to his attorney. As of October, Hendren refused to discuss the investigation, except to say that it was ongoing.

The de Villers family is still trying to come to terms with Greg's murder. In April 2003, Jerome was honored by the San Diego District Attorney's Office with a Citizen of Courage Award for his relentless pressure on the authorities until they arrested Kristin Rossum.

At a special luncheon to honor him and six others, Jerome told the two hundred guests that his real award came when Rossum was brought to justice.

A couple of months later, Jerome quit his job as an insurance adjuster, taking time off to recover from the psychological effects of his ordeal. But this summer, there was even more tragedy for the de Villers family when Greg's mother Marie died from an asthma attack, never having fully recovered from the murder of her eldest son.

The de Villerses' civil trial against Rossum, Robertson and the San Diego County Medical Examiner's Office is scheduled for early 2004.